Political intellectuals
and
public identities
in Britain since 1850

MANCHESTER
UNIVERSITY PRESS

Political intellectuals
and
public identities
in Britain since 1850

Julia Stapleton

Manchester University Press

Manchester and New York

distributed exclusively in the USA by Palgrave

Published by Manchester University Press
Oxford Road, Manchester M13 9NR, UK
and Room 400, 175 Fifth Avenue, New York, NY 10010, USA
http://www.manchesteruniversitypress.co.uk

Distributed exclusively in the USA by
Palgrave, 175 Fifth Avenue, New York,
NY 10010, USA

Distributed exclusively in Canada by
UBC Press, University of British Columbia, 2029 West Mall,
Vancouver, BC, Canada V6T 1Z2

British Library Cataloguing-in-Publication Data
A catalogue record for this book is available from the British Library

Library of Congress Cataloging-in-Publication Data applied for

ISBN 0 7190 5511 3 *hardback*

First published 2001

10 09 08 07 06 05 04 03 02 01   10 9 8 7 6 5 4 3 2 1

Typeset in Sabon
by Servis Filmsetting Ltd, Manchester
Printed in Great Britain
by Bookcraft (Bath) Ltd, Midsomer Norton

For D. P. O'B.

Contents

Preface and acknowledgements

This book attempts both to consolidate some of the growing literature on British intellectuals and British political thought in the last 150 years, and to develop it further. Its main, although by no means sole, concern is to emphasise the influence of conceptions of England/Britain in these two spheres, and to explore the reformulation of such conceptions in turn. Thus I hope that the book will appeal both to advanced undergraduates – anxious for short-cuts through a rich body of work – and to established scholars interested in new perspectives. I also hope that it will assist in bringing the study of British political thought and intellectual history more generally into closer proximity. However, I do not make any claim to have achieved an exhaustive analysis; nor have I attempted to impose clean chronological and thematic breaks on resistant material.

I have been greatly assisted in the writing of this book by an ESRC grant (R000222402) for a collaborative project entitled 'Intellectuals and Political Culture'. I am particularly indebted to the principal grantholder – Jeremy Jennings – for including me, and for providing much stimulus and encouragement along the way. I would also like to thank Peter Stirk and Philip Williamson, both of whom took an interest in the book, read some of the chapters and generously shared their knowledge of relevant sources. At a later stage of the research, I also benefited greatly from comments by Reba Soffer and Ewen Green. Needless to say, none of the above bear any responsibility for the final product.

It is a pleasure to record my thanks to colleagues in the Politics Department at Durham, not least for granting me a sabbatical term at the start of the project, but also for supporting my research generally. I am much indebted, too, to the inter-library-loan service of Durham University Library, which I am conscious of having overloaded throughout the course of writing this book.

I am extremely grateful to the following individuals and libraries for making available, and/or granting me permission to use, unpublished material: the Liddell Hart Centre for Military Archives at King's College London, particularly Kate O'Brien; the Trustees of the Liddell Hart Centre for Military Archives; the Clerk of the Records, House of Lords Record Office (*The Parliamentary*

Archives); Sue Donnelly, British Library of Political and Economic Science; the Librarian, Harvard Law School Library; Helen Langley, Department of Special Collections and Western Manuscripts, the Bodleian Library, Oxford; Simon Bailey, Oxford University Archives, Bodleian Library; Helen Burton, Keele University Library; Leo Greenbaum, YIVO Institute for Jewish Research, New York; Danelle Moon, Yale University Library; Merav Segal, Weizmann Archives, Rehovot, Israel; the Librarian, *The Spectator* for permission to publish a brief extract from a letter by J. St. Loe Strachey; Professor Christopher Seton-Watson; Mr Raleigh Trevelyan; the Library of Congress; and David Higham Associates Limited, on behalf of the Estates of Arthur Bryant and Francis Brett Young. The extract from Edmund Blunden's letter of 18 February 1940 to Arthur Bryant is reproduced by kind permission of PFD on behalf of the Estate of Mrs Claire Blunden. Although every effort was made, I was unable to contact the owners of the copyright in the estates of H. J. Laski, Alfred Zimmern and Jack Lawson.

Chapter 8 is an expanded version of an article which appeared in the journal *The European Legacy*, 5:6 (2000). I hereby acknowledge the copyright of the International Society for the Study of European Ideas, and thank Taylor & Francis Ltd (http://www.tandf.co.uk) for permission to reproduce the article.

Finally, I owe an especial debt of gratitude to my husband, whose unfailing support made possible the completion of this book.

Introduction

The idea that leading scholars, thinkers (and artists) should serve their national community is one that has become increasingly alien in intellectual life today. With the rise of global society and the development of discourses which marginalise, where they do not openly deny, the reality of the local, the concept of 'national intellectual' would seem to subvert the calling of the intellectual itself. The duty of the intellectual to oppose all national interests and champion the interests of the oppressed in the arresting voice of reason and humanity has been forcefully underlined recently by such self-appointed professional spokesmen as Edward Said.[1] In so far as Said harbours lingering doubts about the accessibility of universal truth – unmediated by local commitments and influences which inevitably undermine or compromise it – these have been vigorously combatted by Martin Hollis, for whom 'intellectuals betray their calling, unless they stick to Reason through thick and thin'.[2] Such arguments signal the revival – but paradoxically in the cause of political commitment rather than scholarly detachment – of the legacy of Julien Benda. In his *La Trahison des clercs* of 1927 the contemporary intellectual's propensity to cultivate local attachments is unambiguously denounced for the 'racial' and 'political' passions which were, he believed, its inevitable concomitants. Still smarting from the cultural wounds inflicted on France by the Dreyfus affair, for which he held figures such as Zola responsible, Benda denounced the 'modern "clerk"' for

> entirely ceas[ing] to let the layman alone descend to the market place. The modern clerk is determined to have the soul of a citizen and to make vigorous use of it; he is proud of that soul; his literature is filled with his contempt for the man who shuts himself up with art or science and takes no interest in the passions of the state.[3]

Those in England who have lately expressed concern for the beleaguered state of its national identity would underline the success of Benda's critique of the perfidy of intellectuals in deserting what should be their 'humanitarian' trademark. Simon Heffer, for example, sees no scope for the reinvention of England among the 'civilised and educated' classes, a task made necessary by the combined forces of Scottish independence, European encroachment upon national

1

sovereignty, and the heavy demands of multiculturalism on the historic national culture of Britain. He regards contemporary intellectuals as largely character-ised by a

> repudiat[ion] and cring[ing] at the very idea of nationalism. There is the problem that many in this class no longer feel that England should have its own interests, or identity, but that these should be submerged in the interests and supposed identity of a larger, multi-national state.[4]

For such commentators the 'treason' of intellectuals has reverted to the ordinary meaning of the term as harming the interests of one's country: Heffer and others find it inconceivable that national interests can be furthered by bartering national sovereignty itself.

However, intellectuals in Britain have not always been so concerned to dis-tance themselves from the historical culture of their country. Indeed, this has been a relatively recent phenomenon, the illustration of which is one of the primary objectives of this book. The popular journalist Peter Hitchens main-tains that British intellectuals have long since ceased to identify with their com-patriots, certainly since before the Second World War.[5] He draws support from George Orwell's famous denunciation of the intellectual left in interwar Britain for separating 'patriotism and intelligence'.[6] By contrast, the following chapters emphasise that up until as late as the 1970s, there was a strong, albeit receding, tradition among intellectuals of positive engagement with English/British nationhood.[7] Chapter 1 makes clear that this engagement developed from the late Victorian intelligentsia's sense of national responsibility in eschewing the chauvinism and jingoism of the masses, on the one hand, and the indifference and opportunism towards nation and empire that often characterised politicians and statesmen, on the other. The bond between intellectuals and nation was con-solidated by a conception of scholarship as an uplifting and unifying influence on society at large, its fruits requiring the widest dissemination rather than monopolisation by an elite. It was a conception which endured well into the twentieth century, against all the pressures exerted by the specialisation and institutionalisation of learning. The informality of British intellectuals as a class, because of their diverse professional roots and their close integration into public life more widely,[8] was a leading factor in the formation of a national iden-tity that was restrained rather than belligerent, inclusive rather than exclusive, and social rather than political in emphasis (although its social nature was to be made much of politically). Consequently, British intellectuals complicate the idea – deriving from Benda – that national partialities serve only to warp the intellectual imagination and distract it from its mission of attaining pure truth and understanding. Indeed, the stimulus of national character, culture and tra-ditions has been central to that imagination in Britain for much of the twentieth century, enriching rather than impoverishing it in the process. Certainly, the 'public' intellectual and the national intellectual have been largely inseparable, which is little appreciated among those who champion the former but disdain the latter.[9] This applies not only to 'establishment' intellectuals of an earlier period – H. A. L. Fisher and Ernest Barker are obvious instances – but those, like E. P. Thompson, who have been central to a radical, dissenting tradition in the postwar period.[10]

Of course there have been intellectuals in Britain who took up positions of high moral and cultural detachment. An obvious instance from the early period covered by this book is Lord Acton, whose wholesale condemnation of all national figures in the past who had flouted the universal moral code caused much chagrin in his ageing teacher, the German patriot intellectual Ignaz von Döllinger, in the early 1880s.[11] But, as Reba Soffer has argued, 'Acton was always more cosmopolitan than British'.[12] A later example is Philip and Lady Ottoline Morrell's circle at Garsington which attracted intellectuals such as Bertrand Russell, John Middleton Murry, Katherine Mansfield and D. H. Lawrence who opposed Britain's involvement in the First World War.[13] However, their defence of culture and 'pure intellect' against the seemingly barbarian passions of politicians and populace alike underlined their minority status in the intellectual elite of their day.[14] They certainly held little sway over the young, who – while respecting their conscientious objection – remained unconvinced that the gifted and privileged in society should be exempt from bearing the full weight of the war's burden.[15]

Undeniably, too, there have been 'antagonistic' intellectuals in Britain. Most obviously, the interwar period spawned an intelligentsia that was alienated from national life to a degree unknown previously, and in thrall morally and – in some cases financially – to foreign governments. However, it is little remarked upon that in these years not only did a left intelligentsia which was marked by a contempt for country signally fail to dominate intellectual and cultural life in Britain – the phenomenal success of Vaughan Williams's 'national music' is an obvious refutation of any such presumption;[16] it also generated a vibrant intellectual opposition movement centred on Arthur Bryant which was motivated by deep-seated concern about the damage to national morale inflicted by the left. Moreover, scholars and thinkers who joined forces with the left on such issues as appeasement or unemployment or Spain – for example, R. G. Collingwood and A. D. Lindsay – could be highly sensitive to 'English' themes such as that of the countryside in the case of the former and Nonconformity in the case of the latter. They helped to make these themes central to the repudiation of foreign political and intellectual styles in interwar Britain. The strength of Christian conviction in the political thought of the period also modified the influence of the intellectual left, and in some cases – principally, but not exclusively, that of T. S. Eliot – directly reinforced the notion of a 'national' community.[17] Further, it will become clear in this book that vigorous opponents of Marxism who devoted themselves instead to an ideal of world federalism – A. E. Zimmern, for example – failed to shake themselves free of English images, standards and foibles in envisaging the shape and character of the new world polity. Finally, it will be seen that even in such hard Marxist cases as that of John Strachey, the patriotic impulse – the call to defend an historic ideal of Britain – on the eve of the Second World War undermined his commitment to the theory of international class struggle directed by the Soviet Union.

In underlining the positive contribution to both nation and intellect of some of this country's 'national intellectuals', this book focuses mainly on the work of political intellectuals. In previous work I have argued that political thought has been a primary vehicle of national identity in Britain, as much as the canon of English literature whose role in this respect has attracted far more attention.[18] I develop the thesis further in this book, while occasionally extending it to figures who fall outside the immediate category of 'political intellectual' but whose work engaged – sometimes supportively, sometimes critically – with the policies, values and institutions of a perceptibly national state. My aim is to draw out the contribution which such thinkers and writers have played in shaping the public identities of Britain since the end of the nineteenth century, emphasising, in particular, the strong national flavour those identities had been accorded throughout much of this period.

One side of the national character that they have constantly addressed is the low premium accorded to intellect, and while the virtues of this quality in a long record of practical and political achievement have often been acknowledged, the corresponding defect of a largely untutored nation – with all the potential for a revolution by default that has accompanied it – has proved a source of often deep concern. The importance of education has impressed the intellectual elite at every turn, but it has been acutely sensitive to the need for tailoring that task to the national type. Notoriously, intellectuals have not found a natural home in Britain and, indeed, have rarely sought a privileged place in the national culture. The authority they have exercised has been rooted as much in a sense of common citizenship as the claim to intellectual expertise.

However, while they have often readily identified with the nation in this way, their association with the citadels of power has never been cosy and rarely happy. Undoubtedly, as Chapter 1 emphasises, an intimate relationship developed between intellect and politics in the later decades of the nineteenth century, not least because of the common background of both worlds in liberal learning. But even a prominent intellectual such as H. A. L. Fisher, at the centre of government as Lloyd George's Minister of Education, felt keenly the tension between the independence required by the life of the mind and the compromises demanded by political service.[19] In this sense the claim that 'the oppositional and independent stance of a Bertrand Russell or George Orwell was always less typical' (than those intellectuals such as Laski, Cole and the Webbs, who attained influence through the Labour Party and Fabian Society) is somewhat inaccurate.[20] It both underestimates the number of Russells and Orwells in the British intelligentsia, their commitment notwithstanding a lack of party affiliation, and the dilemmas which their more politically active peers experienced in holding office.

Indeed, sometimes the movement of intellectual opposition has taken place inside the establishment itself, in counteracting the growing cultural antagonism of other opinion makers. For example, later in life Lord Annan had cause to regret the failure of his generation, who came of age after 1918, to provide leadership for postwar Britain; while de Gaulle and Adenauer were giving their countries self-confidence and pride, Annan's intellectual contemporaries in positions of power did nothing to halt the slide of Britain into a state of syndicalism.[21] In 1988, he berated broadcasters for their lack of patriotism.[22] Although he did not say as much, this was a direct consequence of the neglect of country for which his age was responsible in its early reaction against the 'hypocrisy' which had sustained imperial Britain.[23] Greater maturity might well account for these changing responses; certainly by 1996 he was much inspired by the example of the later Keynes's expression of unease at Bloomsbury's detachment from indigenous cultural traditions and its irreverence towards 'the past and towards institutions'.[24] But the episode emphasises, too, the way in which 'opposition' to cultural opposition was still evident among the intellectual elite, even as late as the 1980s – his comments were not well received at the BBC – and the way in which conflict between 'intellect' and 'society' can take any number of political forms.

When, therefore, the critical role of the intellectual is underscored, confining such criticism to national (local) states and discourses is unduly restrictive. Intellectuals discharge an equally legitimate and important duty of criticism when they serve their nation, attempting to ensure its survival and integrity against those who would attenuate its deepest cultural foundations in the interests of more inclusive and expansive social ideals for which the majority of their fellow countrymen feel little sympathy.[25] There is no reason why this essentially local commitment should not co-exist with the censorial role of intellectuals in combatting sharp political and cultural practice, both in their own country and elsewhere. Of course, there are humanitarian norms and international treaty obligations which it is the duty of the intellectual to emphasise whenever and wherever they are violated. (Although in the nineteenth century, intellectuals who agitated on the so-called 'Eastern Question' were not coy about resting their case against oppression on another criterion of justice than the humanitarian and the legal: the 'historic merits' of oppressed peoples such as the Armenians themselves.[26]) But national attachment and commitment have often been an essential springboard to effective critical effort, and a crucial basis of trust, respect and influence between intellectuals and the wider public – whether at home or abroad. It was upon such a foundation that, for example, Gandhi won support for the cause of Indian independence among the British people and intellectuals alike in the interwar period. He was not locked into native Indian traditions, however, and by acknowledging the validity of other paradigms and experiences at the same time as asserting those of his own, he was acclaimed by one leading British intellectual as a crucial 'bridge' and 'reconciler' between East and West.[27] Similarly, Gandhi and other leaders of colonial independence were favourably impressed by the patriotism of British intellectuals and their associated support for liberal nationalism abroad, responses which they used not only to legitimate but also to inspire their own struggles for national liberation.[28]

In this country, intellectuals have attained wide social acceptance when, in pursuing this course, they have heightened national self-knowledge. This self-knowledge has not always taken the form of a myth of exceptionalism: the idea of a 'European inheritance' in Britain is by no means exclusive to the contemporary heyday of the European Union.[29] However, the more that intellectuals have played down Britain's uniqueness and denigrated its achievements, the more such a myth has developed in response. But far from lacking any critical edge, proponents of the latter have been powerfully subversive of the kind of progressive opinion which associates the diurnal with the neanderthal.

The heritage of the 'national intellectual' enjoyed an extended lease of life well into the postwar era, but in oppositional and iconoclastic rather than the establishment mode it had assumed previously, as Chapter 9 makes clear. There have been moves to revive the figure recently; but these attempts are largely situated in the world of journalism,[30] and lack the stimulus and support of the intellectual elite. The alternative – multicultural and internationalist – preoccupations of intellectuals are explored in Chapter 10. This development may seem inevitable given the radically diverse nature of British society compared with the first half of the twentieth century. Intellectuals nowadays can no more be expected to produce a nationalist discourse in the old, 'exclusive' sense than their predecessors could have questioned the cultural homogeneity of the society they served. The age of minority cultures and of devolution, on the one hand, and of supranational organisation, on the other, appears inimical to the very concept of a national intellectual in a nation of nations such as Britain. Such developments have given much succour to those scholars who believe that the enlightenment project of universal criticism provides the sole basis of intellectual intervention. How can intellectuals operate within 'national-popular' cultures when such cultures are fast losing whatever semblance of meaning and reality they once had? Surely their efforts will reinforce the interests and interpretations of the 'hegemonic' classes only?[31]

However, the existence of minority cultures presupposes the existence of majority or mainstream cultures, and these will not dissolve readily. In this country, social and political stability has depended greatly upon the entrenched character of the latter; never exclusive or static, it has – with skilful cultural articulation and adaptation – absorbed elements previously shunned such as those of provincialism[32] through the work of John Betjeman, and hostile forces such as those of socialism through a plethora of thinkers on the left. It still exists in a recognisable, English form – the form which once, unobtrusively, played a disproportionately larger role than Scotland, Wales and Ireland in shaping the identity of 'Britain' more widely.[33] It would be wrong to assume that this culture is or once was wholly inclusive; public cultures can never be such and are therefore constantly open to the charge of being unrepresentative. If sufficiently broad and well established, and therefore secure, they can, however, tolerate a wide range of practices and beliefs. Those who seek the revival of an England which once took this form – whether within a composite Britain or as a devolved nation – could do worse than study the work of intellectuals in the past who helped to create it.

Notes

1 E. Said, *Representations of the Intellectual: The 1993 Reith Lectures* (London, Vintage, 1994).

2 M. Hollis, 'What truth? For whom and where?', in J. Jennings and A. Kemp-Welch (eds), *Intellectuals in Politics: From the Dreyfus Affair to Salmon Rushdie* (London, Routledge, 1997), p. 289.

3 J. Benda, *The Betrayal of the Intellectuals*, trs. R. Aldington (Boston, The Beacon Press, [1927] 1955), pp. 32–3.

4 S. Heffer, *Nor Shall My Sword: The Reinvention of England* (London, Weidenfeld & Nicolson, 1999), pp. 132–3.

5 P. Hitchens, *The Abolition of Britain* (London, Quartet Books, 1999), p. 22.

6 G. Orwell, *The Lion and the Unicorn: Socialism and the English Genius* (London, Penguin, [1941] 1982), pp. 64–5.

7 This is especially evident if what Roger Scruton terms 'the privileged rebels' are set against 'less prominent, more modest, and more worthy intellectuals who have become priests, civil servants, dons, and schoolmasters, humbly accepting their place in the *status quo*'; R. Scruton, *England: An Elegy* (London, Chatto & Windus, 2000), p. 249.

8 W. C. Lubenow, *The Cambridge Apostles, 1820–1914: Liberalism, Imagination, and Friendship in British Intellectual and Professional Life* (Cambridge, Cambridge University Press, 1998), p. 2.

9 M. Ignatieff, 'The decline and fall of the public intellectual', *Queen's Quarterly*, 104 (1997), 395–403; and *The Warrior's Honor: Ethnic War and the Modern Conscience* (London, Chatto & Windus, 1998), p. 167.

10 See M. Kenny, 'Reputations: Edward Palmer (E. P.) Thompson', *Political Quarterly*, 7:3 (1999), 319–27.

11 R. Hill, *Lord Acton* (New Haven, Yale University Press, 2000), p. 322.

12 R. N. Soffer, 'Intellectuals and intellectual history', *Journal of British Studies*, 39:4 (2000), 529.

13 Russell's opposition has been sensitively explored by J. Vellacott, *Bertrand Russell and the Pacifists in the First World War* (Brighton, Harvester, 1980).

14 On the overwhelming support of academics and writers for Britain's participation in the First World War, see S. Wallace, *War and the Image of Germany: British Academics, 1914–1918* (Edinburgh, John Donald, 1988).

15 May Cannan, daughter of the Secretary to the Oxford University Press delegates – and niece of the economist Edwin Cannan – accused Lady Ottoline Morrell of 'opting out' in a very moving memoir of her youth. May Wedderburn Cannan, *Grey Ghosts and Voices* (Kineton, The Roundwood Press, 1976), pp. 113–14. The younger members of the elite social set of Edwardian Britain known as the 'souls' – whose 'philosopher-king' was no less a figure than the former Conservative Prime Minister Arthur Balfour – were equally supportive of the war, albeit on a 'romantic' plane. See J. Mackenzie, *The Children of the Souls: A Tragedy of the First World War* (London, Chatto & Windus, 1986).

16   See Simon Heffer, *Vaughan Williams* (London, Weidenfeld & Nicolson, 2000).

17   M. Grimley, *Citizenship, Community and the Church of England: Anglican Theories of the State, c. 1926–1939*, PhD dissertation, University of Oxford, 1998.

18   J. Stapleton, *Englishness and the Study of Politics: The Social and Political Thought of Ernest Barker* (Cambridge, Cambridge University Press, 1994); and 'Political thought and national identity in Britain, 1850–1950', in S. Collini, R. Whatmore and B. Young (eds), *History, Religion, and Culture: British Intellectual History, 1750–1950* (Cambridge, Cambridge University Press, 2000), pp. 245–69. For an account of 'the rise of English' as the wellspring of national identity in the early decades of the twentieth century, see B. Doyle, *English and Englishness* (London, Routledge, 1989). On the imperial claims that came to be made for English – as an 'arbiter' not just of national identity but 'social thought' more widely – see the discussion by S. Collini in 'How the critic came to be King', *The Times Literary Supplement*, 8 September 2000, pp. 11–12.

19   D. Dean, 'The dilemmas of an academic liberal historian in Lloyd George's government: H. A. L. Fisher at the Board of Education, 1916–1922', *History*, 79 (1994), 57–81.

20   J. Jennings and A. Kemp-Welch, 'The century of the intellectual: from the Dreyfus Affair to Salman Rushdie', in Jennings and Kemp-Welch (eds), *Intellectuals in Politics*, p. 3.

21   N. Annan, *Our Age: The Generation that Made Postwar Britain* (London, Fontana, [1990] 1991), p. 485.

22   Obituary, *The Daily Telegraph*, 24 February 2000, p. 33.

23   Annan, *Our Age*, pp. 43–4.

24   N. Annan, '*Our Age* revisited', in W. R. Louis (ed.), *More Adventures with Britannia: Personalities, Politics, and Culture in Britain* (Austin, University of Texas Press, 1998), pp. 277–8.

25   On the desertion of this duty by intellectuals and other elites – business, artistic and scientific – in an America plagued by postmodernist discourse and practice, see Christopher Lasch's compelling study, *The Revolt of the Elites and the Betrayal of Democracy* (New York, W. W. Norton, 1995).

26   H. A. L. Fisher, *James Bryce (Viscount Bryce of Dechmont, O. M.)* 2 vols, I (London, Macmillan, 1927), p. 184.

27   See Ernest Barker, 'Gandhi, as bridge and reconciler', in S. Radhakrishnan (ed.), *Mahatma Gandhi: Essays and Reflections on his Life and Work* (London, George Allen & Unwin, 1939), pp. 58–62.

28   For example, Gandhi admired Gladstone; Sun Yat-Sen learned from his teacher the Scotsman James Cantlie; and Nehru drew strength from Trevelyan's studies of Garibaldi. See N. Scott, 'The influence of british political thought in China and India: the cases of Sun Yat-Sen, Mahatma Gandhi and Jawaharlal Nehru', PhD thesis, University of Durham, 2000.

29   See, for example, G. Clark, P. Vaucher and E. Barker (eds), *The European Inheritance* (Oxford, Clarendon Press, 1954).

30   For example, Geoffrey Wheatcroft, Minette Marrin, Daniel Johnson, Simon Heffer, Simon Jenkins, and Peter Hitchens.

31   R. Bellamy, 'The intellectual as social critic: Antonio Gramsci and Michael Walzer', in Jennings and Kemp-Welch (eds) *Intellectuals in Politics*, p. 31.

32 Coleridge's opposition in the early nineteenth century between the national and the provincial is remarked upon by H. S. Jones, *Victorian Political Thought* (London, Macmillan, 2000), p. 22.

33 As J. H. Grainger has written of the early twentieth century, 'the consciousness of Britain was predominantly English. England, as J. G. A. Pocock has written, paradigmatically defined the pattern by which the British thought . . . In the matter of Britain the consciousness of England dominated even among the Welsh and the Scots,' Grainger, *Patriotisms: Britain 1900–1940* (London, Routledge, 1986), p. 53.

Part I

The late Victorian inheritance

The rich creativeness of Victorian politics and statesmanship has been explored in fascinating detail by J. H. Grainger. Writing in 1969, when a diametrically opposite political world seemed lamentably apparent, Grainger emphasised the energy and conviction of nineteenth-century politicians and their success in grounding the activity of politics securely in the idea of a public interest. Grainger maintained that, at the dawn of the era of democratic politics, the versatile British politician found the potentially conflicting spheres of party, parliament and nation easily reconcilable. Drawing upon the writings of Sir Ernest Barker in the 1940s, he identified party as a particularly fertile source of the politician's basis of power in the country, inspiring political debate and producing 'a succession of contrasted yet complementary statesmen who diversify and enrich the general national record.'[1] Before parliament became simply a seal on policies which had been worked out previously by specialist ministers, civil servants and interest groups, 'parliamentarianism was based on the assumption that political questions could be resolved in the same way as proposals in a debating society'.[2] The result was that public life acquired 'a repute which it had never had before and has never had since'.[3]

This presumed heyday of the English politician coincided with the heyday of the British intellectual, particularly during the third quarter of the nineteenth century. Like the politician of Grainger's historical imagination, the intellectual was greatly animated by the notion of a public interest whose meaning he sought to amplify through wide and earnest debate, not least in the redoubtable periodical press of mid Victorian Britain.[4] The high intellectual and national ideals which informed the latter are well illustrated in the opening sentences of the first issue of the Unitarian journal *The National Review* in 1855. Its editor, R. H. Hutton, wrote that

> The Periodical Press has many high functions and many solemn obligations. To it belongs the duty of courageous but temperate exposition of national grievances, and the ready reception, the conscientious sifting, and the cautious publication of individual wrongs. To it belongs the privilege of protecting the weak against oppression and rescuing the obscure from oblivion or neglect. It has to tear the mask from successful charlatanry, to expose incapacity where incapacity has been foisted into dangerous and unseemly eminence, and to denounce iniquity and corruption in those high places where only purity and principle should reign. It has to allay popular passion when excessive or astray, and to moderate popular expectations when rushing into wild and irrational schemes. It is sometimes called upon to interpose to save victims as well as to point out criminals, to mitigate the severity of the sentence as well as to furnish evidence and insist upon a trial. It has often to plead the cause of high principle and of common sense in an arena where both are too apt to be trodden under foot. And, most frequently of all, are efforts needed to remind legislators and statesmen of those great objects which are so incessantly smothered and lost sight of in the confused multiplicity of small details and daily strife.[5]

As this manifesto would suggest, intellectuals such as Hutton felt duty-bound to rise above the everyday political fray to address the needs of the nation more widely. Yet, to a large degree, their motivation lay in reaction against the apparent failure of politicians to assert their independence from the popular movements and sectarian interests of a modern democratic society. The post-Reform era of British politics seemed far less healthy to contemporary intellectuals than to those who looked back upon it as a Golden Age from the era of political stalemate after the Second World War. The hallmarks of the earlier age, as perceived at the time, were fundamentally those of political fragmentation and the exploitation of popular sentiments. Far from praising the party system, as Barker was to do in the middle of the twentieth century, those intellectuals such as Sir John Seeley who came of age in the 1870s and 1880s were openly nostalgic for the weak party ties of earlier decades. Looking back to the period of Evangelical reform, in which his father had been a keen participant, Seeley admired the initiative which elites had been able to take in social improvement such as the introduction of factory legislation, unencumbered by the rigidities of party divisions. As Deborah Wormell has argued, Seeley's study of national history – as focused through diplomacy and foreign policy – was a conscious mechanism for overcoming party conflict in the late nineteenth century.[6] His support for Ethical Societies just before his death in 1895 was premised upon a similar understanding.[7]

It is clear from the work of Jeffrey Von Arx that other leading intellectuals of Seeley's age – Leslie Stephen, John Morley, William Lecky and James Froude – were equally dismayed by the hold of party on the popular mind.[8] For Morley, under this stimulus, the political spirit of 'respect[ing] what is instantly practicable' was becoming increasingly divorced from the intellectual spirit of pursuing truth for its own sake.[9] In the view of such leading intellectual liberals, the grip of party on popular thinking owed much to the play of sectional clerical interests associated with the resurgence of Roman Catholicism and the High Church party in the Church of England. They had feared the pernicious influence of the latter in the 1850s and 1860s, an anxiety which proved well grounded after the passage of the 1870 Education Act.[10] Morley's opposition to the combined forces of religious sect and political party underpinned his considerable sympathy for the Oxford Movement. Despite his entrenched agnosticism, he hailed the latter for daring to challenge 'the undisturbed way of the majority as the way of salvation'.[11]

The foundation of the intellectual's growing authority in society after 1850 in an animus against religious orders was explained by a writer in *The Nineteenth Century* in 1877. He was sympathetic to the Church's ministry but was under no illusion about the role it had played in its own decline, particularly the declining authority of the pulpit. The priest as preacher had sounded his own death-knell by overstepping his domain, assuming that

> the place of theology in the sphere of man's knowledge . . . confers the right of speaking with a certain decision on all kinds of topics; . . . there has always been a sort of omniscient tone in the pulpit method of handling intellectual questions which stirs fierce rebellion in cultivated minds and hearts.[12]

The author admitted that this theological arrogance was particularly intolerable in a 'scientific' age.

Not so much arrogance as the Church's acute sense of vulnerability was also recognised as unacceptable and unnecessary by Lord Acton, a leading Catholic intellectual who attempted to bring English Catholicism out of its spiritual ghetto in mid Victorian Britain, not least through urging its engagement with, rather than denunciation of, contemporary intellectual culture, heavily rooted as it was in science. While Acton failed to carry the English Catholic Church with him, closing the *Home and Foreign Review* in which he had promoted his ideas after just eight issues in 1864 and having incurred the full wrath of the Holy See, he assumed a place of high honour among the secular intelligentsia.[13]

The new generation of agnostic liberals who attacked the Church attempted to justify the imperatives of rationalism and explain why they had become so systematically eschewed at its expense. One may doubt, however, whether their emancipation from religious categories and ideals was as complete as they believed. This is clear in Morley's reference to the need for 'truth' and the ignominy of 'error'; the contempt in which intellectual (i.e. secular) 'zeal, faith, and . . . trenchancy' is currently held; the inferiority of 'the disciples of the relative' (i.e. compromise) to 'the disciples of the absolute' (i.e. truth); and majority opinion as 'superstition'.[14]

Intellectuals reached a greater accommodation with organised religion, democracy and party politics towards the end of the nineteenth century. Their ideas became less militantly secular in tone, and their social ideals more solidly rooted in popular aspirations and tendencies. They aimed to confer intellectual coherence and public significance on the latter, which would be elevated at the same time. For example, it was said of Thomas Hill Green by a fellow Balliol college tutor of the late 1860s that 'He was drawn to plain people, to people of the middle and lower class rather than of the upper, to the puritans of the past and the nonconformists of the present, to Germans, to all that is sober-suited and steady-going.'[15] Accordingly, 'the common good' which his political philosophy enshrined was imbued with the efforts of humanity to realise larger and non-material ideals through executing the duties of everyday life.

Yet whether expressed through negative or positive attitudes towards democracy, it is clear that intellectuals assumed greater importance with its advent, and at the expense of the clerical class with whom they now competed for cultural authority in an age dominated by a crisis of faith. Those among the clerical class – such as the *Lux Mundi* group which emerged in High Church circles in 1889 – whom they carried with them conceded more in terms of doctrine than they received in turn from philosophies such as Idealism which anchored an ethic of self-sacrifice in Christian example rather than theology and worship.[16] In essence, British intellectuals attempted to correct democracy's divisive and manipulative potentialities through assuming custodianship of a truly 'national' culture rooted in an ethic of free thought, duty, and the disciplined cultivation of both private and public well-being. They may have formed something of the order of a self-perpetuating elite, whose impact on the lives of the non-university population was limited accordingly.[17] At the highest level, their custodial role was played out in parliament; failing that, in intellectual intimacy with members of the governing class, who shared a common educational and professional background with the leading thinkers of the day.[18] But their widening impact from the beginning of the twentieth century through Extension Lectures and writings for an emergent 'middlebrow' public was not insignificant; nor did it always lack depth and diversity.[19] Furthermore, their aim to introduce aristocratic virtues into democracy was laudable, and something for which many worked tirelessly. It was certainly recognised as such by foreign observers such as Wilhelm Dibelius after the First World War, and, moreover, as a peculiarly English quality.[20] In turn British intellectuals such as A. D. Lindsay were greatly strengthened in the pursuit of this goal by reflections of themselves in such foreign mirrors. They were fully aware, as Lindsay expressed the matter in his farewell speech as Master of Balliol in 1949, that the 'prepar[ation] of the governing class to play its part in a classless society' was far from complete. But, he argued,

> surely a democracy without aristocratic virtues, without a high sense of quality and distinction, and something corresponding to noblesse oblige, becomes, as Plato said long ago, and as we have sadly experienced, a tyranny; and an aristocracy which is not inspired by democratic ideals becomes selfish and arrogant, and eventually decadent and inefficient.[21]

The public role of intellectuals was enhanced by three characteristics that they developed after 1850: an aspiration towards scholarship that was widely accessible; a marked homogeneity of purpose and outlook; and a strong sense of English/British national identity. These features of British intellectuals in the decades following the Second Reform Act will provide the structure of discussion in Chapter 1. The survival, although shifting basis, of these characteristics in the 'civic' context of Edwardian political thought will form the subject of Chapter 2.

Notes

1 E. Barker, 'British statesmen', in *Essays on Government* (Oxford, Clarendon Press, [1945] 1951), p. 32.
2 J. H. Grainger, *Character and Style in English Politics* (Cambridge, Cambridge University Press, 1969), p. 15.
3 Grainger, *Character and Style*, p. 10.
4 Quoting M. M. Bevington, author of a study of *The Saturday Review*, John Roach has written that, 'By the 1850s journalism had ceased to be mere hackwork, and had become . . . "the chosen means of expression, partly vocation and partly avocation, of brilliant young men who wished to influence public opinion."'; Roach, 'Liberalism and the Victorian intelligentsia' (1957), reprinted in P. Stansky (ed.), *Government and Society in Victoria's Britain* (New York, New Viewpoints, 1973), p. 327.

5   'On the just and the unjust in the recent popular discontent', *The National Review*, 1:1 (1855), 1.

6   D. Wormell, *Sir John Seeley and the Uses of History* (Cambridge, Cambridge University Press, 1980), pp. 138, 131.

7   J. Seeley, 'Ethics and religion', in The Society of Ethical Propagandists (ed.), *Ethics and Religion* (London, Swan Sonnenschein, 1900), pp. 23–5.

8   J. P. Von Arx, *Progress and Pessimism: Religion, Politics, and History in Late Nineteenth Century Britain* (Cambridge, Ma., Harvard University Press, 1985), p. 8.

9   J. Morley, *On Compromise*, ed. J. Powell (Edinburgh, Keele University Press, [1874] 1997), p. 98.

10 Von Arx, *Progress and Pessimism*, p. 8.

11 Morley, *On Compromise*, pp. 100–1.

12 J. Baldwin Brown, 'Is the pulpit losing its power?', *The Nineteenth Century*, I (1877), 109–10.

13 R. Hill, *Lord Acton* (New Haven, Yale University Press, 2000), pp. 122–3, 138. Matthew Arnold's tribute to Acton is quoted on p. 153. Acton, of course, became a confidante of Gladstone, and in 1895 Regius Professor of Modern History at Cambridge.

14 Morley, *On Compromise*, pp. 60, 75, 101.

15 R. L. Nettleship (ed.), *Works of Thomas Hill Green*, 3 vols, III (London, Longman, 1889), p. lxii.

16 M. Richter, *The Politics of Conscience: T. H. Green and his Age* (Bristol, Thoemmes Press, [1964] 1996), ch. 4, esp. pp. 122–35.

17 Reba N. Soffer, *Discipline and Power: The University, History, and the Making of an English Elite, 1870–1930* (Stanford, Stanford University Press, 1994), p. 205.

18 S. Collini, *Public Moralists: Political Thought and Intellectual Life in Britain, 1850–1930* (Oxford, Clarendon Press, 1991), pp. 33–4.

19 To take just three examples, the private papers of A. D. Lindsay (Keele), Ernest Barker (Peterhouse, Cambridge) and A. E. Zimmern (Oxford), testify to the range of individuals, organisations, and publications they served. Their writings also testify to significant diversity and, frequently, depth, contrary to the suggestion of Reba Soffer that 'dissent, independent or reflective thought, and critical, subversive analysis were not encouraged because greater value was given to a stable, common culture justified by a historical evolution of personal and communal goods'; *Discipline and Power*, p. 206. Considerable divergence emerged over the interpretation of this 'stable common culture', even among historians. The historical scholarship of George Unwin, educated at Oxford and Professor of Economic History at Manchester from 1910 to 1926, is a case in point. See J. Stapleton, 'English pluralism as cultural definition: the social and political thought of George Unwin', *Journal of the History of Ideas*, 52:4 (1991), 665–84.

20 W. Dibelius, *England*, trs. M. A. Hamilton, introduced by A. D. Lindsay (London, Jonathan Cape, [1922] 1930).

21 A. D. Lindsay, 'The Master's letter', Balliol College, September 1949, Lindsay Papers, Keele University Library, L179.

1

Public scholarship, professional homogeneity and patriotism: the emergence of a national intelligentsia

I

The search of an emergent intellectual elite for influence peaked in the last quarter of the nineteenth century. In this period intellectuals perceived themselves as scholars whose first duty was to educate the newly literate and political classes of late Victorian Britain. They framed their interests and activities accordingly. On the one hand, they were polymaths who straddled across the disciplinary barriers of the humanities with comparative ease; on the other, they engaged fully in the wider activities of public life, performing a variety of work which their scholarship both informed and was stimulated by in turn. This era of close integration between the worlds of thought and action has been illuminated by Asa Briggs in his study of Seebohm Rowntree, and more recently by Stefan Collini in exploring the close connections between the intellectual, professional and governing elite of the second half of the nineteenth century.[1] An exemplar of this world was Lord Bryce, of whom it was said at his death that he occupied

> a unique position in the esteem of his fellow countrymen. He was, as it were, their moral referee, and his judgement on any question of public morality was accepted without question. His position was due not only to his wide experience, his extraordinary knowledge and natural impartiality. It was, I suppose, the deep moral purpose which directed every thought and every action of his life.[2]

So prominent a role for intellectuals in the public life of their country is explained in large part by the persistence of the clerisy ideal of S. T. Coleridge earlier in the century, whether consciously embraced, as in the case of John Stuart Mill and Matthew Arnold, or as the assumption underlying a particular, hierarchical model of interaction between the learned and ignorant in society. Seeley well illustrates the latter form in which the clerisy was advocated. He brought forward the Coleridgean heritage, as it had developed through the Broad Church tradition of Liberal Anglicanism associated with Thomas Arnold and F. D. Maurice, to the end of the nineteenth century, and applied it to an age that was fast losing its religious faith.[3] Shortly before his death in 1895 he wrote that 'there is a gap, there is a wheel wanting in our machinery of culture. We have an apparatus for the discovery and testing of truth and an apparatus for communicating it to a certain small part of the people, but no apparatus for spreading it everywhere.'[4] On this model, the clerisy ideal became the means for rehabilitating religion, although in such a way that the personal and social aspects of the latter were obscured in the vision of national greatness it was primarily made to serve.[5]

After their reform in the middle of the century, the universities assumed a key role in turning the energies of intellectuals to good public account. Oxford, in particular, came to pride itself upon the ease of access to the public ear enjoyed by its graduates, not least those who had been trained in *Literae Humaniores* or 'Greats'.[6] Certainly, the universities of Oxford and Cambridge dominated the landscape of higher education, providing a model of liberal education to which many of the new civic universities of the nineteenth century aspired. Manchester and Liverpool, in particular, pursued a broad balance of arts and science subjects, eschewing the narrowly technical curricula of Birmingham, Sheffield and Leeds.[7] They received precious little encouragement from their institutional betters: writing of his undergraduate days at Oxford in the 1880s H. A. L. Fisher recalled that the new universities hardly touched the consciousness of his contemporaries.[8] Nevertheless, the consensus which prevailed across the intelligentsia that the aim of the university was to produce men (and women[9]) of character, intelligence and high sense of duty rather than 'intellectuals' considerably softened the ambitions of leading thinkers to assert any claim to the possession of esoteric, 'abstract' knowledge. This was despite increasing pressure from more knowledge-based criteria on the concept of a liberal education as 'preparation for life' or 'living with others' which the Georgians had bequeathed to the Victorians.[10] The influence of great Oxford humanists such as J. H. Newman, Benjamin Jowett and Mark Pattison ensured that the German ideal of *Wissenschaft* – however attractive – was harnessed to an ideal of general culture which alone made specialist fields of inquiry intelligible. This implied continued commitment to the inspirational communication of received truth.[11] Their attitudes and values permeated the learned professions of medicine and the law, as well as those of government and administration. In those areas, apprenticeship and practical experience following the traditional liberal education of the university became the preferred alternative to the narrowness and pedantry associated with specialised professional education. In time, this intellectual foundation came to be appreciated by the newer occupations of engineering, accountancy, architecture and dentistry too. Even when pressures increased to introduce professional subjects into the university in the 1860s and 1870s – not least, in response to German industrial competitiveness – their more theoretical side was cultivated in accordance with traditional values in British higher education.[12]

As Christopher Stray has pointed out in relation to classics, the shift from liberal education to 'liberal learning' (scholarship) was accomplished through attempts to relativize value rather than method – insisting on the rigour, discipline, and authority of the latter rather than the subject-matter of specific disiplines such as classics.[13] Yet assumptions of value remained central to academic scholarship, particularly in response to the continuing concerns in schools for classics as a benchmark of status. The decline of an Anglican consensus among elites in British society led not to the downgrading of the classical education on which it was based but to the new role of the latter as the 'semi-sacred substitute' for, rather than handmaiden of, religion. This was achieved in large part by liberal scholars such as Gilbert Murray – inspired by the approach to Greek tragedy of the Cambridge classicist, Jane Harrison, which emphasised the progressive process at work in the classical world rather than the reified status of the latter as a fixed and unrepeatable human attainment. The humanities more generally came to be included in this scheme for studying the emergence of a transcendent ideal in society in the cause of human betterment. This was particularly the case when classics came under threat, not only from rival forms of human inquiry but more seriously from the physical sciences following the perceived success of German superiority in this field during the First World War. In the aftermath of the First World War Bryce could thus stress the nature of the university as 'Organised Thought, organised for practical as well as for theoretic aims . . . Universities exist largely for the purpose of clarifying and testing not only ideas but schemes looking to the moral and social welfare of mankind. Whatever strengthens them and extends their influence, benefits a nation.'[14] Along with Fisher, Murray and John Mackail, Bryce campaigned vigorously for the preservation of classics, albeit in specialist public and grammar schools and with Latin rather than Greek as their exemplar.[15]

Bryce's conception of the role of the university reflects an acute sense among members of the intellectual elite that they were as much public servants as those whom they regarded the duty of universities to nurture for the high offices of church and state. A classic instance in this regard is G. P. Gooch. Gooch was an eminent historian, trained by no less a figure than Lord Acton. But while a much acclaimed scholar – for example, he was elected a Fellow of the British Academy – he fulfilled a lifelong 'sense of mission' to society through social work, as a Member of Parliament, and as Editor for fifty years of one of the few surviving Victorian periodicals, *The Contemporary Review*. As Gooch's biographer has written, 'his historical work was closely connected with and nourished by his other activities'.[16]

The strong motive of public service is also evident in the ambition which intellectuals entertained of educating their fellow citizens by example as well as by opinions propagated through writings which achieved wide circulation. For instance, Leslie Stephen, in concluding the biography of his brother, James Fitzjames Stephen, found himself lamenting that the capacities of so able a mind had been ill-spent on 'comparatively ephemeral objects' and incomplete projects. Yet, suppressing his regrets in order to end on an appropriately positive note, he remarked,

> It often appears to me . . . that a man does good less by his writings or by the mark
> which he may make upon public affairs than by simply being himself. The impres-
> sion made upon his contemporaries by a man of strong and noble character is
> something which cannot be precisely estimated, but which we often feel to be inval-
> uable.[17]

Where influence through a great work had failed, it was evidently thought that
biography could succeed.[18]

The aspiration of intellectuals towards disinterested public service – by deeds
as well as words – was especially characteristic of an emergent profession of
political thinkers and scientists. Significantly, the latter were not the exclusive
occupiers of a distinct disciplinary domain. Rather, in the ill-defined state of
academic boundaries at the turn of the century which particularly affected
Politics, the subject was developed by classicists, sociologists, philosophers, historians and lawyers. The sustained amorphousness of academic political science
in turn generated a broad interest in political debate. As Jose Harris has
remarked,

> Down to the 1930s in Britain political theorising of one kind and another occurred
> not merely in an academic context; it was virtually a national sport of British intel-
> lectuals of all ideological and professional complexions. It was engaged in not just
> by professors of philosophy and by practising statesmen, but by economists, his-
> torians, scientists, doctors, clergymen, social workers, soldiers, business men,
> labour leaders, fellow-travellers and a host of others who saw themselves as having
> a finger in the pie of the body politic.[19]

In leading public dicussion of things political, the position of academic political
thinkers during the first half of the twentieth century came to resemble that
which an increasingly specialist community of historians had lately abandoned:
the ideal of literary scholars who sought to influence public opinion in the widest
possible sense. While a new generation of academic historians at the turn of the
century did not abnegate such a role, as Rosemary Jann has shown, they now
pursued it indirectly – through provision of the moral and mental resources by
which a 'liberally educated ruling class could command society'.[20] As conducted
under a variety of academic umbrellas, political science in the universities shared
this dispensation. But at the same time its practitioners joined a rump of historians from Belloc to G. M. Trevelyan and Churchill – and including Gooch – who
were institutionally independent.[21] These figures maintained contact with a
public that stretched well beyond, while at the same time including, the privileged elite and even professional scholars.[22] This shared sense of purpose is clear,
for instance, in the role which political thinkers such as John Stuart Blackie and
Henry Jones played in staunching the separatist tendencies of celtic nationalism
in Scotland and Wales in the late ninetenth and early twentieth centuries.[23]
Inspired by the 'organicist' imperatives of the political philosophy of Idealism
and also historicist visions of the community of the land, these thinkers pursued
the same twin goals of intellectual accessibility and national inclusiveness as the

'amateur' historians of mid to late Victorian Britain: Thomas Arnold, T. B. Macaulay and Edward Freeman, for instance.

II

The success of intellectuals as 'public' thinkers is intimately linked to the solidarity and common sense of purpose which prevailed between them. They enjoyed close personal, professional and family links, broadly shared the same values and concerns and, perhaps of greatest importance, were united in a commitment to liberalism, which became almost a definitional aspect of intellectual life at the end of the nineteenth century. It was, however, in a large number of cases a commitment which became increasingly at odds with political Liberalism as the latter seemed to career down a populist Gladstonian path, particularly after 1886. This was despite Morley's vehement defence of Gladstone's liberal project in his biographical monument to the latter published in 1903, a work which sold 130,000 copies in ten years.[24] As John Roach has argued, the once 'exalted political principles' of mid Victorian liberalism – the emphasis on reform and efficient government so admired by prominent liberal intellectuals and politicians such as Robert Lowe – seemed to have become employed in the justification of 'self-interested conclusions'.[25] The New Liberalism offered intellectuals the opportunity to return to, and reshape, Liberalism as a political force along the lines of a non-sectarian creed which recognised the disabilities individuals might suffer in an unstructured market society. But not only did old doubts resurface about the need to maintain the purity of such quintessential liberal values as truth, conviction and personal responsibility if its civilising mission was to be accomplished; the new, more egalitarian face of intellectual liberalism often disguised a 'continuing, gut-level confidence in the traditional governing classes'.[26]

This unity of the intellectual elite was maintained in the face of sharp differences over such controversial issues as democracy, religion and the extension of the state, both in relation to national society and to Britain's empire overseas. It was especially fostered by the growth of undergraduate societies devoted to intellectual inquiry in the universities, such as the Old Mortality at Oxford and more famously that of the Apostles at Cambridge. In turn, the Apostles and other literary figures helped to make Letters a central and harmonising feature of cultural and political life through their membership of the London clubs and their contributions to leading periodicals and reviews.[27] Since the formative influence of F. D. Maurice the Apostles had encouraged the utmost sympathy with opposing opinions in select and intimate company.[28] The period between 1854 and 1871 witnessed the erosion of the Anglican monopoly of the universities, a development which greatly enhanced the development of a sense of common identity among the intellectual elite. The contrast with an earlier generation of intellectuals whose university links were necessarily looser is apparent in a remark of John Stuart Mill in a letter to Maurice in 1865:

> I sympathize with the feeling of (if I may so call it) mental loneliness which shews itself in your letter & sometimes in your published writings. In our age and country, every person with any mental power at all, who both thinks for himself and has a conscience, must feel himself to a very great degree alone.

Significantly, however, Mill went on to assert that:

> I sh[d] think you have decidedly more people who are in real communion of thoughts, feelings & purposes with you than I have. I am in this supremely happy, that I have had, & even now have, that communion in the fullest degree where it is most valuable of all, in my home. But I have it nowhere else . . .[29]

Maurice's Broad Church views were no less repugnant in some circles than the free-thinking opinions of Mill. But even though he was Mill's contemporary, his university base and the network of intellectual companionship and support which this spawned were chief factors in the very different circumstances of the two men at a time when religious controversy was at its most intense.

Again, it is Bryce who best strikes the new, more consensual temper of the intellectuals who came of age in the 1860s; for example, the authors who were clustered around *Essays on Reform* of 1867. His book, *Studies in Contemporary Biography*, which was published in 1903, reviewed the life and work of a wide range of contemporary thinkers and politicians, many of whom could not have been more distant from his own intellectual and political circles. Yet there was not one to whom he took exception for serving causes that seemed alien to him. The term most used in connection with his subjects is 'warmth'. Even Cardinal Manning – something of a hate-figure for James Fitzjames Stephen, who represented the deep hostility of many British intellectuals towards Catholicism in the 1860s[30] – could be praised thus: 'he sincerely cared about temperance, the welfare of children, the advancement of the labouring class, and *the greatness of England*.'[31] The characteristically generous tone of the book is explained by H. A. L. Fisher in terms which illuminate the leading role which the universities played in British intellectual culture at the turn of the century, and the social as much as the intellectual source of this influence. Bryce, claimed his biographer,

> was full of the minor loyalties. It counted with him that a man should have come from Ulster or Glasgow, that he should have been a scholar of Trinity or a Fellow of Oriel . . . These pleasant preferences and partialities, albeit tempered by the cooling fluid of experience, Bryce preserved with that constancy which the corporate tradition in British educational life does so much to promote.[32]

These small but overlapping circles of loyalty provided powerful intellectual cement, especially before new divisions spawned by academic specialisation began to weaken their force.

Despite the homogeneity of background and outlook which drew late Victorian intellectuals together, they were not impervious to outside contacts and influences. The periodical press which provided much of their food for thought evinces an astonishing array of contributors, extending – most notably – to foreign intellectuals resident in London and pleading such diverse political causes as that of democracy, national independence, socialism, anarchy and a free European Church.[33] Also, members of the British intellectual elite readily engaged, for example, with the ideas of Herbert Spencer, whose agnosticism and liberalism – albeit with very different intellectual roots – touched their own beliefs at crucial points. Henry Sidgwick, Leslie Stephen, T. H. Huxley and J. S. Mill are only a few of the many examples which could be given of leading Victorian thinkers who took seriously Spencer's utilitarian and evolutionary theories. Spencer, characteristically, rarely returned the compliment of this attention, and declined all invitations from the ruling elite which would compromise in any way his political and social nonconformism.[34]

The openness of the intellectual elite is also illustrated in its patronage of Sir James Knowles, who fulfilled something akin to the role of their agent in his capacity as founder of the Metaphysical Society (1868) and the periodical *The Nineteenth Century* (1877). By profession an architect with few initial connections to the great minds of Victorian England, Knowles was never a scholar. But he achieved extraordinary influence, not only with the foremost intellectuals of his day but also among royalty, whom he frequently entertained at his London home. As a facilitator, it has been said that he 'not only assemble[d] but . . . unite[d] for years on end the best brains in England', and was able to do so through an 'infallible grasp of the uncertain temper of his age'.[35] The entrance which Knowles made into the circles of the intellectual elite was mirrored by John Morley and in the twentieth century by scholars such as Sir Ernest Barker, George Unwin and A. L. Rowse – the first recruit to All Souls from the ranks of the working class. But the openness of this elite was conditional upon acceptance of its clear intellectual standards: wide learning – a requirement that was maintained even in the early stages of specialisation – and the eschewal of doctrine and political associations that required the suspension of intellectual autonomy. As Joseph Hamburger noted some time ago, and drawing on an approving observation by Walter Bagehot for support, doctrinaire politics have been the exception rather than the rule in Britain, and have been invariably short-lived.[36] An 'outsider' such as Rajani Palme Dutt ruled himself out of Britain's intellectual elite in the interwar period, not on account of his ancestral roots in the dependent empire but because of his intimate association with the Communist Party in the interwar period. Although a Greats graduate with a gift for languages, his belief expressed in 1930 that 'First and foremost he [the intellectual] *should forget that he is an intellectual* (except in moments of necessary self-criticism) *and remember only that he is a Communist . . . such as any other Party member*'[37] was the antithesis of the belief that intellectuals should serve wider causes than narrow party interest. This was maintained even on the left, providing the basis of the (New Left) revolt of E. P. Thompson against such 'King Street intellectuals' as Dutt in the 1960s.[38]

III

A broad and deeply felt patriotism is another marked characteristic of English intellectuals after 1850, one which lasted up until 1914 and, although subject to increased challenge thereafter, retained much of its former buoyancy well into the twentieth century. Here, the reformed universities led the way, infusing a gentlemanly ideal of liberal education as the cultivation of mind and taste with patriotic purpose as a means of safeguarding their power and independence.[39] Patriotism was by no means absent earlier in the nineteenth century: as the basis of a commitment to liberty and constitutionalism, it provided powerful fuel for the movements of Catholic Emancipation and political and social reform in the 1820s and 1830s.[40] It was also, as Paul Langford has convincingly argued in a recent landmark study, 'drenched in self-characterization. The cult of John Bull, assiduously promoted from at least the 1790s, had no parallel elsewhere.'[41] But in the 1840s, a patriotism that was strongly rooted in a conception of the exceptional nature of English historical development (and not just English character) rather than the pursuit of a transnational ideal of freedom emerged in the popular historical writings of T. B. Macaulay, albeit within a Scottish Enlightenment framework of the 'progress of civilisation' which embraced all nations, at however low a stage. This converged with a Coleridgean ideal of nationhood within an organic state – actively engaged subsequently by liberal Anglicans such as Thomas Arnold – that was beginning to eclipse the individualist and interest philosophy of early nineteenth century utilitarians and evangelicals, now regarded as inadequate social plinths. Again, the nation provided a stepping-stone to a universal, divine order rather than a negation of the latter, although its particularity was heavily underscored.[42] Macaulay's work was loudly acclaimed, and nowhere more so than in the *Saturday Review* following his death in 1859. There, James Fitzjames Stephen instantly discounted criticisms of Macaulay's work as 'narrow and shallow'. He could neither 'regret nor wonder at its popularity'. Had Macaulay lived to complete his *History of England*, Stephen hypothesised, the outcome would have been 'not indeed the greatest of histories, but a book which would have done more than almost any other to delight his countrymen, and to teach them to love as he did the land over which he rejoiced and exulted with an admiration as passionate as it was manly'.[43]

Stephen is an important figure in the development of English patriotism in the nineteenth century.[44] Not only did he draw a close and explicit connection between patriotism and a socially – if not, regretably for him, a religiously – inclusive English nation; he also applied this potent dual force to a vigorous defence of the empire, particularly post-Mutiny India. The courageous response of the entire British community in defending the garrisons at Lucknow and Cawnpore itself exemplified the vast hidden resources of the national character, giving the lie to Mill's conception of its studied mediocrity.[45] Events at these two garrisons confirmed Stephen's sense that the British Empire in India was wholly justified as the modern successor to *Pax Romana* in bringing order and justice – and all the 'arts of life' they made possible – to the unruly populations of the East. Stephen had no compunction in comparing the Indian peoples to the Jews, '"a people terrible from the beginning", and most terrible of all in matters of religion'. Given the awesome task bestowed upon his compatriots (he does not say by whom, or what), he could confidently declare unenviable 'the Englishman whose heart does not beat high as he looks at the scarred and shattered walls of Delhi or at the union jack flying from the fort at Lahore'.[46]

The weight of the analogy with Rome suggests that, for Stephen, empire was far more than just a consequence of accidental forces such as favourable geographical position. In this respect, he points forward to Seeley in the 1880s, for whom the recent movement of domestic reform was entirely peripheral when compared with the main and exclusive theme of modern English history – the foundation of a 'Greater Britain'. The destiny of the latter, Seeley felt sure, 'will not be decreed arbitrarily' but was already written into the historical record and required only painstaking commitment to the discovery of the laws by which it was governed for its meaning to become apparent, and the public mind – and common sense of nationhood – concentrated.[47] Stephen's deployment of the rhetoric of patriotism, like Seeley's, was focused squarely on the virtues of the English as an imperial race, and constituted in large part a reaction against radical liberalism's indifference to, and sometimes contempt for, country in its zeal to institute popular rule.[48] In the face of this development, Stephen's patriotism may be seen as an attempt to convert the *individual* pride that Englishmen had increasingly taken in being English over the previous two centuries into the *collective* national pride that could be found in France.[49] Stephen here took the language of patriotism far beyond the political characteristics of the nation outlined by Burke and which, Peter Mandler has argued, continued to provide the limits of the English sense of nationhood in mid Victorian political thought.[50] At the same time, Stephen did so by using the products of what little elite interest there had been in English history in early Victorian Britain – for example, the work of Macaulay and Hallam on the constitutional history of the country since the seventeenth century – to stimulate a much wider and deferential appreciation. With evident concern for the poor esteem in which the upper classes were held, he asserted in his essay on liberalism in 1862, 'A powerful and splendid aristocracy is to a nation what his house and grounds, his picture gallery and library, are to a nobleman.'[51] The revival of elite history would counteract the growing tendency for historical studies to develop along the popular, romantic, but dangerously radical, lines of 'Merrie England', with its folk customs and vernacular literature so well evoked by Sir Walter Scott. In so far as the inspiration behind Scott's work was drawn from modern times as well as 'the Olden Time', from a flourishing early nineteenth-century market in a popular literature that was riddled with 'sentimentalism' as well as such high medieval practices as chivalry, courtly love and martial heroism, they would have attracted Stephen's ire.[52] If Stephen's conception of nationality did not go quite as far as the racial definitions which became common on the European continent, it nevertheless emphasised a moral character and outlook that were exclusive to the English people – as much as their political institutions and accomplishments – and which had persisted across great expanses of time. Such an approach presumed the working of deep conservative rather than progressive forces in history, particularly the history of Britain, and in this respect Stephen and his mentor Macaulay could not have been further apart.[53] Coupled with his concern for the increasing hostility towards the native Protestant creed following the Catholic revival of the 1860s and 1870s, his disdain for radicalism fuelled his efforts to shift liberalism on to the higher grounds of national loyalty. The resultant contrast with the intellectual liberalism of J. S. Mill is marked; whereas Mill was noticeably antipathetic to all things English, Stephen basked unashamedly in the glory of English achievements. It was the duty, he maintained, of intellectual and political leaders to instil similar attitudes into the working and middle classes as a primary condition of the success of democratic institutions. In other words, for Stephen, a strong dose of nationalism was essential to counteract the egalitarian trends of democracy in Britain, not – as in France and Germany – to promote them. In time, it became vital to the Unionist cause as well.

James Fitzjames Stephen's brother, Leslie Stephen, was far less receptive to the kind of instinctive patriotism which his elder sibling had found so attractive since boyhood. Along with John Morley, Leslie Stephen considered Macaulay's patriotism narrow and philistine, qualities which resulted from his courting of a large middle-class audience.[54] Leslie Stephen also disliked the compromising effect of Macaulay's patriotism, most notably in his condemnation of Warren Hastings as a 'great criminal' but praise for the services which the latter's 'crimes' had rendered to the British Empire. He himself, he maintained in his biography of his brother, would have treated Macaulay with more severity than Fitzjames Stephen had done in his *Story of Nuncomar and the Impeachment of Sir Elijah Impey* of 1885: while Fitzjames Stephen – on the basis of rigorous sifting of the judicial evidence – had absolved Hastings from any involvement in the prosecution of Nuncomar, and was therefore free to admire him unreservedly, his sympathy with Macaulay's patriotism induced him in turn to overlook his mentor's 'lax morality' evident in this question.[55] Yet Leslie Stephen himself was not impervious to the basis of Macaulay's patriotism in 'the manliness, the spirit of justice, and the strong moral sense of his countrymen'.[56] This was entirely consistent with the hopes of cultural unity against sectarian religion and party strife he increasingly built up as the disintegrating effects of post-Reform politics took their toll on national life.[57] Such sentiments highlight the natural affinity which English intellectuals had come to feel for their native *patria*, even when they disliked its robustious, popular expression, perceived (as Leslie Stephen did) its deepest expression in literary rather than political culture – and a progressive one at that – and disapproved of the duplicity to which it could easily lead.

Indeed, Fitzjames Stephen was not an isolated figure in the new intellectual liberalism of second-generation Victorians in his apparent willingness to sacrifice dignity of style in order to convey high patriotic messages. Stephen's concern to offset the destructive potential of an ever-expanding democracy by seeking popular acclaim for the longevity and distinctions of English national life was echoed by A. V. Dicey. It is certainly significant that Dicey, like Stephen, was vociferous in his support for Macaulay upon the publication of the latter's *Life and Letters* in 1876. Discounting Macaulay's lack of analytical capacity and extolling instead his power of narrative, Dicey played up the great patriotic service he had performed in chronicling the national history of England. He wrote that 'to interest ages or multitudes in the past is in itself a feat which no one but men of genius can achieve, and in the achievement of which genius, however high, may find full satisfaction'.[58]

At the outset of his career as a political intellectual, Dicey was one of the young university liberals who contributed to the pro-Reform manifesto, *Essays on Reform* in 1867, a work whose authors – it has been persuasively argued – 'owed more to Whiggish historical arguments than to utilitarian deductions from the laws of human nature'.[59] Seeking to allay progressive Whig fears about the fitness of working men to exercise the vote, Dicey denied the existence of sharp social cleavages which would give rise to class rule should the majority of the British nation become arbiters of its destiny in line with the policy of Radicalism.[60] Here, along with some of his fellow essayists, he can be seen to have inverted Radicalism by substituting something approaching a Mazzinian concept of organic nationhood for class as its analytical starting point: for Radicals such as Cobden and Bright, the case for an extension of the suffrage arose far more from the necessity of empowering individuals against the self-interested rule of the aristocracy than the achievement of a unified national ideal.

In the 1860s, then, Dicey was not ashamed to associate himself with what he termed 'so-called unphilosophic and vulgar Radicalism',[61] duly transformed in the patriotic manner indicated above. This populist/patriotic cast of Dicey's mind is nowhere more evident than in the great pride he took in the absence of national pride in Britain. 'Happy', he wrote in his *Lectures on the Relation between Law and Public Opinion in England* of 1905,

> from a Benthamite view, is the nation which is not haunted by the dream or nightmare of past or traditional glory. The singular absence in England of all popular traditions causes some natural regret to poets and even to patriots. Yet it has assuredly favoured the growth and the preservation of English freedom.[62]

In such ways British intellectuals after the middle of the nineteenth century began to look with sympathy rather than disdain upon the inherited nation. They did so not only out of concern for the fragmentary and destabilising potential of democracy, but also in response to the increasing imperialist profile of their country. This, together with the threats from other imperial powers, seemed to demand a more forceful sense of national identity and purpose than that which existed hitherto.

IV

There was by no means a consensus among intellectuals on the nature, value and requirements of the British nation's growing imperial connections. However, an overriding concern of all who contributed to this debate – which was raised to a 'higher level' with the publication of J. R. Seeley's *The Expansion of England* in 1883[63] – was to emphasise and enhance the essential unity of its people, however far-flung, in the interests of a common patriotism. This issue shaped attitudes towards the most desirable limits of geographical expansion, and the nature of the ties that would bind together the empire's constituent parts. The pages of the leading periodicals were notably consumed by the discussion of empire in the 1870s and 1880s, and opinion diverged considerably over whether federation, confederation or separation would best maintain the coherence and identity of the British community.[64] One contributor to the debate, Frederic Seebohm – a Liberal Unionist banker and author of *The Village Community* – addressed the three questions of Englishness, democracy and empire together. But he separated the first two sharply from the third. England's chosen destiny, he proclaimed in 1880, was to grapple with the great problem of democracy, not empire, which was a continental notion and led inexorably to socialism. The English people's natural hemisphere was West, not East; the exercise of 'individual freedom and responsibility' which the establishment of homesteads in America afforded, not the search for imperial ascendancy in Asia.[65]

Seebohm's antipathy to empire echoed Gladstone's substantial essay on 'England's mission' which had appeared two years earlier. Although Gladstone was happy to acknowledge that 'the sentiment of empire may be called innate in every Briton', he denounced unequivocally the expansionist, militarist, aggrandising conception of empire pursued by his Tory opponents currently in office. Anxious, on the one hand, about the mismatch between territorial gains and the resources and capacities necessary to govern them, and, on the other, about the ethics of 'dominion', Gladstone attempted to turn the imperial spotlight inwards on Britain itself – on the energetic qualities of its people which had been responsible for rearing the fabric of empire. Only then would it be possible to dispatch with honour the three great tasks of 'the Imperial State of the United Kingdom: government at home, government in the Colonies, and the exercise of foreign influence as a member of the great community of Christendom'. A fourth great task, the government of India, Gladstone mentioned with evident unease and concern that its affairs failed to attract anything like the skill and attention they deserved on the part of the British authorities. Certainly, he believed that Britain's role in India was to exercise tutelage until such time as the latter's 'manhood and faculties of action' had risen to a level necessary for independence: it was not a question of the inferiority of the Indian mind, nor the maturity of Indian civilisation.[66]

In weighing up the benefits and burdens of empire, not the least important consideration was its tendency to inflame popular passions and enthusiasms.

Robert Lowe – Gladstone's Chancellor of the Exchequer and then Home Secretary in 1873 – sought to dispel Britain's imperialist delusions in the wake of Disraeli's Eastern campaign in 1877–78 on precisely this ground.[67] Nevertheless, a deeply felt patriotism based on alternative conceptions of England easily survived the qualms which many intellectuals felt about the tendency of imperial propaganda to defile the public mind at its lower levels. Obvious examples here are the 'Little Englanders' of the early twentieth century: J. M. Robertson, J. L. Hammond, J. G. Godard, L. T. Hobhouse and J. A. Hobson.[68] L. T. Hobhouse celebrated his native land in his book *Democracy and Reaction* (1904), thus:

> The question might be raised whether the British Empire as a whole has any history to show which compares with the history of 'Little England'; any science, any literature, any art; in fact, any great collective military achievement, worthy to be weighed in the scales against the resistance of Little England to Philip II or Napoleon. A great imperialist once coupled the name of Little England with the policy of surrender. It was a libel. Little England never surrendered. On the contrary, she three times encountered powers which aspired to the mastery of the world, and three times overthrew them. The genuine pride of patriotism is surely lost when littleness of geographical extent can be construed as a term of reproach.[69]

Similarly, the historian of England, G. M. Trevelyan, was dismayed by the 'orgy of relieved feelings and relaxed dignity' shown by the urban crowds of England following the routing of the Boers at Mafeking. His feelings were shared fully by many other liberal intellectuals, some of whom – such as Gilbert Murray – were so appalled by such scenes that they renounced (temporarily) patriotism and all kindred instincts entirely in favour of 'the voice . . . of civilized Humanity'.[70] But the loss of perspective at the root of such revulsion was by no means universal, and was certainly not shared by a younger generation of intellectuals, conservative and liberal alike.[71] Trevelyan himself was satisfied that the offending behaviour represented no more than an aberration in the nation's history, where patriotism, though strong, had been largely unobtrusive. Mafeking night for Trevelyan represented an ugly interlude between the 'rural John Bull who had lit his quiet bonfire after Waterloo' and the restrained spirit of the English people during the First World War. Then, to their credit, they had reserved their 'mafficking' for the moment when 'the news arrived of its termination'.[72] Still, the damage had been done by Britain's pursuit of imperial splendour, however short-lived: from the even later and deeply disconcerting vantage point of the 1930s, it seemed that the British Empire had been morally defensible until the days of Joseph Chamberlain. While the latter could be credited with stimulating interest in the empire,

> he and the Conservatives of those days mucked it up and made it suspect by connecting it with a *racial* imperialism, of Anglo-Saxondom, refusing self-government to the Irish and the Boers and giving a jingoistic colour to the Empire in English minds. The reaction was most unfortunate in many respects.[73]

Just as the strong anti-imperial voices of the so-called 'little Englanders' were rarely anti-nationalist, so many supporters of Britain's imperial extension eschewed a narrow, bigoted and aggressive nationalism. It is true that in Britain's high imperial phase, in the last three decades of the nineteenth century, empire tended to be crudely opposed to internationalism. The contrasting liberalism of this period and that of the radicalism of John Bright a few decades earlier is evident in the protest of a Liberal writer in the 1880s against Bright's seemingly facile view that trade and propinquity alone will bring peace and understanding between nations. The only unifying force was 'common interest', interpreted as 'the union of a kindred and sympathetic race'.[74] Similar sentiments had been expressed by the historian J. A. Froude in 1870, when upbraiding the Gladstone government for prioritising trade and manufacture over the retention of the colonial empire as an integral part of Britain. In attacking the Radical prejudice against over-burdening the people with taxes in so frivolous a cause as that of empire, he echoed the arguments of James Fitzjames Stephen in the 1860s. However, Froude was less interested in engendering pride in the British achievement of governing so unruly a country as India than in emphasising the genuine solidarity of purpose that pertained between British settlers – and exclusively British settlers – the world over. Recognition of this solidarity was particularly urgent in the face of the threat which the enveloping democratic culture and gargantuan resources of the United States posed to the integrity of small states such as Britain. In other words, it was possible to support the British Empire as an essential defence mechanism rather than an engine of world conquest. The cosmopolitanism of the ascendant industrial and urban culture, Froude believed, had not only rendered unfashionable the patriotism in which the English had always excelled; it had also corrupted a people whose natural habitat was the land and the organic social ties which farming alone made possible. But this community of the land was not a passive, static one. What Froude termed 'a hardy and abundant peasantry' was essential to the strength of any nation, and had been the central force behind England's expansion. While Gladstone was to claim that it was high time the English turned their naturally energetic nature back upon themselves, Froude maintained that their 'unusual vigour' was destined to decay, unless the (imperial; that is, colonial) conditions in which those energies had flourished were studiously upheld.[75]

But just after the middle of the century and almost a half-century later, many such defences of empire were notably less Anglo-centric, as well as eschewing assumptions of racial superiority and territorial expansionism that became marked features of imperialist thought elsewhere. Imbued with the 'civilisational' conception of England's place in world history and repelled by the narrow and chauvinistic nationalism that had fuelled the 1848 revolutions in Europe, the liberal intellectual establishment in the 1860s emphasised the ecumenical nature of empire.[76] The young John Acton perceived empire as a counterforce to the narrow spirit of nationalism, enhancing the bonds of international society in the same way as the Catholic Church in medieval Europe. In his famous essay on

'Nationality', Acton contrasted the despotic, exclusivist form of nationalism in post-revolutionary France with the historical and federal tradition of nationalism in England and the British empire. He asserted that

> If we take the establishment of liberty for the realisation of moral duties to be the end of civil society, we must conclude that those states are substantially the most perfect which, like the British and Austrian Empires, include various distinct nationalities without oppressing them.[77]

In this sentiment Acton was close to John Stuart Mill, who defended multinationalism in relation to the English imperial idea, while reverting to a narrower form of nationalism in specifying the conditions of 'free institutions'.[78] Mill's orientalist sympathies and his concern for the 'internal culture' of the native people of India produced a model of imperial rule that was starkly opposed to the authoritarian prescriptions of James Fitzjames Stephen in the 1860s.[79] Several decades later, the Idealist thinkers would offer similar justifications of the British Empire to those of Mill and Acton, although on the basis of very different philosophical premises.[80] There was no reason for the empire to be a vehicle of materialist greed and jingoistic sentiments, argued J. H. Muirhead, a prominent second-generation Idealist, in 1900. On the contrary, it contained the unifying seeds of a far higher purpose which would require all the courage and imagination of its servants to fulfil: that is, 'the development of human faculty in one quarter of the globe'.[81] Again, there could not have been a greater contrast with attitudes towards India in the 1870s, when writers such as George Chesney affirmed the importance of India to Britain purely on the grounds of self-interest – not least that of providing a much-needed outlet for middle-class employment – and 'prudent investment'.[82] Even the aggressive and racially hegemonist ideal of empire associated with Joseph Chamberlain in the 1890s was really a Conservative ruse for absorbing Ulster within the United Kingdom in the wake of Irish Home Rule rather than the spearhead of large-scale territorial expansion.[83]

V

Whether imperialist or anti-imperialist, British intellectuals were distinguished by their attempt to forge an inclusive national culture capable of holding together the increasingly diverse and potentially hostile forces in their society. (They were not just English intellectuals: many of the efforts to forge a British ethos in the century and a half up to 1950 came from Scotsmen, as Robert Crawford has recently reminded us in emphasising such quintessentially British items of culture that were nonetheless of a Scottish provenance as the novels of Scott and Buchan, *Encyclopaedia Britannica* and Reith's British Broadcasting Corporation.[84]) In this sense, they might be seen as taking the first of what Maurizio Viroli has depicted as two 'distinct, though partially overlapping pathways to civic virtue: the path of homogeneity and that of liberty', or nationalism and republican patriotism. In this perspective, while an attachment to one's national culture can sometimes strengthen the commitment to civil and political liberty which is the true meaning of patriotism, there is always the danger that it will 'degenerate into the zealot's love of oneness, not the citizen's political love'.[85]

However, this approach to patriotism discounts the way in which 'love of liberty', if it is not to become vacuous, is itself expressed in different cultural voices in accordance with the self-images of character, history and outlook entertained by particular peoples. The propensity to 'domesticate' liberal ideals in this way was especially true of Britain in the second half of the nineteenth century, and it was carried forward well into the twentieth century. An analysis of the activities and beliefs of British intellectuals in their heyday emphasises the artificial nature of the distinction which Viroli draws between politics and culture as divergent routes to patriotism. Without the focus of national character and culture, mere political bonds provide an ineffectual basis of cohesion. The intellectual elite of Victorian Britain was acutely conscious of this deficiency in a political nation whose boundaries were rapidly expanding but which was sailing dangerously close to the shores of Radical national denial. It hence made energetic, collective attempts to provide a cultural underpinning, not least one that would incorporate its own ideals of liberal learning. It was aware of the associated dangers, particularly that of a vulgar, unthinking chauvinism. But the benefits of an ideal of liberty that was grounded in, rather than abstracted from, Britain's history and traditions were well worth the inherent risks involved in such an undertaking.

Notes

1   A. Briggs, *Social Thought and Social Action: A Study of the Work of Seebohm Rowntree, 1871–1954* (London, Longman, 1961); S. Collini, *Public Moralists: Political Thought and Intellectual Life in Britain, 1850–1930* (Oxford, Clarendon Press, 1991).

2   Lord Cecil of Chelwood, quoted in H. A. L. Fisher, *James Bryce*, 2 vols, II (London, Macmillan, 1927), p. 292.

3   H. S. Jones, *Victorian Political Thought* (London, Macmillan, 2000), pp. 57–8.

4   J. R. Seeley, 'Ethics and religion', in The Society of Ethical Propagandists (ed.), *Ethics and Religion* (London, Swan Sonnenschein, 1900), pp. 16–17.

5   Reba N. Soffer, 'History and religion: J. R. Seeley and the burden of the past', in R. W. Davis and R. J. Helmstadter (eds), *Religion and Irreligion in Victorian Society* (London, Routledge, 1992), p. 141.

6   E. Barker, *Age and Youth: Memories of Three Universities and Father of the Man* (London, Oxford University Press, 1953), p. 183.

7   M. Sanderson, *The Universities and British Industry, 1850–1970* (London, Routledge, 1972), pp. 105–6.

8   H. A. L. Fisher, *The Place of the University in National Life* (London, Barnett House Papers No. 4, 1919), p. 4.

9   On the lack of a gender distinction in framing the purpose of higher education for men and women towards the end of the nineteenth century, see R. N. Soffer,

'Authority in the university: Balliol, Newnham and the new mythology', in R. Porter (ed.), *Myths of the English* (Cambridge, Polity Press, 1992), pp. 192–215.

10   S. Rothblatt, *Tradition and Change in English Liberal Education: An essay in History and Culture* (London, Faber, 1976), p. 196.

11   E. Ashby, 'The future of the nineteenth-century idea of a university', *Minerva*, 6 (1967), 5. See also Mark Pattison's defence of Mill's conception of a liberal education in his 'Address on education' of 1877, an extract of which is included in M. Sanderson (ed.), *The Universities in the Nineteenth Century* (London, Routledge, 1975), pp. 133–4. The don as the educator of cultivated opinion has been richly explored by Noel Annan in *The Dons: Mentors, Eccentrics, Geniuses* (London, Harper Collins, 1999).

12   A. Engel, 'The English universities and professional education', in K. H. Jarausch (ed.), *The Transformation of Higher Learning, 1860–1930: Expansion, Diversification, Social Opening, and Professionalization in England, Germany, Russia, and the United States* (Chicago, University of Chicago Press, 1983), pp. 293–305.

13   C. Stray, *Classics Transformed: Schools, Universities, and Society in England, 1830–1960* (Oxford, Clarendon Press, 1998), pp. 111–12.

14   Bryce to Charles W. Eliot, 7 August 1919, quoted in Fisher, *James Bryce*, II, p. 223.

15   Stray, *Classics Transformed*, pp. 113, 203, 223, 266–70.

16   F. Eyck, *G. P. Gooch: A Study in History and Politics* (London, Macmillan, 1982), p. 50.

17   L. Stephen, *The Life of Sir James Fitzjames Stephen* (London, Smith, Elder & Co., 1895), p. 481.

18   Collini, *Public Moralists*, pp. 195–6.

19   J. Harris, 'Political thought and the state', in S. J. D. Green and R. C. Whiting (eds), *The Boundaries of the State in Modern Britain* (Cambridge, Cambridge University Press, 1996), p. 16.

20   R. Jann, *The Art and Science of Victorian History* (Columbus, Ohio State University Press, 1985), p. 232.

21   V. Feske, *From Belloc to Churchill: Private Scholars, Public Culture, and the Crisis of British Liberalism, 1900–1939* (Chapel Hill, University of North Carolina, 1996).

22   For example, Eyck has written that 'Like G. M. Trevelyan, Gooch helped to develop further and in many ways to perfect the writing of popular history of the best kind, capable at the same time of satisying the specialist and of interesting, stimulating and often fascinating the educated layman'; Eyck, *G. P. Gooch*, p. 229.

23   E. F. Biagini (ed.), *Citizenship and Community: Liberals, Radicals and Collective Identities in the British Isles, 1865–1931* (Cambridge, Cambridge University Press, 1996), pp. 6, 15.

24   John Powell, Introduction to John Morley, *On Compromise* (Edinburgh, Keele University Press, [1874] 1997), p. 4.

25   J. Roach, 'Liberalism and the Victorian intelligentsia' (1957), reprinted in P. Stansky (ed.), *Government and Society in Victoria's Britain* (New York, New Viewpoints, 1973), p. 325.

26   P. Mandler and S. Pederson (eds), *After the Victorians: Private Conscience and Public Duty in Modern Britain, Essays in Memory of John Clive* (London, Routledge, 1994), p. 7.

27   W. C. Lubenow, *The Cambridge Apostles, 1820–1914: Liberalism, Imagination, and Friendship in British Intellectual and Professional Life* (Cambridge, Cambridge University Press, 1998), pp. 207–38.

28   P. Allen, *The Cambridge Apostles: The Early Years* (Cambridge: Cambridge University Press, 1979), pp. 86, 209, 217.

29   Mill to F. D. Maurice, 11 May 1865, in *Collected Works of John Stuart Mill*, XVI, ed. F. E. Mineka and D. N. Lindley (Toronto, University of Toronto Press, 1972), p. 1048.

30   J. F. Stephen, review of H. E. Manning (ed.), *Essays on Religion and Literature*, 3 series, I (London, Longman, Green, Longman, Roberts and Green, 1865), in 'English ultramontanism, I & II', *Fraser's Magazine*, 71 (June 1865), 671–87; and 72 (July 1865), 1–35.

31   J. Bryce, *Studies in Contemporary Biography* (New York, Macmillan, 1903), p. 258. My italics.

32   Fisher, *James Bryce*, I, p. 337.

33   On democracy and national independence, see Sun Yat-sen, 'China's present and future', *Fortnightly Review*, 363 n.s. (March 1897), 424–40; on socialism, see Eduard Bernstein's contributions to *Justice*, the organ of the Social Democratic Federation, 'Amongst the philistines: a rejoinder to Belfort Bax', 14 November 1896, and 'Justice, Bax and consistency', 28 November 1896; on anarchy, see Prince Peter Kropotkin's 'The scientific bases of anarchy', *The Nineteenth Century*, 21:119 (February 1887), 238–52 and 'The coming anarchy', *The Nineteenth Century*, 21:126 (August 1887), 149–64; on a free European Church, emancipated from the Papacy and Protestant individualism alike, see Mazzini's essay, 'A letter to the members of the œcumenical council: from the council to God', *Fortnightly Review* (June 1870), 725–51.

34   For example, he refused the free admission he was offered to the opening of the Great Exhibition in 1851 as a journalist for *The Economist*, 'neither then nor at any time caring to be a spectator of State-ceremonies or royal pageants'. Thereafter, however, 'many days and half days were passed with pleasure and profit in studying the arts and industries of the various European peoples'; H. Spencer, *An Autobiography*, 2 vols, I (London, Watts & Co., 1904), p. 373. On another occasion, in 1874, he was invited to an 'at home' at the Foreign Office in honour of the Emperor of Russia. However, he felt compelled to decline the invitation on account of the dress code. When the hostess permitted him to attend in 'ordinary evening dress', he again sent his apologies, pointing out that 'to make himself a solitary exception in so conspicuous a manner on such an occasion would be even more repugnant to him than conformity itself'; D. Duncan, *The Life and Letters of Herbert Spencer* (London, Methuen, 1908), p. 185.

35   Michael Goodwin (ed.), *Nineteenth Century Opinion: An Anthology of Extracts from the First Fifty Volumes of* The Nineteenth Century, *1877–1901* (Harmondsworth, Penguin, 1951), pp. 11–12. See also Priscilla Metcalf, *James Knowles: Victorian Editor and Architect* (Oxford, Oxford University Press, 1980).

36   J. Hamburger, *Intellectuals in Politics: John Stuart Mill and the Philosophic Radicals* (New Haven, Yale University Press, 1965), p. 1.

37   Quoted in T. W. Heyck, 'Myths and meanings of intellectuals in twentieth-century British national identity', *Journal of British Studies*, 37:2 (1998), 212.

38   Quoted in E. A. Roberts, *The Anglo-Marxists: A Study in Ideology and Culture* (Lanham, Ma. Rowman & Littlefield, 1997), p. 68.

39 See R. N. Soffer, *Discipline and Power: The University, History, and the Making of an English Elite, 1870–1930* (Stanford, Stanford University Press, 1994).

40 M. Viroli, *For Love of Country: An Essay on Patriotism and Nationalism* (Oxford, Clarendon Press, 1995), pp. 140–4.

41 P. Langford, *Englishness Identified: Manners and Character, 1650–1850* (Oxford, Oxford University Press, 2000), p. 11.

42 Jones, *Victorian Political Thought*, ch. 2, esp. p. 49.

43 J. F. Stephen, 'Lord Macaulay', *The Saturday Review*, 7 January 1860, pp. 9–10.

44 See J. Stapleton, 'James Fitzjames Stephen: liberalism, patriotism, and English liberty', *Victorian Studies*, 41:4 (1998), 244–61.

45 J. F. Stephen, 'Mr. Mill on political liberty', second notice, *The Saturday Review*, 19 February 1859; reprinted in A. Pyle (ed.), *Liberty: Contemporary Responses to John Stuart Mill* (Bristol, Thoemmes Press, 1994), p. 20.

46 J. F. Stephen, *Liberty, Equality, Fraternity* (Chicago, University of Chicago Press, [1873] 1991), pp. 112–13.

47 J. R. Seeley, *The Expansion of England: Two Courses of Lectures* (London, Macmillan, [1883] 1897), pp. 196–7, 201, 357.

48 G. R. Searle has recently pointed out that not all Radicals were as hostile to patriotism as Richard Cobden and John Bright, being prepared to jettison free trade when the defence of national interests required; for example during the Crimean War; Searle, *Morality and the Market in Victorian Britain* (Oxford, Clarendon Press, 1988), ch. 9. However, the priority that was thus given to patriotism lacked the emotional force and self-idealisation that increasingly became characteristic of English nationalism after 1850.

49 On this distinction, see P. Langford, *Englishness Identified*, p. 315.

50 P. Mandler, '"Race" and "nation" in mid-Victorian thought', in S. Collini, R. Whatmore and B. Young (eds), *History, Religion, and Culture: British Intellectual History 1750–1950* (Cambridge, Cambridge University Press, 2000), p. 226; see also P. Mandler, 'The consciousness of modernity? Liberalism and the English "national character", 1850–1940', in M. Daunton and B. Rieger (eds), *Meanings of Modernity: Britain from the Late-Victorian Era to World War II* (Oxford, Berg, 2001), pp. 119–44.

51 J. F. Stephen, 'Liberalism', *The Cornhill Magazine*, July 1862, reprinted in J. Stapleton (ed.), *Liberalism, Democracy, and the State in Britain: Five Essays, 1862–1891* (Bristol, Thoemmes Press, 1997), p. 54.

52 For this account of the nature of Scott's influence I am greatly indebted to Peter Mandler, 'Against "Englishness": English culture and the limits to rural nostalgia, 1850–1940', *Transactions of the Royal Historical Society*, 6th series, vol. 7 (1997), 158–9; and *The Fall and Rise of the Stately Home* (New Haven, Yale University Press, 1997), p. 24. For Stephen's contempt for popular literature, see his essay on 'Liberalism', in Stapleton, *Liberty, Democracy and the State*, pp. 56–69.

53 See Stephen's review of H. T. Buckle's *History of Civilization in England* (1857–61) in the *Edinburgh Review* (April 1858), 496.

54 Jann, *The Art and Science of Victorian History*, p. 100.

55 L. Stephen, *The Life of Sir James Fitzjames Stephen*, p. 434.

56 L. Stephen, 'Macaulay', *Cornhill Magazine*, 33 (1876), 581. Quoted in Jann, *The Art and Science of Victorian History*, p. 100.

57   J. P. Von Arx, *Progress and Pessimism: Religion, Politics, and History in Late Nineteenth Century Britain* (Cambridge, Ma., Harvard University Press, 1985), pp. 7, 30–1, 50–1.

58   A. V. Dicey, 'Macaulay', *The Nation*, 569 (25 May 1876), 336. Again, I owe this reference to Rosemary Jann, *The Art and Science of Victorian History*, p. 244, n. 51.

59   Jones, *Victorian Political Thought*, p. 55. On *Essays on Reform* see C. Harvie, *The Lights of Liberalism: University Liberals and the Challenge of Democracy, 1860–1885* (London, Allen Lane, 1976), ch. 6; and J. W. Burrow, *Whigs and Liberals: Continuity and Change in English Political Thought* (Oxford, Clarendon Press, 1988), pp. 46–8, 127–8.

60   A. V. Dicey, 'The balance of classes', *Essays on Reform* (London, Macmillan, 1867), p. 74.

61   Dicey, 'The balance of classes', p. 83.

62   A. V. Dicey, *Lectures on the Relation between Law and Public Opinion in England during the Nineteenth Century* (London, Macmillan, [1905] 1940), p. 463.

63   J. R. Seeley, *The Expansion of England: Two Courses of Lectures*, (London, Macmillan, 1883); D. Wormell, *Sir John Seeley and the Uses of History* (Cambridge, Cambridge University Press, 1980), p. 165. See also D. J. Worsley, *Sir John Robert Seeley and his Intellectual Legacy: Religion, Imperialism, and Nationalism in Victorian and Post-Victorian Britain*, D.Phil. thesis, University of Manchester, 2001.

64   Some of the many articles from the periodical press of the 1870s have been republished with a stimulating introduction by P. Cain (ed.), *Empire and Imperialism: The Debate of the 1870s* (South Bend, Indiana, St. Augustine's Press, 1999).

65   F. Seebohm, 'Imperialism and socialism', *The Nineteenth Century* (April, 1880), 726–36; reprinted in Cain (ed.), *Empire and Imperialism*, pp. 297–310.

66   W. E. Gladstone, 'England's mission', *The Nineteenth Century* (September 1878), reprinted in Cain (ed.), *Empire and Imperialism*, pp. 241, 252–3.

67   R. Lowe, 'Imperialism', *Fortnightly Review* (October 1878), reprinted in Cain (ed.), *Empire and Imperialism* pp. 262–3.

68   Grainger, *Patriotisms*, p. 141.

69   L. T. Hobhouse, *Democracy and Reaction* (London, Fisher Unwin, 1904), p. 17.

70   G. Murray, 'National ideals: conscious and unconscious', *The International Journal of Ethics* (October 1900), reprinted in *Essays and Addresses* (London, Allen & Unwin, 1921), pp. 180–2, and 8. Murray's reversal of his position in 1900 on war and patriotism is explored in S. Wallace, *War and the Image of Germany: British Academics, 1914–1918* (Edinburgh, John Donald, 1988), Ch. 6.

71   As a Conservative, May Cannan (see the Introduction, note 15) emphasised the exaggeration of the jingoism of both the crowds and the Army in accounts of the Boer War victory celebrations. May Wedderburn Cannan, *Grey Ghosts and Voices* (Kineton, The Roundwood Press, 1976), p. 12. Similarly, already a Liberal, the young Keynes distanced himself from both the jingoist and what he nicely termed the 'patrophobist' who had become all too evident at the time of the Boer War; see R. Skidelsky, *John Maynard Keynes*, vol. 1, *Hopes Betrayed, 1883–1929* (London, Macmillan, 1983), p. 91.

72   G. M. Trevelyan, *British History in the Nineteenth Century (1782–1901)* (London, Longmans, 1922), p. 421.

73   Trevelyan to Arthur Bryant, 12 January 1940; Bryant Papers, Liddell Hart Centre for Military Archives, King's College London, Box E3.

74 H. O. Arnold-Forster, 'The Liberal idea and the colonies', *The Nineteenth Century*, XIV (1883), 399–400.

75 J. A. Froude, 'England and her colonies', *Fraser's Magazine*, 81 (January 1870), reprinted in Cain (ed.), *Empire and Imperialism*, pp. 27–49.

76 Mandler, '"Race" and "nation"', p. 230.

77 Lord Acton, 'Nationality', *Home and Foreign Review*, 1 (1862), reprinted in Stapleton (ed.), *Libralism, Democracy and the State in Britain*, p. 94.

78 J. S. Mill, *Considerations on Representative Government* (London, Parker, Son, & Bourn 1861), ch. XVI.

79 L. Zastoupil, *John Stuart Mill and India* (Stanford, Stanford University Press, 1994), pp. 201–6.

80 As John Gibbins has remarked, while the generation of Idealists who followed Green and Bosanquet – Jones, Mackenzie, Collingwood, Muirhead, Haldane and Asquith – 'were more prone to nationalism and imperialism, none abandoned and most utilised [the] tradition of internationalism'; Gibbins, 'Liberalism, nationalism and the British Idealists', *History of European Ideas*, 15 (1992), 494.

81 J. H. Muirhead, 'What imperialism means', *International Journal of Ethics*, reprinted in D. Boucher (ed.), *The British Idealists* (Cambridge, Cambridge University Press, 1997), p. 247.

82 G. Chesney, 'Value of India to England', *The Nineteenth Century*, 3 (1878), reprinted in Cain (ed.), *Empire and Imperialism*, pp. 288, 291.

83 James Loughlin, 'Joseph Chamberlain, English nationalism and the Ulster question', *History*, 77:250 (1992), 219.

84 R. Crawford, 'Redefining Scotland', in S. Bassnett (ed.), *Studying British Cultures: An Introduction* (London, Routledge, 1997), p. 94.

85 Viroli, *For Love of Country*, pp. 170, 184–5.

2

The civic ideal and the state: coming to terms with democracy

I

Chief among the concerns of intellectuals in Britain in the early years of the twentieth century were the nature and conditions of the exercise of 'true' citizenship. As Frank Turner has written,

> Democracy, empire, military preparedness, international economic rivalry, an expanding bureaucracy, national insurance, school lunches, and national education, to mention only a few political developments, had made citizenship a category of thought and association to which an increasingly large number of values and experiences adhered.

A new category of public discussion emerged in the wake of these developments: that of the 'civic'. In essence, it denoted a changing understanding of the point at which individuals were most vitally related to the larger community: at the intersection of society and state rather than in the smaller, early Victorian worlds of religion, estate, county, city and class.[1] To define this intersection more closely, the state was conceived less as an exclusively political organisation than as – in the words of L. T. Hobhouse – 'the social union based on citizenship.'[2]

Certainly, a new and typically moral discourse on citizenship flourished at this time. This is reflected in the publication of a plethora of books on the topic, bearing such titles as *The Principles of Citizenship*, *Ethical Democracy*, *The Citizen's Choice*, *Citizenship* and James Bryce's *The Hindrances to Good Citizenship*.[3] The latter illustrates well the way in which an ideal of citizenship that was linked closely to social reform was used to undermine jingoistic notions of patriotism, although not patriotism itself. Addressing an audience at Yale, Bryce dwelt on the challenge of imbuing modern democracy with the spirit of 'human fellowship' necessary to its strength:

> If you and we, both here and in Britain, are less active than we should be in this and other forms of civic work, the fault lies in our not caring enough for our country. It is easy to wave a flag, to cheer an eminent statesman, to exult in some achievement by land or sea. But our imaginations are too dull to realize either the grandeur

of the State in its splendid opportunities for promoting the welfare of the masses, or the fact that the nobility of the State lies in its being the true child, the true exponent, of the enlightened will of a right-minded and law-abiding people.[4]

The ideal of citizenship inspired much new creative scholarship, not least in the study of Greek and Roman antiquity. Leading classicists such as Alfred Zimmern and Ernest Barker sought counsel on the prospects for British democracy from the authorities and the practices of the ancient world. Zimmern, for example, wrote movingly of the basis of Greek citizenship, and 'of all good citizenship since', in 'the plain primaeval emotions of friendship and family'. While the English did not possess these resources in quite the same abundance, nevertheless there were – fortunately – still moments when the 'modern man feels himself stripped bare of his citizenship, when even the statesman used to living such as a Greek, in the world's eye, retires into privacy and feels himself just a man alone with his God or his kin, in a world of strangers'.[5] Into this region the state 'has hardly dared to intrude, or if it has ventured in at all, has crept in on tiptoe', commented Zimmern approvingly. He had been much influenced by his Classics master at Winchester, Graham Wallas, who was later to become the first Professor of Political Science at the London School of Economics in 1906. Wallas's political thought will be discussed later in this chapter. Here, however, it is important to note that Wallas had pointed to a disjunction between man's primitive instincts and the modern environment in which they were repeatedly 'baulked'. For Wallas, as for Zimmern, the key model of harmony between man and his environment was to be found in the ancient city-state, particularly in the 'Golden Age' of Athens under the leadership of Pericles. That community had not only allowed scope for the continued expression of the family and the tribe, out of which it had emerged; its ideal of the 'perfect citizen in the perfect state' had unified politics and morality in a way that had not been achieved since. The only blot on this otherwise exemplary record was a neglect of the material infrastructure which could potentially give, if not comfort then convenience to the lives of citizens. In idealising Athens thus, Zimmern exemplified a peculiar Edwardian conjunction of scholarship, civic-mindedness and liberal concern for national efficiency which compromised neither the privacy of family life nor the virtues of a fiery individualism. Zimmern's fifth-century Athenians heartily disliked the notion of 'system' and 'compulsion' associated with socialism, preferring 'to remain amateurs, to be supreme as they said of perhaps their greatest statesman, in "improvising right remedies for sudden emergencies."' Zimmern sympathised, but if his Athenians had more than a touch of the English ethic of self-help and the spirit of *ad hoc* government about them, they were nevertheless not beyond reproach, and in a highly educative way; for careless of the common material resources necessary to sustain their 'great spiritual adventure', the Athenians fell prey to disease and overcrowding, and hence irreversible decline.[6]

The movement in ethical and political thought which resulted from the broadening of the boundaries of the political nation was also reflected in the growing irrelevance of elite-centred accounts of English history to the needs of a new democratic age. Historians such as Gooch and the Hammonds insisted that history was about the people, not just the rulers – even when the latter formed the ostensible subject of inquiry, as in Lawrence Hammond's book on *Charles James Fox* (1903). It was an approach which was informed by a faith in the capacity of the masses to master democracy. Indeed, these historians believed that histories of the people, rather than the institutions by which they were ruled, could aid the process by which democracy and citizenship would move closer together, greatly strengthening the former as a result.[7]

The language of citizenship was readily deployed across one of the chief fault-lines of early twentieth-century political thought: between self-styled 'progressives' such as Hobhouse and the forces of 'reaction' which they identified as their chief antagonist.[8] 'Progressives' aligned themselves with the rejuvenated radicalism of the late nineteenth century, much of the impetus of which – whether in its Idealist or 'socialist' form – had derived from Liberal legislation since the Irish Land Acts of 1881.[9] They welcomed the further moves towards political reform that had been taken since the Second Reform Act and looked forward keenly to the extension of the reform initiative to social matters as well. They regarded such developments as emblematic of the advancement of British society towards a higher, because 'broader' level of civilisation, one characterised by increasing social harmony and equality.[10] 'Reaction', on the other hand, was constituted in their eyes by those who upheld elitist models of political rule – those who defended the economic and social privileges which had plagued national life in the past. In the words of Sidney Webb, 'the Progressive instinct always exists, and will always, in time, raise up an opposition to the party which strives to maintain the vested interests of the existing order.'[11] But the dichotomy between 'progress' and 'reaction' not only concealed the many internal divisions within these camps themselves; it also glossed over such common inspiring forces as the ideal of 'citizenship' and furthermore, a belief in progress itself.

This confusion of animosities is readily apparent in the 'national efficiency' movement of the early years of the century. The movement found focus in the humiliations which the British Army suffered during the Second Boer War in 1899. This triggered an outbreak of criticism levelled at the methods and organisation of many other areas of British life, which were deemed to have put the country at a severe handicap in relation to its competitors.[12] The campaign for 'national efficiency', however, contained 'progressives' such as Sidney Webb, whose managerialism was considerably at odds with the democratic convictions of fellow progressives such as Hobhouse. It also included within its ranks Eugenicists such as Francis Galton. Galton swore by the aristocratic principle of 'heredity' so much disdained by the progressive camp, but in the new guise of the need for racial survival and improvement. Here, he expressed a reconciliation of the intellectual elite to the aristocratic basis of the existing governing class after the sound beating it had taken in the press during the Boer War.[13] Again though,

Galton made common cause with progressives in combining a statistical approach to selective breeding with the more emotive language of civics. He thus argued in 1901 that 'high civic worth includes a high level of character, intellect, energy and physique, and this would disqualify the vast majority of persons from that distinction'.[14]

What forces had given the concept of citizenship such a high premium; what aspirations for national life and mankind as a whole underlay it; what models of knowledge were promoted in its service; and what insights into the character of society in general and England in particular did it yield? These questions will provide the central framework of this chapter.

II

From a 'progressive' perspective, successive extensions of the franchise had exposed the flaws in the Utilitarian theory of human nature as selfish and atomistic, signalling instead a society that was increasingly unified by a sense of common purpose. At the same time, the challenge posed to Christianity by science stimulated an interest in 'ethical culture', which in turn reinforced the centrality of citizenship as a political ideal. The beliefs, for example, which informed the London Ethical Society during its existence from 1886–97 were grounded in a conception of social cohesion suggested by the universal ties of citizenship which had been explored in the work of T. H. Green. To J. H. Muirhead, a leading figure in the Society who presumed to speak on its behalf in his *Autobiography*, it seemed that the organic nature of society was inadequately conveyed by the recent references of Dicey and Bryce to 'public opinion' as its mainstay. That idea could never amount to anything more substantial than 'views casually picked up from newspapers or from particular social groups'. Muirhead went on to ask, 'if there were no deeper bond, how is it . . . that political societies hold together at all and resist the strain of men's individual stupidity and wilfulness?'[15] Without both the stimulus and challenge of citizenship under conditions of growing religious doubt, this question would conceivably not have been asked.

A distant sympathy with Comte and the ideal of altruism based upon scientific morality drew such unexpected figures as Leslie Stephen to the cause of ethical culture.[16] Stephen's belief in the importance of an intellectual elite to a modern secular culture was antithetical to the Idealist search for a society that was morally integrated by virtue of being more socially integrated. This is evident in Stephen's expression of scepticism – the roots of which were explored in the previous chapter – that between the 'thoughtful' in society who wanted a religion based on philosophy and the 'vulgar' who could yield to religion only at the level of 'superstition' there was an unbridgeable gulf. He certainly made no attempt to conceal his distaste for Salvation Army evangelism.[17] Yet those who perceived morality as human rather than divine in its primary manifestation ultimately had no other option than to join forces with advocacy of an ideal of social inclusiveness at which the Idealists proved so adept. This was especially the case in an era in which sensitivity to class divisions ran increasingly high.

The gradual acceptance of new groups into the constitution served to enhance recognition of the bewildering variety of forms in which membership of society was signified: not just through the traditional agencies of political representation but in the network of organisations which a new Hegelian awareness identified as 'civil society'. At its extreme, this tendency is registered in the 'civics' movement of Patrick Geddes and Victor Branford. Attempting to localise the primary context of citizenship in cities, Geddes and Branford not only rejected the authority of the national state; they also elevated the evolution of local communities as experienced by their inhabitants as the touchstone of knowledge above the 'abstractions' of experts and intellectuals.[18]

However, the 'civic' ideal by no means marked off anti-statist from statist sympathies. It was embraced as warmly by *dirigistes* such as the Webbs as by the Pluralist opponents of Austinianism led by F. W. Maitland and J. N. Figgis. Moreover, it served to attenuate the oppositional stances taken up by these protagonists: a heavy commitment to a state-centred 'civic' vision never excluding more local contexts of citizenship and a group-centred counterpart rarely dismissing the state outright. This will become apparent if Pluralism and the Fabianism of the Webbs are analysed in turn. The parallels and differences between these two quintessential Edwardian perspectives will attain further clarity through a consideration of Wallas's political thought along the way. Wallas stood resolutely between both camps, while reaching out tentatively to their respective concerns and commitments. Towards the end of the chapter, some measure will be taken of the conservative forces of 'reaction', the strength of which prompted the Webbs to despair of science and civic life as a joint and beneficial partnership ever being realised in Britain.

III

In elaborating the 'civic' conception of society advanced by the Pluralists, it is first necessary to note that the homogeneity of this school of thought was constituted merely by a partial overlapping of interests and concerns between its diverse membership. Certainly, all Pluralist thinkers were characterised by a favourable view of the role played by groups in national life. But their justifications differed markedly, as did the extent to which they elevated groups and the obstacles to voluntary association they attacked in the process. To identify the one unifying strand of the Pluralist movement as 'a refusal to pay homage to the established capitalist system of [the] day, and a recognition that the parentalist state was rapidly becoming the chief instrument for its preservation'[19] is to mistake a part for the whole. For while at times this kind of invective is characteristic enough of Laski, Cole and Figgis – particularly when engaged in indictments of large-scale impersonal organisations – it leaves out of the count the strictly political assumptions of state sovereignty which exercised Maitland and Barker.

The various affinities between Pluralist thinkers are best explored at the 'civic' level. What did they contribute to a more expanded conception of citizenship in the high profile they gave to groups, and what problems arose from the new, 'civic' analysis of society they promoted in the process?

Pluralist thought was steeped in historical analysis of the struggles between church and state. This was part of the initial 'historist' impetus of pluralism in exposing the essential contingency of sovereign authority in opposition to the immutable claims to obedience that were frequently made on its behalf.[20] It was Figgis who pre-eminently set the tone for drawing Pluralist conclusions for the present from the many and varied religious confrontations with the secular authorities of past ages. He regarded the modern state – 'unitary, omnipotent and irresistible'[21] – as heir to all the pernicious doctrines of Church supremacy in the Middle Ages, which were themselves the successors of state autocracy in the ancient world. Just as in the medieval period 'citizenship was identified with churchmanship',[22] the contemporary citizen lay crushed under the weight of the state. But modern citizenship was merely superficial so long as it remained inexorably tied to the state. The 'civic standpoint' lay midway between these two extremes. It entailed recognising a sixteenth-century idea, both Jesuit and Royalist in origin, of church and state as institutionally separate entities – both manifestations of the *societas perfecta*.[23] Therein, argued Figgis, lay the path towards more peaceful relations between the two. But while Figgis was primarily defending the cause of Anglican disestablishment, he recognised that the *quid pro quo* would be the termination of the Church's claim to authority in all matters outside of its domain. If the result was a declining membership of the Church, with the establishment of rival systems of morals and education, Figgis was quite prepared to console himself with the prospects of increased intensity of belief among those who remained.[24]

It is significant that Figgis lent heavily on the anti-Ultramontane beliefs of his mentor, Lord Acton, for the basis of this line of 'civic' thought. Ultramontanism developed between the Reformation and the French Revolution, being designated as such by the Gallican party which – seeking the subordination of the Catholic Church in France to the monarch – 'accused their opponents of looking *ultra montes*, across the mountains, to take their cue from Rome'.[25] In the early 1860s, Acton wrote on the subject of Ultramontanism for the liberal Catholic journal which he edited, the *Home and Foreign Review*. He maintained that originally,

the name of Ultramontanes was given in consequence of their advocacy of the freedom of the Church against the civil power; but the characteristic of their advocacy was, that they spoke not specially for the interests of religion, but on behalf of a general principle which, while it asserted freedom for the Church, extended it likewise to other communities and institutions.[26]

He went on to analyse the corruption of Ultramontanism from a form of defence of liberty against the tyranny of the state in the thought of de Maistre and Görres – and more lately, that of Döllinger and Eckstein – to a new form of tyranny itself in the hands of papal zealots. However, he argued in the article on 'Ultramontanism' that while the Church should rightly be powerless against well-founded attacks from within upon the conduct of its 'interests' – that is, secular affairs – this did not extend to its duty to protect 'truth'.[27] At about the same time as he wrote this article, he published a generally approving review of Mill's conception of liberty as 'absence of accountability to any *temporal* authority'; but he went on to insist that 'coercion by ecclesiastical censures, proceeding in the last resort to excommunication, is inseparable from the idea of the Christian Church'.[28]

Figgis defended 'the civic standpoint' in *Churches in the Modern State* on Acton's conception of the early Ultramontane model.[29] He praised his mentor's recognition that the right of the Church to question the authority of the state was not exclusive to it but extended to all lesser societies. But he refused to acknowledge the potential of small societies for oppression, both within their own spheres and without.[30] This can occur when internal and external sources of authority alike are undermined, as well as when internal authority is strengthened unduly. Barker's favourite examples of the Mafia and Camorra, no less than Mormonism, underline the importance of scepticism in attibuting 'real personality' to groups – with its implication that groups thereby have intrinsic value and are above (external) criticism.[31] At the same time, the vulnerability of groups to cliques emphasises the need for clear and often central lines of authority within. This latter aspect is no less true, perhaps all the more so, of religious organisations. In his chapter on 'Ultramontanism', Figgis implied that the propensity towards autocratic centralism within the Catholic Church was a problem exclusive to that organisation. Even the problem in the Church was not insoluble. It would require, however, nothing less momentous than the recognition that

> in the last resort his [the individual's] allegiance to his own conscience is final. In regard, moreover, to the Church, we cannot often enough repeat that the Church of the future must be a laymen's Church (although it still must have its priesthood), that is, the real democracy of God's servants and Christ's brethren, and no exclusive or illimitable power into which they may not look.[32]

This statement unquestionably overstepped the limits to which Acton was prepared to go in loosening the yoke of 'papalism' in the Church, and it underlies the evident disappointment which Figgis felt for Acton's failure to 'discern the logical result and visible embodiment of [his] conception' in a disestablished but high Anglican Church.[33] For Figgis, the ideal of an Anglican Church – liberated from the interference of both state and Papacy and free to pursue its own course within a federal Catholic culture along the lines of the ill-fated conciliarists at Constance in the fifteenth century[34] – was a distinct possibility. How much more so, then, for all other 'small societies' on whose behalf the cause of a rejuvenated Anglicanism was battling too.

It was left to Barker – alone among the Pluralists – to balance the claims of group life against the state, stressing the importance of mutual co-operation and check upon the excesses of the other. Perhaps the greatest synthesiser of early twentieth-century political theorists, Barker constructed a triad of individual, group and state, and argued the case for the maintenance of a delicate balance between them. Defending, in particular, the position of the state in society as 'a general and embracing scheme of life,' he maintained that its function was to

> necessarily adjust the relations of associations to itself, to other associations, and to their own members – to itself, in order to maintain the integrity of its own scheme; to other associations, in order to preserve the equality of associations before the law; and to their own members, in order to preserve the individual from the possible tyranny of the group.

Barker applauded the Pluralist emphasis upon the capacity of English society to form voluntary societies for all manner of purposes, and to ensure their legal protection from the odious 'concession' theory of Roman Law through the 'trust' idea in Equity. But he thought that Pluralist indignation against the presumption of the state in such infamous cases as *Taff Vale* and the Church of Scotland Appeals had more potential for social fragmentation than diversity. In this, it reinforced the movements towards guild socialism and nationalism in the United Kingdom at the turn of the century – *prima facie* trends towards a new federalism whose thrust was not so much the integration of smaller units but the disintegration of 'the great State'.[35]

Barker's more than lingering sympathies with Latin culture rather than the teutonism of Maitland was a pivotal factor in the strong reservations he held about Pluralist ideas. While an ardent critic of the Platonic conception of undifferentiated unity in the state,[36] he nevertheless believed that each national culture should have its 'centre'. This was also a legacy of the Idealist emphasis upon the state as the 'focus' of a national 'general will' which he had imbibed as an undergraduate at Oxford in the late 1890s. Preferably, there should be a spiritual dimension to that centre – a point which is clear from Barker's conception of the way in which Christianity had strengthened the Roman Empire: the empire's capacity for survival was limited so long as it rested upon mere 'worship of the state'.[37] He was drawn to Burke's defence of the Established Church on similar grounds. But at the same time, he was all too aware of the tension between the *regnum* (the sphere of compulsion) and *sacerdotium* (the sphere of spiritual freedom) which had emerged in the politics of Latin Christendom. As a Lecturer in Modern History at Oxford, this was his key historical reference point for considering the problems of a Pluralist polity in the years before the First World War. Yet even while admitting a certain bias towards the *sacerdotium* (and its modern equivalent, the voluntary society) in retrospect, he emphasised in an article that was completed in May 1914 the pull which the sovereign authority would always exercise in times of crisis – a clear anticipation of the war that was soon to come.[38] This concession did not, however, extend to an endorsement of modern dictatorship as that phenomenon manifested itself in the interwar period: Roman dictatorship and modern dictatorship differed in at least this much, that the one came into existence for a short period only, and by due legal process, whereas the other – in Russia, Germany and Italy – originated in a *coup d'état* and showed every prospect of permanence.[39]

These, then, were the terms in which Barker wrestled with the threat of Pluralism to the political and spiritual unity of society. It is important to emphasise that in rallying to the defence of the state, he was not denying but amplifying the civic vision of his contemporaries. The essence of this vision was a recognition of unprecedented social complexity. At the same time, however, it urged the greater magnitude of the state with the proliferation of social ties and loyalties. As Barker expressed the matter when chiding Spencer for his 'administrative nihilism',

> It is easy to say, with Spencer, that voluntary co-operation achieves the vast mass of the world's work, and that the State (in the sense of the government) achieves but little, and that little ill. It is harder, but it is v ery necessary, to see that voluntary co-operation is only made possible by the State, and, what is more, that the more there is of voluntary co-operation, the more need there is of the State.[40]

IV

Barker's wariness of the tendency of Pluralism to defy the state is significant in the light of Sheldon Wolin's thesis of 1960 that much which passed for political thought in the twentieth century was greatly influenced by the demise in the previous century of 'the political' as the principal category of debate.[41] Maintaining that politics had been 'sublimated' into hitherto 'non-political' associations – such as those which the Pluralists championed against the state – Wolin lamented the loss of the sense of individuals as 'whole' beings, an identity exclusively reflected in the state. Wolin's argument rings truer of American than British political thought. The idea of 'the political' – and its corollary, citizenship – exercised a more tenacious hold on the imagination of political thinkers in Britain than elsewhere. Not the least important factor here was the much less developed state of organisation and management theory applied to the corporate firm, and then to a wider, national plane. Equally, the traditional categories of politics were more deeply embedded in British political thought through the prominence of classical studies within the elite culture which shaped it. These reflections are well illustrated in Graham Wallas's analysis of the 'Great Society', the title he gave to a book published on the eve of the First World War.

Wallas had made a considerable mark upon British political thought through exploding the 'intellectualist' myth which had been an unquestioned assumption throughout much of the nineteenth century. The idea that political action is motivated by a rational inference of means appropriate to the achievement of some considered end Wallas assailed from the disturbing vantage point of modern psychological theory. Not only Utilitarianism but Idealism, too, stood condemned by Wallas's theory of the non-rational instincts which move mankind. (The main institutional home of Idealism – Oxford – returned the snub when it rejected Wallas's application for the newly established Gladstone Chair in Political Theory and Institutions in 1912.[42]) Adopting the long perspective of evolutionary analysis in his pioneering *Human Nature in Politics* of 1908, Wallas contended that while man's environment had changed dramatically, his response mechanisms were still largely those which had enabled him to survive in the 'tribal organisation of the Stone ages'.[43]

But Wallas never meant to endorse the 'anti-intellectualism' which had gained considerable ascendancy at this time, both in Britain and other European countries. Hoping to stem that tide, he wrote *The Great Society* (1914), a book which emphasised the importance of thought to human well-being. Like the more familiar instincts, thought was part of mankind's inherited disposition: 'Thought may be late in evolution, it may be deplorably weak in driving power, but without its guidance no man or organisation can find a safe path amid the vast impersonal complexities of the universe as we have learnt to see it.'[44] There are three interesting aspects to Wallas's analysis here. The first is his arresting depiction of the rapidity and scale of change in modern western society, an evocation which was at the root of his conviction that the invention of new forms of organisation was central to the management of further developments. He argued in this connection that 'the old delight in the "manifest finger of destiny" and "the tide of progress", even the newer belief in the effortless "evolution" of social institutions are gone. We are afraid of the blind forces to which we used so willingly to surrender ourselves.'[45] But the new forms of organisation for which Wallas called steered clear of the 'particular', more localised forums with which the Pluralist and syndicalist writers of the early part of the twentieth century were experimenting. In other words, the notion of 'the Great Society' was ultimately inseparable from 'the Great State'. This is the second notable feature of Wallas's outlook – that he never abandoned the vision of social and political unity which he had imbibed from his studies of ancient Greece as a 'Greats' student at Oxford in the 1870s. As M. J. Wiener has remarked,

> Wallas' vision of the good life . . . involved a unified, integrated society, where the political relation embraced all aspects of life and all members of society. Only the political relation was general enough to fulfil this function . . . though Pluralism was as logical a deduction from Wallas' own psychological analysis of society as the ideal of 'the great community', for Wallas himself it was unacceptable.[46]

Third, and linked to the importance of 'wholeness' in society for Wallas, was the special significance which he continued to attach to an intellectual elite in his search for 'scientific democracy'.[47] This was integral to his determination to maintain the primacy of 'thought' – and advanced thought at that – in addressing the complex problems of 'the Great Society'. The latter was an emphasis with which his contemporaries concurred, and undoubtedly assisted the welcome he received from them on returning to the rationalist fold. His analysis of human instincts was now taken with some seriousness.[48] As Barker wrote to Wallas when congratulating him upon *The Great Society*, 'What you say of the instinct to think – what you say of the need to consider a rational purpose . . . is splendid service against the psychological Pan who is invading, as Bosanquet puts it, rational Olympus.'[49]

The invocation of Bosanquet here as the arch-apostle of common identity in the state well illustrates the association between reason and social unity that resonated in early twentieth-century political thought. Clearly, Wallas remained faithful to the 'civic' vision of society which had moved the Idealists, however much he continued to scorn the purer type of intellectualism still practised at Oxford through their auspices, not least of Barker himself.[50] The source of this vision was an ideal view of British democracy refracted through the lens of the Greek *polis*, the same one which moved his pupil, Zimmern. Ultimately, however, his hopes foundered upon a lack of faith, not in the capacity of the masses to 'work' democratic institutions after due education but in the aptitude of all contemporary intellectuals – not just Oxford philosophers – to bring the appropriate 'inventiveness' to bear upon the political system of the new world. The weight of institutionalisation and specialisation was taking its toll on creative thought for Wallas, as is clear in his nostalgic glance backwards to the Golden Age of Bentham. In an essay on Bentham of 1922, he wrote:

> Those who, under Bentham's leadership, transformed the institutions of their time were not English university professors and scholars, but Mill, the poor Scotch student and hack-writer, and his home-educated son, Chadwick, the journalist turned official, Place the tailor, Grote the banker, Wakefield the ex-convict, Dumont the French tutor, Parkes the Birmingham solicitor, and Romilly the Huguenot barrister. [T]heir knowledge, poor and inadequate as it now seems to us, gave them a sense of power and vision by which they overturned mountains of prejudice and invented new paths for civilisation.[51]

Earlier, in *The Great Society*, Wallas had expressed dissatisfaction with all three of the available agents of change in the early twentieth century: the 'special student', with his 'sectional observations'; the 'ever accumulating records of the past'; and the 'practical man', hampered by 'narrow experience'.[52] All three were a product of the professionalisation of learning. The effort to understand society in these modern forms lacked co-ordination, insight, scientific rigour and practical application.

V

Wallas was not the only British thinker to become considerably disillusioned with the intellectual and political establishment in his country for failing the cause of citizenship in the modern state: the analogous 'civic' hopes of Sidney and Beatrice Webb rose, only to slump dramatically over the same period of the first two decades of the twentieth century.[53] Wallas's commitment to democracy was, of course, far clearer than that of his erstwhile Fabian colleagues, and had always been such: experts were needed in his scheme of things largely to devise the political machinery necessary to enable ordinary mankind to control its own destiny. But although neither Sidney nor Beatrice Webb had directly encountered the *polis* ideal that held such great sway over Wallas and his Oxford-educated contemporaries, they yearned for the same combination of order and harmony, if not quite self-government in the state which propelled it.

Initially, in the 1890s, they were confident that the tide of British politics was moving in their favour. Dismissing the Conservative government's half-hearted attempts to pursue social reform under the auspices of Joseph Chamberlain in 1897, Beatrice Webb triumphantly recorded in her diary that 'Social reform is becoming far too complicated for the actor-politician or the accomplished *littérateur*. That fact works our way: the collectivists alone have the faith to grind out a Science of Politics and I think they will prove to have the capacity.'[54] Fired up by their 'National Campaign against Destitution', which they launched alongside the publication of the Minority Report of the Royal Commission on the Poor Law of 1909, the Webbs continued to fight vigorously for this 'scientific' initiative. The policy of prevention alone was 'scientific', building upon the signal achievements of Benthamites such as Chadwick in the nineteenth century; by contrast, the policy of 'paliation' or relief was the helpless resort of unenlightened ages to the problems of social misfortune. It was not that the 'civic' motive was the crucial differential here: both responses were grounded in a belief that local communities, particularly in England, had proved adept at giving expression to a powerful sense of mutual obligation and civic identity. This should now be replicated in the national state. The chief philosophical inspiration behind the Majority Report of the Royal Commission on the Poor Law, Bernard Bosanquet, stressed the importance of his upbringing in the Northumberland village of Rock for his theory of the 'social spirit' constituting the 'completer fact in which the private will finds form and stability'. The essentially personal, 'case work' response to social problems that Bosanquet advanced through the Charity Organisation Society was rooted in such early experiences of a place where, 'for several generations there has reigned a practice of business efficiency together with a spirit of cordial co-operation and neighbourly kindness'.[55]

The Webbs' policy of preventing destitution sought similar legitimation in local practices, specifically the old manorial and common law action against 'nuisances'. Sidney Webb had written early in life on the benign intervention of feudal landowners to ensure the well-being of local communities.[56] This was a heritage to which the modern administrative state was the natural heir, after the reforming impulse had been blown off course in the period since 1688 by the ravages of *laissez-faire* individualism in local government, a process which the Webbs painstakingly traced in their eleven-volume *History of English Local Government* between 1906 and 1929. To the long-standing recognition of the community's responsibility for maintaining a healthy moral and material environment was now added the scientific knowledge – based on 'definitely ascertained facts' – necessary to the most complete attainment of this goal. The Webbs made no attempt to disguise the division of labour which the new possibility of preventing destitution entailed – between, on the one hand, the maintenance and 'perpetual enlargement' of social purpose by the whole community and, on the other, the acquisition of a 'larger and larger measure of foresight, invention, and technical efficiency on the part of specialised groups of brain-workers on whom, for the most part, the execution of this social purpose will necessarily devolve'.[57] This mirrored the chasm which other leading Fabians conceived between a socialist intellectual *avant-garde* served by the Society and a mass socialist party. Shaw, for example, railed against Wells's suggestion that this chasm should be bridged:

> As to the statement that we do not ask the nation to join the F.S., you imagine this is a jibe. It is not . . . The old cry, 'Proletarians of all lands, unite – in our organisation; and we will lead you to victory' is the folly that has damned every Socialist Society that ever existed. We have absolutely nothing but our ideas to offer; and to sell them in exchange for votes & subscriptions is "the idea of gain" at its maddest.[58]

However, in the next few years the Webbs were to grow pessimistic about the future of their proposal for a National Minimum level of Civilised Life, supported by scientific investigation and provision, upon which preventive policies would be based. They recognised, in terms similar to those of Wallas, that the intellectual and political culture of Britain was considerably opposed to their blueprint for social and administrative change. As Germany seized the initiative on the western front in March 1918, confounding the complacency of the Allies that victory was now theirs, Beatrice Webb wrote in her diary of this – yet another – instance of the Germans' 'superiority in forethought'. 'What', she queried,

> is the explanation of the paralysis of British brains which shows itself in the War Office, in the Admiralty, in Parliament, and in private enterprise?
>   The answer is a complicated one. The British governing class, whether aristocratic or bourgeois, has no abiding faith in the concentrated and disinterested intellectual toil involved in the scientific method. Science to them is a sort of intellectual adventure to be undertaken by a rare type of man. The adventure may or may not turn out worthwhile, but in any case it is silly to expect this adventurous spirit from ordinary men in the conduct of daily life. Indeed, applied to social, economic and political questions the scientific method is to be shunned as likely to lead to experiments dangerous to liberty and property and the existing order of society. . . . The Englishman hates the impersonality of science.[59]

Indeed, what the Webbs perceived themselves as having come up hard against was the immense wall of prejudice in favour of the hereditary principle, which was so ably defended by the Conservatives they despised and which had lost touch with the spirit of mutual obligation that had once sustained it in England. That spirit now needed to be annexed to scientific inquiry and bureaucratic expertise in the organisation of society, but to this the Conservative interest proved irreconcilably opposed. This outlook is well illustrated by the Webbs' growing differences with R. B. Haldane, who, for all his concern to import science into the business of government, remained steadfastly committed to the existing elite, with all its aversion to change. Haldane's condescending review of their *Methods of Social Study* in 1926 prompted a vengeful attack in the pages of Beatrice's diary. She specifically lighted upon his 'idols' – 'The City' and 'good society' – which she went on to describe as 'the tip-top circle which includes the Court (more especially the entourage of Edward VII) and the greater and more distinguished aristocrats, plutocrats and social charmers. His adoration of and subordination to Roseberry, in the days of that hero's glory, shocked us.'[60]

VI

Faced with this kind of opposition, the Webbs loved to play the democrat, 'eager to raise the standard of the mass of men', embattled against the aristocrat, 'caring for the free development of the select few'. But, as was shown above, the forces of 'reaction' were just as capable of speaking the language of disinterested politics in the service of citizenship, without all the connotations of wire pulling which cast such a comic shadow across the work of the Webbs. Lord Hugh Cecil provides a further example of this tendency, staunchly defending the basis of the House of Lords in 'exalted rank' as a crucial impetus to public service throughout society. For Cecil, the existence of the House of Lords lent strong support to the notion of the 'dignity of civic life which makes many Englishmen spend time and trouble, labouring without reward in the public interest'.[61] Democracy in Britain, argued Cecil, was much less about the substitution of a populist for an aristocratic order than 'the constant extension of an aristocracy until it has included almost the whole people'. He meant by this that the working class would eventually embrace the value of individual liberty with the defence of which the English aristocracy were indelibly associated. 'I hope', he argued, that

> the people of our country will inherit to the full that great tradition of fighting for the individual's rights, the great tradition which teaches each man to look for help and progress to himself, to his own capacity and his own strength, trained by self-discipline and self-control, and not to the State's enervating hand.[62]

The forceful individualism which underpinned Cecil's defence of the hereditary principle was enlisted in the same cause by a variety of groups in the first two decades of the twentieth century – all formed to resist the collectivist menace: the British Constitution Association (which, ironically, counted T. H. Green's widow among its members), the Anti-Socialist Union and the Industrial Freedom League.[63] In this way, attempts were made to rejuvenate the increasingly discredited libertarianism of Spencer by transferring its constituency from the industrial to the 'militant' sector of society.[64] Like Cecil, too, the other stalwart champions of the new Spencerianism could not be impervious to the powerful evocations of civic-mindedness in defending hereditary privileges. This is especially apparent in a book published in 1911 when, under the dual pressures of the National Insurance Act and the Parliament Act, the resurgence of 'militancy' in an industrial guise came into its own. Under the title *Rights of Citizenship*, a number of notable political writers loosely associated with the British Constitutional Association evidently sought to tilt the balance of emphasis in civic thought back from 'duties' to the more traditional and traditionally English notion of 'rights'. This entailed an insistence on the primacy of constitutional over legislative consciousness. One such writer was A. V. Dicey, active in the campaign to introduce the referendum as a necessary corrective to the power of party and interest group in parliament.[65] Heartily committed to the idea of 'national sovereignty', Dicey insisted that not only the referendum but a House of Lords constituted on a hereditary basis was essential to its safeguarding. Triumphantly pointing to the defeat of Home Rule in the election of 1895 after the Bill of 1893 had been defeated in the Lords, Dicey proclaimed:

> This condemnation [by the people of the United Kingdom of the whole policy of Home Rule] should never be forgotten; it is of infinite significance, it means that at a great crisis in the fortunes of England, the hereditary House of Lords represented, whilst the elected House of Commons misrepresented, the will of the nation.[66]

Such forceful statements were wholly in keeping with his views on the merely temporary ascendancy of 'collectivism' – as he saw it – over the more solid and, again, fundamentally English, paradigm of individualism that had existed unchallenged until the 1860s. These were expressed in his *Law and Public Opinion* of 1905. In the second edition of 1914, Dicey took the opportunity to admonish the collectivist worship of expertise in politics. Once again, he linked political to epistemological argument, and grounded both in an appeal to English national character. The Benthamite heritage was crucial to Dicey's case against collectivism, as it was to the Webbs' claim in its favour. However, Dicey exalted Bentham for the 'amateur' approach which he brought to reform, a quality that – in seeking to enlarge the sphere of liberty by cutting through the 'fetters' on individual action in law and custom – was firmly linked to the essential individualism of the English people in all their social, cultural and moral traditions. 'Rarely, indeed, does reform come from even the best among professional men. Bentham gained the ear of some eminent lawyers, but the conception of Benthamite reform did not come from the leaders of the Bar, nor generally from the judges.'[67] Pointing to the inferiority of scientific understanding to intuitive common sense, Dicey reverted to a distinctly Burkean form of political argument that drew anti-intellectualism and *laissez-faire* into an indissoluble unity. 'Our democrat', he maintained,

> if he is a man of sense, ought to have one inestimable virtue. He may lack the knowledge possessed by the ablest of specialists; but he knows and feels that the prosperity of men and nations has its source in self-help, energy, and originality. He is thus saved from that belief in formulas which has now and again wrecked the plans of enthusiastic socialists.

Elsewhere in the introduction to the second edition, Dicey made it abundantly clear that this conjunction of individualism and anti-intellectualism was a distinctively English quality, and recognised as such by envious authorities labouring under more oppressive systems of government.[68]

VII

There can be little wonder that Beatrice Webb despaired of her native land (an attitude which will be explored further in the introduction to Part II). The battle over citizenship had exposed a yawning gap between liberal culture, now attached firmly to Conservative constitutionalism, and scientific government committed to substantial political as well as social transformation. Yet the choice of a common, 'civic' battleground is evidence of the Edwardian intellectual elite's shared sense of purpose and 'national' identity, in which they situated themselves among, rather than apart from, their fellow citizens. As Beatrice Webb wrote in response to Haldane's review, 'we have, in fact, never claimed to be otherwise than useful citizens'.[69]

Notes

1 F. M. Turner, *The Greek Heritage in Victorian Britain* (New Haven, Yale University Press, 1981), p. 368; see also J. Harris, *Private Lives, Public Spirit: A Social History of Britain, 1870–1914* (Oxford, Oxford University Press, 1993), pp. 17–23. On the liberal and Idealist contribution to this movement of simultaneously redefining and rehabilitating the notion of community, see S. den Otter, '"Thinking in communities": late nineteenth-century liberals, idealists and the retrieval of community', in E. H. H. Green (ed.), *An Age of Transition: British Politics 1880–1914* (Edinburgh, Edinburgh University Press, 1997), pp. 67–84.

2 L. T. Hobhouse, 'The growth of the state' (1906), in J. Meadowcroft (ed.), *L. T. Hobhouse: Liberalism and Other Writings* (Cambridge, Cambridge University Press, 1994), p. 145.

3 H. Jones, *Principles of Citizenship* (London, Macmillan, 1915); S. Coit (ed.), *Ethical Democracy: Essays in Social Dynamics* (London, Swan Sonnenschein, 1900); E. Barker, *The Citizen's Choice* (Cambridge, Cambridge University Press, 1937); H. Hadow, *Citizenship* (Oxford, Oxford University Press, 1923). J. Bryce, *The Hindrances to Good Citizenship* (New Haven, Yale University Press, 1909).

4 Bryce, *Hindrances to Good Citizenship*, p. 41.

5 A. E. Zimmern, *The Greek Commonwealth: Politics and Economics in Fifth-Century Athens* (Oxford, Clarendon Press, [1911] 1924), p. 72.

6 Zimmern, *The Greek Commonwealth*, pp. 432, 292–8.

7 On Hammond and Fox, see V. Feske, *From Belloc to Churchill: Private Scholars, Public Culture, and the Crisis of British Liberalism, 1900–1939* (Chapel Hill, University of North Carolina Press, 1996), pp. 106–8. On the Hammonds see Stewart A. Weaver, *The Hammonds: A Marriage in History* (Stanford, Stanford University Press, 1998). On Gooch's conception of 'public history', see F. Eyck, *G. P. Gooch: A Study in History and Politics* (London, Macmillan, 1982), p. 228.

8 On the primacy of the analogous democracy/Reaction dichotomy in Hobhouse's thought after 1900, see J. Meadowcroft, *Conceptualizing the State: Innovation and*

Dispute in British Political Thought 1880–1914 (Oxford, Clarendon Press, 1995), p. 233.

9   On T. H. Green's attempt to provide a theoretical rationale for Gladstone's reforming administrations, see 'Liberal legislation and freedom of contract' (1881), reprinted in J. Stapleton (ed.), *Liberalism, Democracy, and the State in Britain: Five Essays, 1862–1891* (Bristol, Thoemmes Press, 1997). On the effect of the new face of Liberal administration on socialism, see S. Collini, *Liberalism and Sociology: L. T. Hobhouse and Political Argument in England, 1880–1914* (Cambridge, Cambridge University Press, 1979), p. 33.

10   L. T. Hobhouse, 'Government by the people' (1910), reprinted in Meadowcroft (ed), *L. T. Hobhouse* p. 123.

11   S. Webb, 'Lord Roseberry's escape from Houndsditch', *The Nineteenth Century* (1901), reprinted in E. J. T. Brennan (ed.), *Education for National Efficiency: The Contribution of Sidney and Beatrice Webb* (London, Athlone Press, 1975), p. 64.

12   G. R. Searle, *The Quest for National Efficiency: A Study in British Politics and Political Thought, 1899–1914* (Oxford, Basil Blackwell, 1971), pp. 34, 54.

13   Searle, *The Quest for National Efficiency*, pp. 80–1, 88.

14   F. Galton, 'Sociology as eugenics' (1901), reprinted in P. Abrams, *The Origins of British Sociology* (Chicago, Chicago University Press, 1968), p. 260.

15   J. H. Muirhead, *Reflections by a Journeyman in Philosophy on the Movements of Thought and Practice in his Time* (London, George Allen & Unwin, 1942), p. 87.

16   T. R. Wright, *The Religion of Morality: The Impact of Comtean Positivism on Victorian Britain* (Cambridge, Cambridge University Press, 1986), pp. 142–4, 156.

17   L. Stephen, 'The aims of ethical societies', in The Society of Propagandists (ed.), *Ethics and Religion* (London, Swan Sonnenschein, 1900), pp. 251–2.

18   See P. Geddes, *Cities in Evolution: An introduction to the Town Planning Movement and to the Study of Civics* (London, Williams & Norgate, 1915), pp. 247, 255. On Geddes, see H. Meller, *Patrick Geddes: Social Evolutionist and City Planner* (London, Routledge, 1991).

19   D. Nicholls, *The Pluralist State: The Political Ideas of J. N. Figgis and his Contemporaries* (London, Macmillan, [1975] 1994), p. 11.

20   The displacement of 'historist' (recognising the contingency of the state's role in history) by 'historicist' (determining its future path of development) accounts of the state by the Pluralist-turned-Marxist thinkers, Laski and Cole, after 1918 has been perceptively explored by D. Runciman in *Pluralism and the Personality of the State* (Cambridge, Cambridge University Press, 1997), p. 259.

21   J. N. Figgis, *Studies of Political Thought from Gerson to Grotius, 1414–1625* (Cambridge: Cambridge University Press, [1907] 1916), p. 13.

22   J. N. Figgis, *Churches in the Modern State* (London, Longmans, 1913), p. 106.

23   Figgis, *Churches in the Modern State*, pp. 109–10.

24   Figgis, *Churches in the Modern State*, p. 119.

25   R. Hill, *Lord Acton* (New Haven, Yale University Press, 2000), p. 142.

26   See Lord Acton, 'Ultramontanism', *Home and Foreign Review*, 3 (July 1863), 192. On the German background to Acton's theory of Ultramontanism – the treatment of the Catholic Church after 1815 by the Hapsburgs and Wittelsbachs alike as 'part of their civil service' – see Reba Soffer, 'The historian, catholicism, global history, and national singularity', *Storia della Storiografia*, 35 (1999), 118–19.

27 Acton, 'Ultramontanism', p. 203.

28 Lord Acton, 'Mill on liberty -1', *The Rambler* (November 1859), 68, 75.

29 Figgis, *Churches in the Modern State*, pp. 111–12.

30 One of the most startlingly frank statements of the potential of 'self-created' groups for harm is by C. A. R. Crosland, *The Future of Socialism* (London, Jonathan Cape, [1956] 1963), pp. 74–5. This echoed the sentiments of an earlier revisionist socialist, E. F. M. Durbin. See p. 75n.1.

31 E. Barker, 'The discredited state', *Political Quarterly*, (February 1915), 113, 118.

32 Figgis, *Churches in the Modern State*, pp. 154–5.

33 Figgis, *Churches in the Modern State*, p. 264.

34 Figgis, *From Gerson to Grotius*, ch. 2; *Churches in the Modern State*, pp. 146–7.

35 E. Barker, *Political Thought from Spencer to the Present Day* (London, Williams & Norgate, 1915), pp. 178–9, 182.

36 See E. Barker, *The Political Thought of Plato and Aristotle* (London, Methuen, 1906), p. 159.

37 E. Barker, 'The conception of empire', in C. Bailey (ed.), *The Legacy of Rome* (Oxford, Clarendon Press, 1924), p. 78.

38 E. Barker, Preface to *Church, State, and Education* (Ann Arbor, University of Michigan Press, 1957).

39 E. Barker, 'The prospects for democracy' (1934), reprinted in *The Citizen's Choice*, pp. 46–7.

40 Barker, *Spencer to the Present Day*, p. 119.

41 S. Wolin, *Politics and Vision: Continuity and Innovation in Western Political Thought* (London, George Allen & Unwin, 1961), ch. 10.

42 On this episode see J. Stapleton, 'Academic political thought and the development of political studies in Britain, 1900–1950', unpublished PhD thesis, University of Sussex, 1986, pp. 166–8. On Wallas's undergraduate rejection of Idealism see M. J. Wiener, *Between Two Worlds: The Political Thought of Graham Wallas* (Oxford, Clarendon Press, 1971), pp. 6–7.

43 G. Wallas, *Human Nature in Politics*; London, Constable, [1908] 1929), p. 59.

44 G. Wallas, *The Great Society: A Psychological Analysis* (New York, Macmillan, [1914] 1921), p. 45.

45 Wallas, *The Great Society*, p. 14.

46 Wiener, *Between Two Worlds*, p. 182.

47 Wiener, *Between Two Worlds*, p. 198.

48 Gilbert Murray wrote of *The Great Society* that 'no one before had seriously observed and thought out the effects produced on the natural human instincts and cravings by the conditions of a "Great Society." That book is one of the very few of which I could say that it made a permanent difference in my outlook on human conduct, and I believe Wallas's disciple, Walter Lippmann, has said the same'; Murray, Preface to *Men and Ideas: Essays by Graham Wallas*, ed. M. Wallas (London, Allen & Unwin, 1940), p. 7.

49 Barker to Wallas, 15 July 1914; Wallas Papers, British Library of Political and Economic Science, London, 4/2/111.

50 G. Wallas, 'Oxford and political thought', *The Nation*, (15 May 1915), 227–8.

51 G. Wallas, 'Bentham' (1922), reprinted in Wallas (ed.), *Men and Ideas*, p. 32.

52 Wallas, *The Great Society*, p. 15.

53 On the 'civic' dimension of the Webbs' Fabianism, particularly as reflected in their interest in rejuvenating English local government, see J. Stapleton, 'Localism versus centralism in the Webbs' political thought', *History of Political Thought*, 12:1 (1991), 147–65; and A. J. Kidd, 'The state and moral progress: the Webbs' case for social reform, c. 1905–1940', *Twentieth Century British History*, 7:2 (1996), 189–205.

54 N. and J. Mackenzie (eds), *The Diary of Beatrice Webb*, 4 vols, II, 1892–1905, *All the Good Things in Life* (London, Virago, 1986), p. 106.

55 B. Bosanquet, 'Life and philosophy', in J. H. Muirhead (ed.), *Contemporary British Philosophy* (London, George Allen & Unwin, 1924), p. 52.

56 Feske, *From Belloc to Churchill*, p. 78.

57 Sidney and Beatrice Webb, *The Prevention of Destitution* (London, Longman, 1911), ch. 10 and p. 334.

58 Shaw to Wells, 5 May 1907, in J. Percy Smith (ed.), *Bernard Shaw and H. G. Wells* (Toronto, University of Toronto Press, 1995), p. 51.

59 N. and J. Mackenzie (eds), *The Diary of Beatrice Webb*, III, 1905–24, *'The Power to Alter Things'* (London, Virago, 1984), pp. 304–5.

60 N. and J. Mackenzie (eds), *The Diary of Beatrice Webb*, IV, 1924–43, *'The Wheel of Life'* (London, Virago, 1985), pp. 71–3.

61 Lord Hugh Cecil, *Conservatism* (London, Williams & Norgate, 1912), p. 232.

62 Lord Hugh Cecil, *Liberty and Authority* (London, Edward Arnold, 1910), pp. 66–7.

63 W. H. Greenleaf, *The British Political Tradition*, 3 vols, 2, *The Ideological Heritage* (London, Routledge, [1983] 1988), pp. 285–6.

64 The relationship between the political thought of Spencer and Cecil is explored in Meadowcroft, *Conceptualizing the State*, pp. 102–12.

65 See J. Meadowcroft and M. Taylor, 'Liberalism and the referendum in British political thought 1890–1914', *Twentieth Century British History*, 1 (1990), 35–57; and M. Qvortrup, 'A. V. Dicey: the referendum as the people's veto', *History of Political Thought*, 20:3 (1999), 531–46.

66 Sir William Anson *et al.*, *Rights of Citizenship: A Survey of Safeguards for the People* (London, Frederick Warne, 1912), p. 86.

67 A. V. Dicey, *Lectures on the Relation between Law and Public Opinion in England during the Nineteenth Century* (London, Macmillan, [1905] 1914), pp. 90, lxxvii.

68 Dicey, *Law and Public Opinion in England*, pp. xcii–iii.

69 N. and J. Mackenzie (eds), *The Diary of Beatrice Webb*, IV, p. 72.

Part II

Political thought and public values, 1918–50: the perspectives of civilisation

The civic vision which dominated the political thought of the earlier part of the twentieth century rapidly declined after the First World War. The emollient vision of belonging which was central to it – whether in small and local circles or in a more all-embracing national community invariably focused upon the state – seemed to crumble in the face of a far more hostile attitude to political power, class, nation and democratic institutions than had prevailed previously. A. L. Rowse spoke for a new generation which complained of the inadequacy of the 'worn coinage of an exhausted idealism' that passed for political thought after the War.[1] The ideals of prewar Britain – not least, the faith in reform through piecemeal concession and organisation that was held by socialists and New Liberals alike – were rapidly losing their former sheen.[2] Similarly, the Edwardian view of thinkers such as Masterman, Hobhouse and Wallas, who clustered around the *Nation* that the human world was as open to scientific intelligibility as the natural world – yielding a progressive and largely democratic political consensus in its train – found fewer defendants among a new generation of thinkers.[3] Now, the cause of 'science' was more likely to be upheld by openly elitist writers such as H. G. Wells and Bertrand Russell in utopian perspectives. These writers shunned the conventional world of politics – and work as well – and unlike their New Liberal forbears, divorced rigidly the business of organising production on a scientific basis from the maintenance of cultural values.[4]

The political thought of the 1920s, certainly, was much impoverished as a result. It must be emphasised that this assertion applies largely to the work of secular political thinkers because, as Matthew Grimley has convincingly argued, a considerable and influential body of political ideas was developed by Churchmen and devout laymen from the middle of the decade in response to such divisive issues in the state as the General Strike, the revised Prayer Book and, in the 1930s, unemployment and the crisis of the monarchy.[5] Some of the theorists who helped to give this movement of Christian political thought its momentum will be encountered in the following chapters, most notably A. D. Lindsay and Ernest Barker. But the fragmented efforts that were made by secular thinkers in the 1920s possessed none of the energy and complexity of the ideas of Hobhouse, Hobson and Maitland in the first decade of the twentieth century. Indeed, political thought – as in the period immediately after the Second World War – seemed to atrophy and live off, without replenishing, the capital it had acquired in the years before war broke out. Political thought in the 1920s is not notable for pathbreaking works. A possible candidate might have been Laski's comprehensive *Grammar of Politics*, published in 1925, whose point of departure was the recognition that 'a new political philosophy is necessary to a new world'.[6] But for all its wealth of knowledge and suggestion regarding contemporary social organisation, Laski's efforts to marry political theory and science did not advance far beyond the prewar Fabian paradigm, suitably modified by his equally prewar Pluralist convictions.

One factor in the malaise of political theory in the 1920s was the malaise of liberalism. This was felt keenly by liberal intellectuals such as Keynes. In his view, liberalism – and the creativity of thought associated with it – was fast becoming eclipsed by socialism, a force led by 'sentimentalists and pseudo-intellectuals'. In this he made common cause with openly elitist writers such as Wells. But the challenge of the time, he maintained, in an otherwise favourable review of Wells's *The World of William Clissold* in 1927, was to re-harness the creative, and essentially liberal, force of 'Brahma' to politics and government in place of its present master, the world of science and business represented by Clissold. Liberalism had to die, but in order to 'be born again with firmer features and a clearer will'.[7] Only then could Siva – in the form of the passionate destructiveness of Labour – be overcome. The problem with businessmen as the potential servants of Brahma was that they lacked a creed. 'They would so like to be apostles. But they cannot. They remain businessmen.'[8] Keynes did not believe that the captains of industry would ever part company with the profit motive sufficiently to join the 'open conspiracy' against the ascendancy of Labour: his contact with business circles was minimal, and – as his biographer emphasises – he was a 'typical product of the ancient universities in ranking business activity very low in his scale of values'.[9] By contrast, there was still potential in the universities – denuded of business studies – thought Keynes, to become temples of Brahma, 'which even Siva will respect'. However, by the end of the 1930s Keynes had come to recognise that in the communism of that decade lay the closest embodiment of the true spirit of liberalism in which alone salvation could be found:

> There is no-one in politics today worth sixpence outside the ranks of liberals except the post-war generation of intellectual Communists under thirty-five. Them, too, I like and respect. Perhaps in their feelings and instincts they are the nearest thing we now have to the typical nervous nonconformist English gentleman who went to the Crusades, made the Reformation, fought the Great Rebellion, won us our civil and religious liberties and humanised the working classes last century.[10]

From the opposite perspective of the socialist left, the main factor in the paucity and relatively sterile nature of 1920s' political thought was the lack of humanity and sympathy among intellectuals which Beatrice Webb constantly remarked upon in her diary. Even allowing for the gloom which beset her character generally and the sense of distance from contemporaries who now held the field which old age inevitably wrought, there certainly was among younger intellectuals such as Cole, Russell and Keynes an emotional as well as political detachment – a discounting of the role of creeds, ideals and character in society in favour of abstract ideas.[11] She remarked upon the 'creedlessness' of the modern world – a creedlessness which was bound to issue in fanaticism – in a letter to John St Loe Strachey, Editor of the *Spectator*, in 1926.[12] To judge by the warmth of this correspondence she felt closer to some of her peers – even those of a Conservative persuasion – than to younger socialist and liberal intellectuals. Strachey, for his part, had written appreciatively of *My Apprenticeship*, not least because it emphasised

how false is the view which the present generation – I mean the post-War generation – has of our particular set of Victorians. Of course, their view is true of a great
part of the population, but they never seem to remember that there was quite a considerable body of people, Potters, Stracheys, Mallets, and others, who were quite
different.[13]

Strachey was evidently speaking from the bitter experience of his son – John
Strachey – who had recently become a convert to the Labour Party, as much in
generational as in political revolt. According to John Strachey's biographer,
Hugh Thomas, the younger Strachey 'looked on [his father] with disapproval, as
a very old-fashioned intellectual'. Strachey's communism forms the subject of a
later chapter.[14]

  Beatrice Webb's sense of the 'creedlessness' of the contemporary world was
mirrored in modern art, literature and music, which she denounced for its yearn-
ing after the 'sub-human'.[15] The modernist movement should not be confused
with Bloomsbury in this respect: Bloomsbury's deserved reputation for elitism
co-existed with some major improving initiatives from that quarter in the interwar period.[16] But there certainly was a diminished concern for the problem of
poverty which had animated much prewar political thought and helped to
increase contact between the educated and the non-educated classes. Noting, in
January 1928, good progress with the second volume of their *English Poor Law
History*, she nevertheless reflected that

> few would buy these ponderous volumes: Who today is interested in the question
> of 'Poverty in the midst of riches'? The rich seem to be more callous than of old;
> fear of Communism, of increased taxation and diminished privilege, has become
> their dominant emotion; pity for the misery of poverty is dead; indeed, there is a
> certain resentment at the rise in wages, following the rise in prices, and also at the
> 'dole'.[17]

The loss of interest in the 'social questions' which had fired the imagination of
the prewar political and cultural elite is certainly evident in Kenneth Clark's rec-
ollections of his Oxford days in the early 1920s: 'When I read a paper on Ruskin
to the College literary society, the only response was one of astonishment that
anyone should take him seriously.'[18]

  Yet within a decade or so after 1918, British political thought seemed to
recover some of its former vitality. The 1930s – often regarded as a 'Red decade'
in thrall to foreign ideologies and parties – is increasingly appearing in a more
diverse light. Against political extremism of both the right and the left, a liberalism that found focus in English national identity was ably defended from positions right across the ideological spectrum of British politics.[19] In the same vein,
David Blaazer has drawn attention to the flourishing socialist progressivism of
the decade and emphasised its independence from Moscow.[20] Even the Marxism
of the 1930s is now commended for its creativity.[21] It was not simply a case of old
ideals being intoned, but with more vigour than in the 1920s. Instead, although
much of the new thought built upon a prewar heritage of ideas, these were

considerably reworked and adapted to the political and cultural exigencies of the time. What is especially notable, however, about the political thought of the 1930s is the reassertion of the authority of the intellectuals who articulated and disseminated it, and their determination to make it a crucial vehicle of public values once more. An instrumental force in this respect was the development of new media – particularly public service broadcasting after its inauguration in 1927 under the auspices of John Reith. Reith himself exemplified a view which had struggled against the forces of intellectual specialisation and professionalisation earlier in the century but which was to be reactivated in the 1930s: in the words of D. L. LéMahieu, a 'rationalist faith in the liberating potential of great ideas'.[22] The revival of this view is also evident in a work published at the end of the decade and reissued five times by 1952: a volume of essays by leading thinkers, mainly but not solely British, and most with a political dimension to their various philosophies, entitled *I Believe*.[23] The pressures of the period encouraged intellectuals to think on a large philosophical and historical canvass; to assume, sometimes, the mantle of prophet; and to reflect on ordinary experience – its shortcomings and its higher possibilities.

The following three chapters explore the work of intellectuals who took up this challenge within broadly cosmopolitan frameworks of belief between 1930 and 1950. Subsequently, I turn to scholars and thinkers who reacted against the loss of national perspective which they believed was entailed by such intellectual agendas, but who were equally concerned to exert moral, cultural and political leadership. However, it must be stressed at the outset that the universal perspectives of analysis that will be considered here were firmly embedded in local debates and idioms and framed by the perception of cultural 'others'. Similarly, the more nationalistic notes struck by those who reacted against these perspectives rarely abandoned the humanitarian gestures that had been inherent in British political thought since the middle of the nineteenth century, imperial and anti-imperial alike.

Notes

1   A. L. Rowse, *Politics and the Younger Generation* (London, Faber & Faber, 1931), p. 213.

2   See, for example, the Webbs' *The Decay of Capitalist Civilisation* (London, The Fabian Society, 1923), in which they spoke of the 'catastrophic reaction' after the Great War to the 'acquiescence' that took place before it 'in the progressive development of political and industrial democracy'; pp. 174–7.

3   On the *Nation* group see Christopher E. Mauriello, 'The strange death of the public intellectual: liberal intellectual identity and the "field of cultural production", *Journal of Victorian Culture*, (6:2001), 1–26.

4   See P. Ironside, *The Social and Political Thought of Bertrand Russell* (Cambridge, Cambridge University Press, 1996), pp. 170, 175.

5   M. Grimley, *Citizenship, Community, and the Church of England: Anglican Theories of the State, c. 1926–1939*, PhD dissertation, University of Oxford, 1998.

6 H. J. Laski, *A Grammar of Politics* (London, Allen & Unwin [1925] 1941), p. 15.

7 J. M. Keynes, ' Clissold' (1927), in *Essays in Persuasion* (London, Macmillan, 1972), pp. 318–19.

8 Keynes, 'Clissold, p. 320. Keynes would inevitably have been aware of, although perhaps not impressed by, the considerable public ice which several notable business-men had cut in the early decades of the twentieth century. Two such businessmen are mentioned in this book – Lionel Hichens and F. S. Oliver. Both were influential figures within the Round Table movement and also, via that movement, within the Astors' 'Cliveden Set'. The nature of the latter as a 'ginger group' carrying substantial weight within foreign policy-making circles is the subject of an excellent recent study by N. Rose, *The Cliveden Set: Portrait of an Exclusive Fraternity* (London, Jonathan Cape, 2000).

9 R. Skidelsky, *John Maynard Keynes*, 2 vols, II, *The Economist as Saviour, 1920–1937* (London, Macmillan, 1992), pp. 259–60, 248.

10 Keynes, *New Statesman*, 28 January 1939, quoted in D. Winch, *Economics and Policy: A Historical Study* (London, Hodder & Stoughton, 1969), p. 348.

11 N. and J. Mackenzie (eds.), *The Diary of Beatrice Webb*, 4 vols, IV (1924–43), '*The Wheel of Life*' (London, Virago, 1985), pp. 94, 97, 113.

12 Beatrice Webb to John St Loe Strachey, 10 December 1926, in N. Mackenzie (ed.), *The Letters of Sidney and Beatrice Webb*, 3 vols, III, *Pilgrimage, 1912–1947* (Cambridge, Cambridge University Press, 1978), pp. 277–8.

13 Strachey to Beatrice Webb, 7 December 1926 Webb MSS, II.4.h.77, British Library of Political and Economic Science, London.

14 H. Thomas, *John Strachey* (London, Eyre/Methuen, 1973), p. 64.

15 Mackenzie (eds), *The Diary of Beatrice Webb*, 4, pp. 152–3.

16 The complexities of the relationship between Bloomsbury and modernism are briefly but succinctly explored by Peter Clarke in *Hope and Glory, Britain 1900–1990* (Harmondsworth, Penguin, 1996), pp. 166–74.

17 Mackenzie (eds), *The Diary of Beatrice Webb*, 4, p. 136.

18 K. Clark, *Another Part of the Wood: A Self-Portrait* (London, Murray, 1974), pp. 112–13.

19 J. Stapleton, 'Resisting the centre at the extremes: "English" liberalism in the politi-cal thought of interwar Britain', *British Journal of Politics and International Relations*, 1:3 (1999), 270–92.

20 D. Blaazer, *The Popular Front and the Progressive Tradition: Socialists, Liberals, and the Quest for Unity, 1884–1939* (Cambridge, Cambridge University Press, 1992).

21 E. A. Roberts, *The Anglo-Marxists: A Study in Ideology and Culture* (Lanham, Ma., Rowman & Littlefield, 1997).

22 D. L. LeMahieu, 'John Reith, 1889–1971: entrepreneur of collectivism', in S. Pederson and P. Mandler (eds), *After the Victorians: Private Conscience and Public Duty in Modern Britain: Essays in Memory of John Clive* (London, Routledge, 1994), p. 196.

23 W. H. Auden *et al.*, *I Believe: Nineteen Personal Philosophies* (London, George Allen & Unwin, 1940). Contributors included Auden, Forster, Laski, Lin Yutang, Jules Romains, Thomas Mann, Russell, Thuber, Wells, West and Van Loon.

3

The secularisation of liberalism and political decline: R. G. Collingwood, A. D. Lindsay and T. S. Eliot

I

Perhaps the most obvious stimulus to political thought and the strengthening of its prewar association with public values from the end of the 1920s was the advent of political extremism in both its fascist and communist forms. Concern for this development was not narrowly confined to the centre ground of liberal opinion; rather, it became increasingly apparent across a broad spectrum of political belief, from the speeches of Conservative leaders such as Baldwin and Halifax to the socialist theory of Evan Durbin.[1] Such concern was also characteristic of university thinkers, forcing a deep questioning of their professional role and influencing their political philosophy accordingly. The distance of academic study from the problems of the wider society in which it took place preoccupied philosophers in particular. In 1935, for example, in response to an invitation from the Editor of the journal *Philosophy* to stimulate discussion of contemporary issues, Sir Herbert Samuel – President of the Institute of Philosophy – urged his fellow philosophers to give up their obsession with epistemology for the time being and to consider, instead, the urgent 'practical questions' of the time. By this he meant questions of 'personal and social morality, of economic organisation, of international relationship'.[2] Similarly, C. E. M. Joad called in 1940 for fresh contact to be made with the 'classical tradition' of philosophy. This had a dual purpose: 'to clarify the wisdom of common-sense people, and to increase it'. He deplored the effects of the analytical revolution in the subject, whereby the philosopher had 'draw[n] in his horns and content[ed] himself with the scrutiny of sentences through an intellectual microscope'.[3]

This narrowing of the philosopher's horizons was of particular concern to two seminal political thinkers of interwar Britain – R. G. Collingwood and A. D. Lindsay – and also their contemporary, the poet and critic, T. S. Eliot. Despite very different backgrounds, interests and values, all three traced the political crises of the 1930s and 1940s to a common source: the erosion of Christian ends and ideals, either by liberalism as an independent force, as in Eliot's case, or by a liberalism and associated form of democracy which had progressively bitten

63

the Christian hand by which it had initially been fed, as Collingwood and Lindsay believed. The significance of this feature of their thought lies in its questioning of the secular character of the liberalism which had been such a defining feature of British intellectual life since the middle of the nineteenth century. The crisis of religious faith which had thus made intellectuals central to British culture was resolved anew in some quarters in favour of Christianity rather than agnosticism.

II

R. G. Collingwood welcomed Samuel's challenge to enhance the contemporary relevance and accessibility of philosophy. In an article written in 1940, he maintained that the 'classical tradition' of philosophy involved the deployment of 'trained faculties' on facts, 'and primarily . . . facts of practical importance in relation to the lives of . . . fellow men'. The most important facts at the present time, in his view, were fascism and Nazism, and the necessity for taking them seriously; he thereby wrote of the need 'to stop flattering ourselves with the belief that they are baseless follies indulged by unaccountable foreigners, or the alternative belief that they are good examples which we should be wise to follow. What our soldiers, and sailors, and airmen have to fight, our philosophers have to understand.'[4]

This Collingwood had struggled valiantly to do throughout the second half of the 1930s and into the 1940s from the distinguished position of Waynflete Professor of Metaphysical Philosophy at Oxford, which he held from 1935 to 1941. The waywardness of politics in the 1930s was, from Collingwood's perspective, a direct result of a crisis in liberalism – a crisis that had beset European liberalism as a whole. But like Keynes, he believed that it was only through a resolution of the crisis in liberalism's favour that an adequate offensive could be mounted. Liberalism had fallen into discredit because it had lost touch with the essentially Christian heritage from which it had been born: under the strain of the Illuminist movement of the eighteenth century, the idea of freedom had become detached from its religious underpinning in 'love of a God who set an absolute value on every human being'.[5] This development had been exacerbated, for Collingwood, by the cutting off of industry from all agricultural roots, thereby constituting 'a kind of madness, which may endure for a time in a feverish and restless consciousness, but can have no lasting vitality'.[6] The result of the tendency which Collingwood identified was that – deprived of the emotional but stabilising force that was once supplied by the values of religion and the countryside alike – liberalism had no means of competing with the heady philosophies of Nazism and fascism which reached back to pre-Christian, pagan religious forms. 'Liberalism or democracy', Collingwood concluded in his article on the two extremist philosophies of the right, 'may be wise, but the people who care for it do not care for it passionately enough to make it survive.'[7]

Collingwood was in no doubt as to the necessity for that survival. David

Boucher has firmly rejected the idea that Collingwood's ideological sympathies lay anywhere else than with liberalism in the 1930s, for all his support for the republican cause in the Spanish Civil War and his opposition to appeasement, commitments which had become integral to the left.[8] He had merely made his liberal commitment more public in the light of these events, applying no further principle from Marx than the indissolubility of theory and practice. As he recalled in his *Autobiography*, the appeasement controversy 'broke up my pose of a detached professional thinker'.[9] Collingwood was quite explicit in a (then) unpublished paper of 1936 that '[h]owever much so-called liberal governments have failed in acting up to their principles, those principles themselves are the most precious possession that man has ever acquired in the field of politics'.[10] They were not in themselves incompatible with socialism, but they were incompatible with forms of socialism which took the class war and dictatorship for its means of implementation. They constituted, in fact, the only true 'public' philosophy in the terms in which Collingwood drew it. The essence of liberalism being 'the dialectical solution of all political problems', its success depended upon the permeation of political life and activity throughout society. Implicit in liberalism was the idea that 'political activity and political education are inseparable, if not identical, that no politician is so expert that he should be allowed to govern without being exposed to the criticism of his fellow experts, none such a beginner or an ignoramus that his opinion is valueless to the community'.[11]

Thus for Collingwood a commitment to liberalism, and only a commitment to liberalism, would ensure the status of political thought as a public rather than a specialist activity. It also ensured a conception of politics as concerned primarily with orderliness and regularity; and the science of politics as concerned with that form of rightness which would secure this end.[12] Political action entailed the formulation and implementation of the rules by which order across a wide range of human actions was achieved. Unity and plurality were hence the indissoluble basis of political life,[13] as was an unbroken continuum of theory and practice. Rules, for Collingwood, existed only in a world of practice where they were creatively applied, an activity which pre-eminently involved freedom of the will.[14] This insistence pointed inevitably towards the need for closing the growing distance between intellectual and political life, and also between the world of the expert and the world of the common citizen. If Plato's proposal for philosopher-kings no longer drew the support it did at one time, argued Collingwood, this was not because 'our opinion of philosophy is lower, but because our opinion of the plain man is higher'.[15] Still, if philosophers had ceased to be 'pilots', they could not rest content with being mere spectators of everyday life. There remained for them a critical role in emphasising the creative possibilities of the human will at particular historical junctures, particularly in eradicating evils from social and political institutions. Collingwood, of course, regarded the 'realist' revolution in philosophy, with its conception of the indifference of knowing to what is known, as an abject twist in the development of modern philosophy.[16]

III

A conception of the arrogance of professional knowledge and a respect for the opinion of ordinary people similarly inspired the political philosophy of A. D. Lindsay.[17] With Collingwood, too, and consciously drawing upon the latter's work,[18] Lindsay attempted to reinstate political activity within a religious framework; in his case one that was essentially defined by his Scottish Presbyterian faith. His maternal grandfather had played a major role in the 'Disruption' of 1843 in which the Free Church broke away from the Established Church of Scotland.[19] While Lindsay's own religious faith appears to have been peripheral to his life and thought before 1925, when he became Master of Balliol, it began to occupy a more central position afterwards.[20] It was certainly from a deep Protestant sense of the divine imperative to pursue spiritual perfection that his interest in strengthening the theory – and practice – of modern democracy after this date developed.[21] His concern to flag the Puritan contribution to democracy stemmed from a belief which he attributed to Idealists such as Green against more secular contemporary viewpoints such as that of Leonard Woolf in the 1930s. Far from being incompatible, as the latter maintained, democracy and Christianity were inseparable: 'democracy was, and must be, based on religion, . . . the doctrine of human equality is a religious doctrine, or it is nothing'.[22]

Religion, for Lindsay, supplied the only possible basis of the secure public values which had proved to be at such a dangerous discount in recent years. This stance is especially significant when compared with that of his Oxford contemporary, William Temple, who became Archbishop of York in 1929 and Archbishop of Canterbury in 1941. By 1939, the latter had recognised the irrelevance of the 'Christo-centric metaphysics' which – even as late as the mid 1920s – he thought might come to dominate the philosophical atmosphere in Britain.[23] Temple, like Lindsay, had been trained as a philosopher by the Idealist thinker Edward Caird. But it was Lindsay who persisted in giving his teacher's creed the fullest religious as well as political application. Temple went no further than 'offer[ing] what religious support he could to a secular attempt to change, or perhaps even to discover the true nature of "British" identity by means of what came to be known as the "welfare state"'.[24] By contrast, Lindsay's much higher, Christian aspirations for politics are evident in a lecture he delivered on Plato in 1934. Plato, he maintained, had

> prepared the way for the Christian theory of democracy by maintaining that the state existed for the sake of the eternal life of all its individual members, and by showing that only through the apprehension of the eternal could a society be built which got beyond the struggle for power and provided for the true interests of all its members.[25]

For Lindsay, this view had become more, not less, compelling in the wake of the note of scepticism that modern liberalism and its Marxist antagonist alike struck during and after the Second World War. He found in this note of scepticism merely a reiteration of the negative, Lockean view that the essence of toleration – and the democratic institutions it later supported – was 'indifference or compromise'. This contrasted with the view of toleration associated with the Puritans of the left, who stressed its roots in a doctrine of 'the priesthood of all believers'.[26] Unlike their Anglican opponents, who were also concerned to attain comprehensiveness, they insisted on a strict separation of the spheres of church and state as the condition of the fulfilment of this notion. But with equal fervour the Puritans – and their nineteenth-century descendants, the Nonconformists – believed in the importance which different contributions could make to the unity of society. Writing in 1941, Lindsay argued that this spirit of reconciliation through the widest possible debate and dedication to a common cause, 'more deeply felt than clearly stated', was evident in the England of Elizabeth and Cromwell. It was 'nourished in times of crisis, [and] is very far from the spirit of the flabby tolerance of indifference which has sometimes so prevailed among us that we did not know who was for our cause and who was against it'.[27]

It was as if he had anticipated E. H. Carr's Cust Foundation Lecture of 1945, and a train in modern liberal and socialist thought which the latter intensified. Carr had argued that the claim of the Soviet Union to be a 'democratic' country was as equally valid as – and in some ways, not least in its greater amenability to planning, superior to – that of its western counterparts, democracy's nature being conceived there as fundamentally 'anti-aristocratic'.[28] Several responses to Carr emphasised the necessity of organised opposition to democracy – visibly lacking in the USSR – however much they conceded Carr's point that western tolerance was rooted in a 'lack of faith' in anything. As the Cambridge political scientist, D. W. Brogan, expressed the matter, the only unity of opinion that was possible in modern society was 'faith in the necessity, the healthy purgative character of scepticism. Doubt is part of our faith.'[29]

But Lindsay was concerned to stress the criterion, not merely of the existence of a government opposition and a culture of pluralism to democracy, but of discussion and the reconciliation of differences which it made possible. For Lindsay, this emphasis upon belief and debate as the basis of social unity was also the vital missing element in the Marxist emphasis upon progress through conflict, and he chose to exemplify it in the attitudes of the devout, from the seventeenth-century Anglican divine – William Chillingworth – to Roger Williams, leader of the 'left' Puritans in Rhode Island, and the Catholic intellectual, Baron Von Hügel. It was a far cry from the democracy of contemporary Russia, and while Lindsay went as far as conceding the existence of a flourishing grass-roots democracy there, he was not ready to shear democracy of all the aristocratic connections which Aristotle had attached to it at its best.[30] Indeed, he maintained, the tolerance by which English Protestants came to set such great store – the recognition that general councils may err – may plausibly be considered an aristocratic virtue. To Lindsay, it certainly seemed worth emphasising that the intellectuals upon whom Carr leant in deriding the 'indifference' that passed for 'tolerance' in the west were a Spaniard – Salvador de Madariaga – and a Russian, Nicolai Berdyaev. The implication here is that the religious inspiration behind toleration was more deeply rooted in England than elsewhere, and should be protected from the corrosion of secular political creeds, not least that of 'pure' democracy as practised in the Soviet Union.[31]

For Lindsay, the belief that tolerance was founded upon indifference would have been a chilling reminder of the progressive de-spiritualisation of the world, with all the opportunities for the manipulation of the masses that had accompanied it, and the origins of which he traced back to the sixteenth and seventeenth centuries. What had essentially gone wrong was that the scientific revolution which had accompanied the religious revolution associated with Protestantism in the pursuit of 'infinite understanding' had become exalted out of all proportion to its merit. Its momentum had been enhanced by the emergence of 'scientific individualism' – the nemesis of 'Christian individualism' – following the atomistic approach to knowledge taken by Descartes. Its progress was further consolidated in the work of Hobbes. As Lindsay argued in a series of lectures delivered at Yale University in 1943,

> Is not the Leviathan a parable of the impact of modern science upon an unregenerate society? Hobbes' men, as I have suggested, are animals in all but the possession of an over-developed intellect. Any lop-sided development of intellect would thus have a Hobbesian result, and any society which encouraged the scientific intellect, as Hobbes understands it, at the expense of other qualities would be so far a Hobbesian society. Do we not read Hobbes with different eyes when we have seen Hitler and learnt how modern scientific development and modern technology can produce in reality Hobbes' Leviathan?[32]

The joint 'great adventure' constituted by science and religion in the sixteenth and seventeenth centuries was finally arrested by industrialism, another antipathy Lindsay shared with Collingwood. Not surprisingly, Lindsay admired those nineteenth-century novelists – for example, Dickens, Mrs Gaskell, Disraeli and Trollope – who protested against the iniquities of modern society in reducing individuals to so many disposable units in the great industrial machine. He also recognised in mass democracy – as conceptualised by de Toqueville and Ortega y Gassett – the triumph of scientific individualism over Christian individualism. All of these ills had culminated in a secular, economic form of liberalism which differentiated between individuals while denying their essential spirituality.

However, Lindsay never ceased to believe in the possibility of salvation from these ills through re-creating the spirit of modern democracy in its truest, Puritan incarnation. Siding with Cromwell against the Levellers' demands for universal suffrage, Lindsay argued that although it was true that the 'will of God' might speak through the conscience of any human being, the claim to have received it must be submitted to the judgement of others. Hence the importance of the Puritan congregation, which Lindsay elevated to the status of prototype of democratic society writ large. In his support of Cromwell's stance, Lindsay followed his mentor, T. H. Green, who had been instrumental in rehabilitating

Cromwell's reputation in the nineteenth century. Green, too, rejected the argument for modern scepticism drawn from misinterpretations of the case for toleration. He upheld Cromwell's legacy, and that of Sir Henry Vane and the Independents to whom he saw Cromwell as closely allied. The principle of toleration which they advanced, Green argued, 'did not . . . rest, as in modern times, on the slippery foundation of a supposed indifference of all religious beliefs, but on the conviction of the sacredness of the reason, however, deluded, in every man, which may be constrained by nothing less divine than itself'.[33] But Lindsay was able to push further the basis of British Idealism in the legacy of the radicals of the English Civil War on account of the publication in 1891 of the Clarke Papers recording debates within the New Model Army at Putney.[34] Through a conjunction of the Idealist conception of the 'general will' with the Puritan conception of the 'Will of God', which would be defined through democratic discussion between equals, he endeavoured to strengthen the religious foundations of that creed. More than this, however, he clearly believed in the crucial role of democratic theory and practice, not only in counteracting the socially isolating effects of industrialism upon individuals, but also in strengthening Christian sentiment. Thus in an introduction to a series of broadcasts by eminent Churchmen of various religious denominations published in 1944, he urged his readers to reflect on the worth of 'devising elaborate democratic machinery to preserve freedom, if men cease to care for "the glorious liberty of the children of God"'. He went on to liken the futility of such a venture to 'building a wall to protect growing plants and finding that what should be life-giving soil is so arid and so full of brickbats that nothing grows inside the wall, and it becomes a place into which men throw tin cans and cigarette ends'.[35]

To the community-based organisations developed by the working class – trade unions, co-operative societies and the Labour Party – Lindsay attached special importance in revitalising democracy along the lines of its original, Puritan form. In the first volume of his *The Modern Democratic State*, published in 1943, he spelt out their role as an antidote to industrialism. His political sympathies were solidly socialist; but his socialism was of a markedly unworldly kind, embracing a conception of equality inspired by the Protestant idea of 'a calling to be free', a 'gift of God' bestowed on all men regardless of their 'station, abilities, wealth, or birth'.[36] It emphatically rejected definitions of equality in terms of wealth or capacity; on the first score, he believed that the material position of the working class had improved rather than deteriorated; and on the second, he insisted that modern government was heavily dependent upon technical expertise for the attainment of policy ends.[37] Although he never completed Volume 2 of *The Modern Democratic State*, the draft chapters indicate a further privileging of working-class organisations as the backbone of the 'public concern groups' whose role it was to supply the new, democratic 'ruling class'.[38] For like Collingwood, Lindsay was keenly interested in emphasising the necessity of an easily permeable boundary between the ruling and ruled classes. But both the first volume, and the draft chapters of the second, were heavily tinged with a pessimistic sense that democracy was seriously threatened by dark forces: on the one hand, the growth of expertise had vastly outstripped the capacity of the 'plain man' to ensure that government fulfilled the common good of society (particularly in the face of the new weapons of mass destruction); and on the other, there was no guarantee that the 'integrative' forces of 'public concern groups' would triumph over the 'dispersive' forces of mere interest groups.[39] Lindsay's failure to complete Volume 2 may well have been rooted in a sense of despair that these threats and uncertainties could ever be overcome; further- more, in a scepticism that the scientific mentality of the expert could yield to the individual approach to human problems that he so much admired in Victorian reformers such as Octavia Hill;[40] and finally, an anxiety that the essential basis of the spirit of democratic equality in religious faith[41] was likely to be wanting in the future.

Lindsay's political thought may have been vulnerable in the face of these pres- sures because of his entrenched antipathy towards Lutheranism. He identified more with Calvinism than Lutheranism.[42] This was not just on the grounds of loyalty to an ancestral Scottish Presbyterian religion but also because of his unease with the supreme authority which Luther bestowed upon the Prince in interpreting the law of the Church, and the passive acceptance of the morality of 'my station and its duties' and retreat into their inner life incumbent upon Christian subjects as a corollary. The role of Lutheranism in hampering the German Churches' protest against Nazism confirmed Lindsay's faith in the great store which Calvinism set by the responsibility of all Christians for interpreting the word of God through human institutions. While he hailed the essentially British practice of congregationalism as the source of modern democracy, it was not a matter in which Lindsay ever indulged any sense of national pride. He dis- trusted nationalism as all of a piece with the industrialism and liberalism that had blighted contemporary society, and he regarded the religious congregation as integral to the survival of democracy worldwide. Nevertheless, the contrast between the independence of the Churches in Britain and their subordination to the state in Germany, and also between the nakedness of political power in Germany and its conditional nature in Britain, gave Lindsay considerable food for philosophical thought. A lasting impression had been made upon him by the publication of Ernst Troeltsch's great study of the way in which the various Protestant sects viewed the problem of the two moralities in the second volume of *The Social Teaching of the Christian Churches* in 1912.[43] His eyes had been opened to the basis of modern politics in force at the time of the First World War when, along with many British academics at the time, he became much exercised by the problem of 'Prussianism'. He continued to recommend A. J. Balfour's elo- quent but critical introduction to Treitschke's *Politics* of 1916 well into the Second World War.[44] It may well be that, as Graham Maddox has persuasively argued, if Lindsay had appreciated the potential in Lutheranism for a reciprocal relationship between the two forms of individual and communal perfection, which were nevertheless sharply distinguished, the ambiguities of his democratic theory might have been resolved.[45] This would have required, however, a more moderate view of the transformative effect of the morality of grace upon the morality of power than his Calvinist political theory enjoined, and to which the bringing up of his political thought sharply against the realities of political power also pointed.

IV

In this respect, the political philosophy of Lindsay reflected a wider trend in the social thought of the Anglican Church in the late 1930s and 1940s, even if he himself was unable to respond effectively. Edward Norman has written of the growth of 'realism' among the Church's leading thinkers which began in these decades – a conscious retreat from the radicalism of the early years of the twentieth century marked by the heyday of the Church's social conscience.[46] Attempts continued to harness Christian and political thought, but with more moderate expectations of the consequences and with the latter rather than the former as the principal driver. Whereas Lindsay had set his sights upon religious revival, an end that could be achieved through political means, Temple had pursued the ideal of national revival using the full force of Anglicanism.

With important qualifications, the same was true of T. S. Eliot. Throughout the 1930s, Eliot was struggling to give expression to the Christian aspirations for society that were developing alongside, but never in association with, his modernist literary criticism.[47] His efforts were consolidated in the company of likeminded Christian intellectuals in small groups such as 'The Moot' – which existed between 1938 and 1947 – and the Christian Frontier Council (1942). His lectures on *The Idea of a Christian Society*, delivered at Corpus Christi College, Cambridge, and published shortly after the declaration of war in 1939, developed from such links. Eliot made far less concession to the 'wisdom of the plain man' as the ultimate repository of society's common will than Lindsay. But like Lindsay, and also Collingwood, he emphasised the responsibility of intellectuals to reverse the moral and spiritual decline of society, through all available Christian means. Like them, too, he was concerned to treat the ills of modern society as a whole, although with indigenous forces such as the Established Church and debates within it assuming disproportionate influence; this naturally diminished the relevance of his model to societies in which such a Church was inappropriate, a limitation which he fully recognised.[48] Also in common with these two contemporary political philosophers, he laid the blame for the present crisis of spirit, thought and politics in western society squarely upon the shoulders of a secularised liberalism. Liberalism had confirmed its potential for transformation into its very opposite: 'the artificial, mechanized or brutalized control which is a desperate remedy for its chaos'.[49] Likewise, in relegating religious matters to a discrete private world – the nemesis of the Puritan emphasis upon religious liberty as a basis for public engagement – Christianity had fallen victim to the toleration it once so urgently sought: it had been tolerated out of existence by the subtle pressures of a non-Christian society.[50] The upshot was the bankruptcy of public life (and language), and a people without convictions. The failure to address this problem concealed the paganism which Britain shared with its fascist foes.[51]

In urging a Christianisation of both state and society, Eliot distinguished his endeavour from that of the Christian sociologists, led by V. A. Demant. Their interest in shaping public policy along Christian lines missed an essential precondition for its success: the need to change social attitudes more widely. Eliot was anxious that his proposals should not be mistaken for mere 'revivalism', or the reintroduction of a Christian morality without the supporting theology in touch with the universal Catholic Church; and he feared that the measures of the Christian sociologists could be easily accepted by anyone of sufficient goodwill.[52] While he advocated national Churches as focuses of Christian belief, he insisted that they should maintain strong links with the universal Church. In the notes at the end of the essay, he distinguished his own position in this respect from that of his contemporary, John Middleton Murry, and Thomas and Matthew Arnold, from whom Murry drew support. The upshot, he claimed, of discounting the need for doctrinal orthodoxy in Christian life and placing greater emphasis upon 'worship', as these authors did, would be the degradation of Christianity to nationalism rather than the raising of nationalism to a Christian level. He asked, 'What does Mr. Murry mean by Christianity in his National Church, except whatever the nation as such may decide to call Christianity?' Equally vacuous in this respect was the 'Moral Rearmament' movement of the late 1930s, which Eliot dismissed as 'no more essentially Christian than the German National Religion of Professor [Wilhelm] Hauer'.[53] The true Christian society, he believed, was much more deeply permeated with religious than national ideals. 'It would be a society in which the natural end of man – virtue and well-being in community – is acknowledged for all, and the supernatural end – beautitude – for those who have eyes to see it'.[54] If the true Christian society were never fully attainable it remained an ideal to strive for, albeit through the institutions and culture of the nation-state.

Naturally, the pursuit of so exalted a goal would require a good deal of leadership, and the elite in whom Eliot placed his trust was designated by the term 'Community of Christians'. This was a conscious adaption of Coleridge's notion of the 'Clerisy'. Coleridge confined membership of the latter to the clerical (and exclusively Anglican) orders. By contrast, Eliot recognised that the educational institutions through which the elite would principally work had outstripped the Church's control. He thus accepted that non-Christians – both secularists and adherents of other faiths – would also hold teaching positions. But they would be directed by a select group of 'consciously and thoughtfully practising Christians, especially those of intellectual and spiritual superiority'. This Community of Christians would ensure at all educational levels that 'Christian presuppositions of what education – as distinct from mere instruction – is for'[55] were implemented. No stronger – and no weaker – a conception of

Christian education was required to realise the Thomist ends which Eliot had outlined for a Christian society. Firmly in the Clerisy tradition which had been sustained since Coleridge by Arnold, Mill and Russell, Eliot insisted on the necessity of a broadly uniform culture to any civilised society, and that a key pre-requisite for attaining that culture was a 'positive distinction – however undem-ocratic it might sound – between the educated and the uneducated'.[56] The Clerisy, however, had consciously to address itself to the spiritual needs of the latter. He deplored the 'refined provincial crudity' in which intellectuals wrote either for a small circle of fellow writers or a vaguely imagined popular audience whose existence was questionable. While not wishing to confine culture and learning to the cloister once more, nor could he contemplate as progressive 'the segregation of lay "intellectuals" into a world of their own, which very few eccle-siastics or politicians either penetrate or have any curiosity about'.[57] To avoid the 'half-baked philosophies' generated by the latter situation, what was needed was a common background of knowledge which presumably traversed the current theological/literary/political divide.[58]

Eliot was attempting to steer a middle way between two sides of contempo-rary Christian opinion in Britain on the relationship of Christianity to society. On the one hand, the Catholic writer Christopher Dawson advocated a 'demo-cratic organisation of culture' which would be stripped of any link with philos-ophy and theology towards which the predominantly lower-middle-class character of modern society was indifferent. This would at least provide a bulwark against the totalitarianism which threatened to obliterate Christian civ-ilisation entirely, without forcing the Church to side with the dominant ideology of the time or, indeed, to set itself up as an ideological rival itself.[59] On the other hand, Christian publicists of the left, such as Maurice Reckitt, pursued a more ambitious course for Christianity, entailing a far greater commitment to spiri-tual holiness for the masses than the mere outward obedience to Christian forms of behaviour favoured by Eliot. To the first, Eliot emphasised the need for an elite of 'thought, conduct, and taste' which would produce the culture of the lower middle class, and presumably with more definite Christian shape than Dawson envisaged.[60] To the accusation of the second – that his 'idea' of a Christian society was 'sub-Christian' – he retorted that his proposals were in keeping with Christendom's experience of the New Testament, not that of utopian humanity's. He added, 'If I risk destruction in Pelagianism, Mr. Reckitt the theologian runs the danger of abandoning the world to Mr. Reckitt the social worker'.[61]

It is significant that Ernest Barker was equally sceptical of Reckitt's aspira-tions to remake the social order along Christian lines, despite his equally strong Christian commitment. He held no brief for Eliot, despite having read a good deal of his verse and prose.[62] But he, too, had increasingly woven Christian themes into his political thought in the interwar period. In 1932 he shared with Reckitt – whom he had taught at Oxford – the reasons why he had recently turned down an invitation from the Dean of Exeter[63] to write a book on the

Christian conception of society and the state, and in the process voiced friendly
criticism of Reckitt's outlook:

> I can only repeat to you my deep feeling that the 'general Christian' underlies all
> human life, but the 'specific Christian' cannot be carried through each of life's
> phases. For we pass into the infinite, when we pass into the vast detail of life; and
> in the region of infinite detail we have to get on as best we can. And if we tie up our
> Faith about this or that solution to the detail, we box it in too small a receptacle.[64]

This response emphasises well the cautiousness with which many secular intellectuals in Britain approached the problem of filling what they regarded as the
dangerous spiritual void that had opened up in the twentieth century, largely
through the separation of modern liberalism from Christianity. It was a caution
to which Eliot could not have been more sympathetic. In many ways, he simply
kept up the pressure for a society marked by a common culture which had been
the aspiration of Britain's governing minds since the second half of the nineteenth century, and which had assumed new urgency in the interwar period at the
same time that it acquired a more definite Christian shape. Like them, he believed
that 'a nation's system of education is much more important than its system of
government'.[65] There is no suggestion in his writings or activities in groups such
as The Moot that compulsion formed any part of his plan for the regeneration
of society. He was not engaged in the production of blueprints for reform or programmes for political change.[66] He was certainly not a devotee of conspirational
politics in reaction against a sense of the futility of revolution, as demonstrated
by the *Action Francaise*, whose spearhead – Charles Maurras – one commenta-
tor has recently argued was the presiding influence over Eliot, both before and
after his 'conversion' in 1927.[67] He was discriminating, too, in the company he
kept, even at the height of the Cultural Cold War, turning down a request by
Stephen Spender to write for the American-backed journal *Encounter*.[68]

Nevertheless, Eliot was virtually disowned by fellow literary critics such as Sir
Arthur Quiller-Couch following the publication in 1934 of *After Strange Gods*,
his earlier condemnation of British intellectuals for straying from the wholesome
path of 'orthodoxy' in morals and values. This work was far less tempered than
The Idea of a Christian Society, although its emphasis on the need for re-
establishing Christian standards in public and cultural life formed a clear bridge
between the two. For 'Q', the triumph of Eliot's proposals would spell little more
than the suppression of free thought by 'dogma' – 'the priestly utterance of a
particular offset of a particular branch of a historically fissiparous Church'.
Eliot's work roused him to an eloquent defence of the 'tradition' embodied not
in 'orthodoxy' but in 'that Liberty which was the ark within the citadel of our
father's soul'. This was his alternative interpretation of the ideal of 'the poet as
citizen', drawing upon the full pantheon of English literature – from Chaucer to
Dickens – in his support.[69] Here, Quiller-Couch well illustrates the reaction
against cosmopolitan strains of interwar political thought – for all their immer-
sion in national institutional models such as the Anglican Church – which will

form the subject of Part III. It was this quality, as much as, if not more than, the religious presumptions of Eliot, that caused offence. Eliot was to redeem himself in this respect in the postwar period by lending considerable intellectual weight to the notion of a 'British way', whose coherence and uniqueness lay in its traditions of internal national diversity.[70]

But in defence of Eliot's stance in the 1930s, it might be said that just as he was the first to recognise that those Christians who were most vociferous in their Christian faith were those most lacking in it, so those most hostile were in some ways the embodiments of the Christian spirit. While the latter category would not be represented in the Community of Christians, nevertheless they were not to be denied influential positions within society.[71] An example of the committed but secular intellectual who might well have been accorded such a position will be considered in the following chapter.

Notes

1   See P. Williamson, *Stanley Baldwin: Conservative Leadership and National Values* (Cambridge, Cambridge University Press, 1999), ch. 10; and 'Christian conservatives and the totalitarian challenge, 1933–1940', *English Historical Review*, 115:462 (2000), 607–42. E. F. M. Durbin's psychological analysis of extremism in terms of group aggression, which led him to catalogue and compare the atrocities of Nazi Germany and the Soviet Union, won him few allies on the left. See his *The Politics of Democratic Socialism: An Essay on Social Policy* (London, Routledge, 1940); also see S. Brooke, 'Evan Durbin: reassessing a Labour "revisionist"', *Twentieth-Century History*, 7:1 (1996), 27–52.

2   H. Samuel, 'The present need of a philosophy', *Philosophy*, 9 (1934), 134–6.

3   C. E. M. Joad, 'Appeal to philosophers', *Philosophy*, 15 (1940), 400, 408.

4   R. G. Collingwood, 'Fascism and Nazism', *Philosophy*, 15 (1940), reprinted in D. Boucher (ed.), *Essays in Political Philosophy: R. G. Collingwood* (Oxford, Clarendon Press, 1989), p. 196, note 2.

5   Collingwood, 'Fascism and Nazism', p. 190.

6   See Collingwood's unpublished paper, 'Man goes mad', begun 30 August 1936, Collingwood MS, Dep. 24/4 Folder 38. The first half of this paper is published as 'Modern politics' in Boucher (ed.), *Essays in Political Philosophy*. On the influence of Ruskin on Collingwood in shaping his rural sensitivities, see D. Boucher, 'The place of education in civilization', in D. Boucher, J. Connelly, and T. Modood (eds), *Philosophy, History and Civilization: Interdisciplinary Perspectives on R. G. Collingwood* (Cardiff, University of Wales Press, 1995), pp. 269–99. The context of Collingwood's concern in significant debate about the role of the countryside in interwar Britain will be seen in Chapter 6.

7   Collingwood, 'Fascism and Nazism', p. 191.

8   Boucher, Introduction to *Essays in Political Philosophy*, p. 30.

9   R. G. Collingwood, *An Autobiography* (Oxford, Oxford University Press, 1939), p. 167.

10 Collingwood, 'Modern politics', p. 180.

11 Collingwood, 'Modern politics', p. 178.

12 R. G. Collingwood, 'Politics', extract from 'Lectures on Moral Philosophy' (1933), in Boucher (ed.), *Essays in Political Philosophy*, p. 119.

13 Collingwood, 'Politics', p. 112.

14 Collingwood, 'Politics', pp. 115–16.

15 R. G. Collingwood, 'The present need of a philosophy', *Philosophy*, IX (1935), reprinted in Boucher (ed.), *Essays in Political Philosophy*, p. 167.

16 Collingwood, *An Autobiography*, ch. 6.

17 See, for example, his lecture *The Good and the Clever*, The Founders Memorial Lecture, Girton College, Cambridge (Cambridge, Cambridge University Press, 1945); and 'Philosophy as criticism of standards', a paper read at the Jubilee Meeting of the Scots Philosophical Club, 29 September 1950, published in E. V. Lindsay (ed.), *A. D. Lindsay, 1879–1952: Selected Addresses* (E. V. Lindsay, Cumberland, 1957).

18 See A. D. Lindsay, 'Christian individualism and scientific individualism', in T. F. Woodlock (ed.), *Democracy: Should it Survive?* (London, Dennis Dobson, 1946), p. 118.

19 D. Scott, *A. D. Lindsay: A Biography* (Oxford, Blackwell, 1971), p. 10.

20 Scott, *A. D. Lindsay*, pp. 174–5.

21 G. Maddox, 'Skirmishers in Advance: A. D. Lindsay and modern democratic theory', in *Balliol College Annual Record* (1997), p. 14.

22 A. D. Lindsay, Introduction to T. H. Green, *Lectures on the Principles of Political Obligation* (London, Longmans, Green & Co., 1941), p. ix.

23 D. Emmett, 'The philosopher', in F. A. Iremonger, *William Temple: Archbishop of Canterbury* (London, Oxford University Press, 1948), pp. 521–2.

24 J. Kent, 'William Temple, the Church of England and British national identity', in R. Weight and A. Beach (eds), *The Right to Belong: Citizenship and National Identity in Britain, 1930–1960* (London, I. B. Tauris, 1998), p. 34.

25 A. D. Lindsay, *The Churches and Democracy*, The Social Service Lecture (London, Epworth, 1934), p. 77.

26 Lindsay, *The Churches and Democracy*, p. 26; and *Christianity and Economics* (London, Macmillan, 1933), p. 15.

27 A. D. Lindsay, *Toleration and Democracy*, Lucien Wolf Memorial Lecture, 1941, (London, Oxford University Press, 1942), pp. 16–17.

28 E. H. Carr, *Democracy in International Affairs*, Cust Foundation Lecture, 1945 (Nottingham: University of Nottingham, 1945), pp. 5–6.

29 D. W. Brogan, contribution to *What is Democracy?*, Peace Aims Pamphlet No. 38 (London, 1946), p. 17. This brought together several contributions to the public debate in the *Manchester Guardian* that was sparked by Carr's lecture. Other contributors included II. J. Laski and S. de Madariaga.

30 See his comments on attempts at Balliol to lay aristocratic foundations for British democracy, p. 15.

31 A. D. Lindsay, 'Democracy in the world today', in R. McKeon (ed.), *Democracy in a World of Tension* (Chicago, University of Chicago Press, 1951), pp. 180–1.

32 A. D. Lindsay, *Religion, Science and Society* (Oxford, Oxford University Press, 1943), p. 23.

33 T. H. Green, 'Four Lectures on the English Commonwealth', in R. L. Nettleship (ed.), *The Works of Thomas Hill Green*, 3 vols, III (London, Longman, Green & Co., 1888), pp. 296–7.

34 C. Firth (ed.), *Clarke Papers*, 4 vols (London, Camden Society, 1891–1901). Lindsay wrote in 1928 that the ideas contained in the Clarke Papers constituted 'the first authentic utterance of modern democracy with which I am acquainted'. A. D. Lindsay, *General Will and Common Mind* (London, Hodder & Stoughton, 1928), p. 4.

35 A. D. Lindsay, 'The Church's concern', in William Temple, *et al.*, *The Crisis of the Western World And Other Broadcast Talks* (London, George Allen & Unwin, 1944), p. 13.

36 See Lindsay, 'Christian individualism and scientific individualism', p. 120.

37 See A. D. Lindsay, *The Modern Democratic State*, (London, Oxford University Press, 1943), pp. 173, 259; See also 'The philosophy of the British Labour Government', in F. C. S. Northrop (ed.), *Ideological Differences and World Order: Studies in the Philosophy and Science of the World's Cultures* (New Haven, Yale University Press, 1949).

38 The draft chapters are in the Lindsay Papers (L214), Keele University Library.

39 Lindsay, draft of *The Modern Democratic State*, Volume 2, Lindsay Papers (L214); *The Modern Democratic State*, vol. 1, ch. XI.

40 Lindsay, *The Good and the Clever*, p. 27.

41 A. D. Lindsay, *I Believe in Democracy*, addresses broadcast in the BBC Empire Programme (London, Oxford University Press, 1940), p. 13.

42 See his Foreword to the German translation of his *The Two Moralities: Our Duty to God and Society* (London, Eyre and Spottiswoode, 1940), in the Lindsay Papers, L204.

43 Lindsay, Foreword to the German translation of *The Two Moralities*. E. Troeltsch, *The Social Teaching of the Christian Churches*, transl. O. Wyon (London, Allen & Unwin, 1931).

44 H. von Treitschke, *Politics*, transl. B. Dugdale and T. de Bille, 2 vols (London, Constable, 1916).

45 See Maddox, 'Skirmishers in advance', p. 16.

46 Edward Norman, *Church and State in England, 1770–1970: A Historical Study* (London, Clarendon Press, 1976), ch. 9.

47 On the disjunction between Eliot's political and religious projects, on the one hand, and his literary criticism, on the other, see L. Menand, 'T. S. Eliot', in A. Walton Litz, L. Menand and L. Rainey (eds), *The Cambridge History of Literary Criticism*, vol. 7, *Modernism and the New Criticism* (Cambridge, Cambridge University Press, 2000), pp. 17–56.

48 R. Kojecky, *T. S. Eliot's Social Criticism* (London, Faber & Faber, 1971), p. 136.

49 T. S. Eliot, *The Idea of a Christian Society and other Writings*, intro. by D. Edwards (London, Faber & Faber, [1939] 1982), p. 49.

50 Eliot, *The Idea of a Christian Society*, pp. 53–4.

51 Eliot, *The Idea of a Christian Society*, p. 52.

52 Eliot, *The Idea of a Christian Society*, pp. 45, 78.

53 Eliot, *The Idea of a Christian Society*, pp. 95, 86.

54 Eliot, *The Idea of a Christian Society*, p. 62.

55 Eliot, *The Idea of a Christian Society*, p. 63.

56 Eliot, *The Idea of a Christian Society*, p. 67.

57 Eliot, *The Idea of a Christian Society*, p. 65.

58 Eliot, *The Idea of a Christian Society*, p. 66.

59 C. Dawson, *Beyond Politics* (New York, Sheed & Ward, 1939), pp. 30–1, 90–1.
60 Eliot, *The Idea of a Christian Society*, pp. 90–2. In 1946, Dawson was more hopeful that – due to the cataclysm of war – the spiritual renewal of which western civilisation was sorely in need could be achieved. See his essay, 'Religion and mass civilization', in Woodlock (ed.), *Democracy*.
61 Eliot, *The Idea of a Christian Society*, p. 115.
62 Barker to Frances Brett Young, 10 March 1948 and 6 April 1953; in Frances Brett Young Papers, Birmingham University Library, FBY 2546 and 2547.
63 The Very Reverend Walter Robert Matthews.
64 Barker to Reckitt, 3 October 1932; Reckitt Papers, Box 10/1, University of Sussex Library, Brighton.
65 Eliot, *The Idea of a Christian Society*, p. 67.
66 D. Edwards, Introduction to *The Idea of a Christian Society*, pp. 18–19.
67 K. Asher, *T. S. Eliot and Ideology* (Cambridge, Cambridge University Press, 1995), p. 85.
68 F. Stonor Saunders, *Who Paid the Piper? The CIA and the Cultural Cold War* (London, Granta, 1999), pp. 186–7.
69 A. Quiller-Couch, *The Poet as Citizen and Other Papers* (Cambridge, Cambridge University Press, 1934), pp. 61–5.
70 See his *Notes Towards the Definition of Culture* (London, Faber & Faber, 1948), ch. III. On the historical significance of this text, see C. Harvie, 'The moment of British nationalism, 1939–1970', *Political Quarterly*, 71:3 (2000), 330–1, 337.
71 Eliot, *The Idea of a Christian Society*, p. 68.

4

Communism and the religious impulse:
John Strachey and the search
for political faith

I

It is salutory to reflect further upon Eliot's remark concerning the spirit of Christianity often being embodied in its intellectual foes. It is particularly worthwhile to consider the extraordinary fertility of Marxism during the 1930s in its light. For without doubt, Marxism and the associated phenomenon of fellow-travelling traded upon the increasing lack of assurance which characterised British intellectual life as the authority previously commanded by liberalism in this sphere was progressively undermined.[1] As we saw in the previous chapter, it was liberalism's association with agnosticism that proved not the least important source of its travails. In some cases, this vacuum at the heart of liberalism redounded all to the benefit of Catholicism, as in the circle of writers and aesthetes which emerged in postwar Oxford and whose Catholic converts included Evelyn Waugh, Christopher Hollis and Harold Acton.[2] Others turned in earnest to alternative faiths of a political variety, but whose strength was equally potent. While maintaining the spirit of denial that had become a central feature of liberalism, no attempts were made to disguise the religious parallels of the new and more exotic forms of political belief, particularly those on the left. As Laski wrote of his conversion to Marxism, it had left him with 'the paradoxical sense that a fighting philosophy confers an inner peace unobtainable without its possession'.[3] Earlier, he had written of the 'compelling strength' of communism: 'that it has a faith as vigorous, as fanatic, and compelling as any in the history of religions'. It was doubtful, he maintained, whether capitalism could inspire 'emotions of similar intensity', even in the hearts of those whom it most benefited.[4] Keynes, as we have had occasion to observe, could only look with envy at the capacity of communism to inspire its followers. Eliot likewise sensed that, unless Toryism could match the discipline and conviction achieved by communism through forging new Christian roots, it too – like liberalism – would be fatally undermined.[5] Indeed, so intertwined did the political and religious impulse become in the communism of the 1930s that a notable school of Christian communism developed,

79

led by the Scottish philosopher John Macmurray and the English analytical thinker John Lewis.[6]

An added attraction of communism as a political faith was the comradeship and 'community of the faithful' it offered to intellectuals. The ideal of intellectual autonomy which had been steadfastly upheld by nineteenth-century thinkers – such as J. S. Mill and John Morley – lost much of its former sheen after the First World War. The basic moral and political certainties which had sustained the much-valued independence of the intellectual were then greatly eroded. To communist converts such as John Strachey in the early 1930s, surrender of the liberal conscience to the unquestionable commands of a centralised party was a small price to pay for the comfort of intellectual rectitude they were assured in return. Conscience also became an easily expendable item of excess baggage from a bourgeois past – an encumbrance that was happily discarded in the attempt to prove the earnestness of their new political commitments.[7] Indeed, one can almost say that the uncompromising defence of intellectual integrity by late Victorian intellectuals such as Morley invited the abdication of any sense of political responsibility in circumstances of economic and political crisis. For all his concern to temper the political spirit ('respect for what is instantly practicable') with the intellectual spirit ('the search after what is important only in thought'), there is no recognition of at least the occasional value of the obverse – of tempering the intellectual spirit with the spirit of (democratic) politics.[8]

Finally, integral to the vision of communism was an ideal of effective party organisation – not unlike the more hierarchical forms of religion – to which the Soviet system gave dramatic expression and which intellectuals of the left applauded. Contemplating the odds that were stacked against the parliamentary route to socialism, Stafford Cripps maintained that a vital precondition was 'party loyalty and solidarity'. He continued, 'once the party is in power it will have to be ruthless as regards individuals. Those who do not devote themselves whole-heartedly to the active propagation of the Plan must not be allowed to have the power to hand over the fortress to the forces of capitalism'.[9]

Some Marxists were of course anxious to disentangle their creed from the taint of religion. John Strachey, for example, denied that the communist dedication to the improvement of mankind was simply a subliminal form of religious longing. The commitment to human betterment and the belief in a deity were two very different ideals, he maintained, and the first should not be confused with theology any more than the second should be confused with philanthropy. Nevertheless, entirely despairing of the hold of religion on the human imagination as Strachey was, he still appealed to the Christian to recognise the essential conformity of his or her ideal, 'mystical' though it was, of a 'united humanity' with that of the communist dedication to the same end. In the face of that common commitment – conspicuously rejected by Nazi philosophers – the communist insistence on class war as a means to that end was, he maintained, irrelevant.[10]

Strachey himself was anything but a narrow class warrior, for all his anxiety to please the communist authorities, and both his interest in the relationship between communism and Christianity, and his communist commitment itself in the early 1930s invite further inquiry. It is not just Strachey's unparalleled ability to present 'contemporary macroeconomics from a Marxian standpoint' or 'the compelling clarity' with which he expounded Marxism that strikes the reader of his writings during this period – the emphasis of a recent study.[11] As the present chapter seeks to show, the politics of so central a communist thinker as Strachey has to be understood in terms of a crisis of authority and belief within Britain's intellectual elite, as much as an extreme response to domestic and world events. In Strachey's Marxism lay not only an attempt to settle accounts with Christianity, now returning to haunt the agnosticism which had attempted to expel it from intellectual culture some half-century previously; but also a critical review of the contemporary British world of letters whose cultural ascendancy and impact on political thought he wished to maintain, albeit through the unorthodox channel of communism. At the end of the chapter it will become clear that in this endeavour Strachey was not alone: Marxism also seemed to A. L. Rowse the key to reviving political thought, letters and public culture in Britain simultaneously. In both cases, however, Marxism fell victim to its own success in this respect.

II

From his first book, *The Coming Struggle for Power* (1932), published by Victor Gollancz's Left Book Club in 1936, Strachey proved himself to be a worthy successor of the cultivated mantle of his father – John St Loe Strachey, Editor of *The Spectator* from 1898 until 1925 – and equally adept at educating public opinion in the political causes he held dear. Faithful to the distinguished intellectual lineage of his family, he encased his political ideas in a broad historical and literary framework of inquiry, acted from a strong sense of duty to bring 'truth' before the general public and kept alive the interlocking world of politics and letters, which had been an integral part of the Victorian tradition of the public intellectual. Indeed, Strachey's application to join the Communist Party in 1932 was turned down, not only because his intellectual interests were still too wide of the strict communist mark (for example, he retained a keen interest in Freud when he turned to Marxism) but also because it was thought that he could perhaps do more for the Party if he were not a paid-up member.[12]

Strachey's concern to become a 'public' intellectual was manifested in 1925 when, with Cyril Joad, he launched a series of radio programmes designed to 'introduce the public to some of the problems of philosophy'.[13] The light-hearted but also didactic nature of these programmes was reproduced at a more serious level in his Marxist works of the 1930s. The latter stemmed from a deep sense of personal intellectual mission – a belief which he expressed to Victor Gollancz in 1934 – that 'I happen to be the only person who is putting over this particular information [that is, Marxism] which people desperately need today, in a form which they can comprehend.'[14] As a doyen of Gollancz's Left Book

Club, he wrote articles – almost continuously over a period of five years – for its monthly organ *Left News*. The style of these articles led his biographer to remark that 'they did for the socialist left what St Loe's *Spectator* had done for the upper class before 1925: they gave ammunition'.[15]

It was undoubtedly the less than orthodox status of Strachey's communism which gave his writings such a high premium. They ranged far wider than the tight economic focus of those of Rajani Palme Dutt – the Communist Party of Great Britain's leading theoretician – who nevertheless remained an intellectual figurehead for Strachey in the 1930s. Strachey had been gravitating further to the left since the early 1920s, when he joined forces with the Independent Labour Party. He became a Labour MP in June 1929, and while he threw in his lot with Oswald Mosley's New Party the following year, the theoretical basis of the Party's policies which he helped to formulate were of a decisively socialist hue.[16] His conversion to communism in 1931 was finally sealed by a sense that what was at stake was nothing less than civilisation itself – not the ending of capitalist exploitation more narrowly. For Strachey, the economic and political crisis of 1931 posed a stark choice between communism and civilisation, on the one hand, and the 'mental and moral suicide of fascism', on the other. This was unaccept-able to at least one communist critic, for whom Strachey had simply opted for 'the policy of the lesser evil'.[17] Neither was it a flippant comment designed to add lustre to what was essentially a philosophy of proletarian liberation. On the con-trary, Strachey took great pains throughout the book to emphasise the damage which capitalism had done to all facets of the arts and sciences, even envisaging the indefinite postponement of death in a communist society, due to the 'full pos-sibilities' it offered for the development of science.[18] Furthermore, despite refer-ences to continental literary figures such as Proust, Nietzsche and Freud, a major, perhaps even the main, concern of *The Coming Struggle for Power* was to con-front the work of contemporary intellectuals in Britain, and their account of British history and culture.

This is evident right at the start of the book, in which Strachey considered the nature of modern British history in terms other than the 'struggle for liberty' in a narrowly political sense which Whig historians such as Trevelyan continued to propagate. Targeting Trevelyan's view – expressed in *England Under the Stuarts* (1904) – that the Glorious Revolution was stirred by the pure passions of patri-otism, religion and love of liberty, rather than class greed, Strachey pulled his opponent up sharp over the middle-class resistance to taxation in the ship money trial of John Hampden. He remarked of this episode, sarcastically, that 'there is nothing like a threat to property for rousing moral splendour in prosperous patriots'.[19] The Whigs were champions of nothing more noble than the market, the freedom to buy and sell, and simply represented one episode in a struggle which had begun at the time of the Reformation and flowered to full conscious-ness in the writings of Smith, Jefferson and Paine. In classic Marxist fashion, Strachey went on in the book to elaborate how ideas were dependent upon the social system which gave birth to them, and while not denying the intellectual achievements of the capitalist age of 'individualistic freedom', he took as his starting point the progressive degeneration of all aspects of human thought – in association with the 'dry rot' at their economic base.[20] In the field of literature, this was evident in the writings of D. H. Lawrence, Marcel Proust and Aldous Huxley, all of whose 'tragic' view of human life failed to appreciate the relevant backdrop in 'a specific system of society in a period of decay'. In the field of poetry, it was evident in the gradual impoverishment of the English tradition – once that nation's 'greatest aesthetic achievement':

> Laggards and dunces at the plastic arts, heirs to a tradition of native music which somehow died before it had had the opportunity to come to maturity, the English have century after century poured their fancy into a golden stream of poetry, which is without rival in the world.[21]

But the stream which had flowed unbroken from Chaucer to Shelley then became a 'trickle'. The drying up of English poetry was illustrated in the slim output of A. E. Housman, 'the very last of the English classical poets'.[22] Literary modernism was similarly condemned: one of its best exemplars – T. S. Eliot – had sought sanctuary from the 'waste land' of capitalist decay in the 'typical position of a highly intellectual reactionary',[23] while James Joyce burst the boundaries of the old literary culture but without any real certainty about the position of the new.[24] As for the country's leading social critics – Wells, Shaw and Keynes – they were notable for failing to recognise the full force of their critical analysis of contemporary society: given the extent of its problems which they all readily identified, it was inconceivable that capitalism could be – in the words of Keynes – 'wisely managed'.[25]

Strachey turned for relief to the literary fountainheads of British communism and socialism – Sir Thomas More, Gerald Winstanley and William Morris – whose work he explored in his next book for the Left Book Club, *The Theory and Practice of Socialism*. Winstanley was judged by Strachey to have lacked the 'polish and elegance of the scholarly More, but he was at least as eloquent a writer and was in many respects a more profound thinker'. He was not, however, a mere *savant* but was acutely alive to the importance of the tie between theory and practice, vilifying the 'clerical philosophers' of his day as '"monsters who are all tongue and no hand"'. The value that Strachey placed upon the literary and intellectual quality of these figures is thrown into sharp relief when he comes to discuss Robert Owen, whose pragmatism in the apparent absence of a directing theory he wholly despised. The Fabians fell into the same doomed category, imagining that socialism could be achieved by a succession of reformist measures to whose cumulative effect the capitalist class would be insensible. It was for Morris, however, in perceiving the consequences of reformism in fascism, that Strachey reserved his ultimate accolade: the genius of the poet who 'may see [far more clearly] into the nature of political reality than can the practical men of his day'. Morris's case was much helped too by the sheer 'lyricism of his ode to the beauty of the English countryside, [and] his denunciation of the odious, crass barbarity of the profit-making process which, in his day (as it is now) was remorselessly destroying that beauty'.[26] Again, we find that Strachey's capitulation to communism had not anaesthetised him totally against such central emblems of cultural identity in England as the landscape.

But perhaps the most striking aspect of *The Coming Struggle for Power* is the frequency with which the subject of religion is raised. As well as devoting a single chapter to a Freudian analysis of the persistence of the religious impulse in advanced capitalist societies – as a vital source of supernatural comfort and also social stability – Strachey traced the changing forms of religious belief following the advent of capitalism. Further, he gave free rein to his speculative powers on the implications in terms of religion should the communist alternative to monopoly capitalism be rejected. There was nothing particularly novel about his attributing the Reformation to the need of a new economic system to measure success in worldly terms, rather than securing the (costly) opinion of the nearest priest as to the prospect of salvation in the next; coupled with the need to break the Church's monopoly of prime agricultural land. (It was, however, a theory that was laid out with great literary panache: 'What are Liberty of Conscience, and the principle of Justification by the unaided Faith of the individual, but claims that every man may go and fetch down God's mercy from on high, if he can, for himself?'[27]) But when Strachey turned from past to future, his prognosis was *sui generis*, and it is hard to escape the conclusion that he had fallen prey to the very same vice of 'project[ing] . . . subjective reactions to present day life' on to the future which he castigated in the work of Wells and Huxley. For in attempting to argue against the idea of 'organized capitalism' – in the form of a 'perfect monopoly' formed by expropriating all small, independent producers – Strachey again invokes the idea, not only of the 'enslavement of nine-tenths of humanity' but, equally important for him, 'the ruin of human civilization'. Monopoly capitalism as a cure for wasteful competition, he maintained, could only result in a succession of 'inter-imperial' wars, the outcome of which in turn was victory to one power. The victor would possess 'the whole earth as its fief'. The lapse into a new form of feudalism would have been eased by the crushing of all resistance mounted in earlier wars by an oppressed proletariat, and their reduction to a state of 'barbarism'. Creativity would also be proscribed for the governing class, lest 'any advance in technics' lead to opportunities for private accumulation. Surpluses would have to be spent, rather than saved, but horror at the orgy of 'pleasure' which would ensue would induce a return flight to the consolations of religion. And here lay Strachey's chief difficulty with monopoly capitalism. Would not such a resort lead, eventually, to a renewal of the union of church and state, and a 'new Constantine . . . approaching down the avenue of the future'? He recalled that once before 'the race' had been 'at that point in history when, in a period of economic decline, the Catholic Church [had] assum[ed] control over the destinies of man'. The prospects, then, as now, were dire – 'a new dark age of ecclesiasticism, in which the knowledge and skill, the culture and civilisation of the world would temporarily disappear'. In time, mankind would come to its senses, as it had done before, and the (Marxist) prophets of Strachey's own age would become the 'antiquity' by whose guidance a future age would seek 'renewal'. But why, asked Strachey, pursue this anguished, circuitous route to communism when following the Russian example now could easily prevent it?[28]

Strachey recognised the 'fantastic' nature of these speculations. Certainly, in *The Theory and Practice of Socialism*, he confined his analysis of religion to a straightforward denunciation of 'religious mythology' as 'profoundly inimical to the specifically scientific attitude to the universe which must be the mental climate of a free, socialist society'. The statement was accompanied by an equally bald defence of the Soviet government's repression of the Russian Orthodox Church for the 'political power' and 'intellectual monopoly' it continued to enjoy.[29] But did the impetus for his indulgence in futurology in the earlier work not stem from more immediate anxieties about the present? There is evidence to suggest that Strachey believed that Catholicism represented a serious competitor with Marxism in a major battle for 'faith' taking place in the 1930s. This sense was later vindicated by the Catholic conversions undergone by several notable communist apostates of the 1930s, shifts of personal belief that were, significantly, influenced by native strains of Catholic thought, such as those embodied in the writings of Belloc, Chesterton and Langland.[30] The test of the worth of this sought-after faith of the 1930s would be its ability to define, and command obedience to, a set of morals that was truly 'public' in scope. Strachey recognised that Catholicism was moving in this direction, and was exerting greater appeal as a result. The Catholic Church, he remarked, 'has been getting more Catholic again'. After the protestantisation of Catholicism which culminated in the Jansenist movement of the seventeenth and eighteenth centuries, Catholicism had turned 'communal' again, reflecting both the need to recover from its 'low-water mark' of the late eighteenth century and also the growth of large-scale production away from the independent trader and producer. He continued,

> Thus, for anyone who can achieve religious belief at all, the Catholic form of Christianity is becoming increasingly appropriate. To-day, the point has been reached where a highly intellectual neo-Catholic, and significantly neo-Thomist, movement is evidently reaching back for the pre-Franciscan, predominantly communal form of faith.[31]

Like Collingwood, Lindsay and Eliot, Strachey was engaged in the process of drawing political thought in close proximity to developments in religious belief, only in the form of a rival rather than an ally. Strachey deliberately made communism imitate the pattern and ideals of religion's most successful expressions in an effort to capture the public imagination and thereby strengthen the public realm. Such endeavours did not pass uncontested from defenders of Christianity. In a debate in *The Spectator* in 1936, Strachey and his fellow communist theorist, Joseph Needham, lined up against articulate defenders of the Christian Church in Britain – Ernest Barker, Father d'Arcy and Dean Inge – who categorically denied the claim of communism to constitute a faith. Certainly, the advent of communism caused some painful reflection on the neglect of urgent matters such as material equality in Christian theology and practice of late. However, as Barker argued vehemently,

> The whole philosophy of Communism is resolutely opposed to faith. It is a philosophy of material causation; and its devotees are vowed to the study of material causes and the production of material effects. . . . In a mechanical and mechanized universe there is no place for God; and where Communism enters, with its jejune aetheism and its crude anti-God propaganda, all forms of faith are under an interdict.[32]

Nevertheless, it was this consciousness of the success of organised religion in creating and sustaining public moral space on the part of political thinkers in the 1930s and early 1940s which helped to give their subject its strikingly expansive quality – both in terms of its epistemological range and in terms of the audience it sought.

After the Second World War, Strachey recognised the spiritual lacunae in communism itself. Reviewing sympathetically the 'literature of reaction' against communism produced by Arthur Koestler, Boris Pasternak, Whittaker Chambers and George Orwell in 1960, he praised the attention they had drawn to the crudity and horror of attempts – communist and fascist alike – to 'rationalise' the sphere of social existence. Yet none of these literary 'reactionaries', Strachey concluded, adequately identified and explored the area of human consciousness that had suffered most from the nightmare of totalitarianism – that which was marked by 'personal, religious, and aesthetic values' and with which all political ideologies had to come to terms, albeit 'wherever at any rate the economic problem is on the way to solution'. Orwell took refuge in the 'assumptions of English empiricism' while the solution of his continental counterparts lay in cults of the supernatural.[33] It would seem from this analysis that Strachey had come to accept the worth of the more conventional responses to the 'mysteries' of human life against which he had waged war in the 1930s, and now embraced religion as a partner in the socialist quest. This his agnostic intellectual inheritance prevented him from doing at an earlier stage, and was heavily implicated in the ease with which he submitted to communist dogma.

Ultimately, however, the literature of reaction led Strachey to reflect upon, and lament, the dissipation of 'rationalism' that had accompanied the retreat from communism. Disillusion with the values of communism had fostered an antipathy towards politics in general, and a misguided elevation of the private sphere in its place. This was illustrated by Dr Zhivago and Orwell's *1984*. Such literature had passed from exposing the reckless failure of a system which had attempted the radical transformation of social and political life to an equally reckless caution about instigating change more generally. Its authors were, consequently, nothing less than 'the enemies of civilised life'.[34]

III

Strachey was by no means alone among British intellectuals in turning towards Marxism in reaction against, on the one hand, a liberalism whose bankruptcy on a variety of fronts had seemed evident since 1918 and, on the other, a resurgent form of Christianity. As an historiographical tool and framework for analysing existing society, for the priority it set upon the values of community and economic security, and as a bulwark against organised religion, Marxism/socialism was also championed by the Fellow of All Souls and political writer A. L. Rowse in the early 1930s. He, too, hoped to forge a link between Marxism and Letters in such a way that the status of political thought as a primary channel of public discourse would be restored. At this time he was closely involved with T. S. Eliot, who made space available to Rowse in his literary periodical, *The Criterion*, for articles of a political nature. Eliot also encouraged the writing of Rowse's second book, *Politics and the Younger Generation*, with its epigraph from the leading French intellectual, Julien Benda, '*L'âge actuel est proprement l'âge du politique*'. Marxism alone seemed to offer a way out of the intellectual impasse caused by a liberalism that had grown fundamentally stale. This Rowse had encountered in his native Cornwall as the Labour candidate for Penryn from 1929 to 1941, a constituency dominated by the negativity and obstructionism of the Liberal Nonconformist conscience.[35] Above all, Marx inspired the conviction in Rowse that the ultimate units of co-operation and conflict alike in human society are group interests formed essentially by the economic structure of society. This view effectively discounted the 'usual liberal rationalism in politics, assuming that you have only to make up your mind what to do and it will be done'.[36] In this light, Churches themselves could be no more than 'sects', at best offering spiritual shelter from the storms of a world economy dominated by the profit imperative of capitalism but by no means the sole or superior purveyor of pastoral service in modern society.[37]

But Rowse was more alive than Strachey to the potential in Marxism for becoming a pseudo-religion, particularly through its central and problematic notion of the 'dialectic'. With him, liberal scepticism deriving from Hume,[38] if not liberal rationalism, remained far more intact. Its greater hold on the English, in stark contrast to the German mind which had produced Marxism and much else of dubious intellectual worth besides, was to be a leading source of Rowse's national pride. The latter wrestled with Marxism for his innermost convictions in the 1930s and 1940s, and national pride eventually triumphed over Marxism far more unequivocally than in Strachey's case.[39] The imposition of the dialectic on history he described in 1946 as 'an obvious relic of the old transcendent claims of idealist metaphysics'. It had led communists down the dangerous road of pragmatism in the wake of Nazism – as witnessed by the Nazi-Soviet pact – although in this they were no worse than the appeasers in Britain whom Rowse equally despised.[40]

Strachey himself was increasingly discomforted by defending the Soviet line of 'revolutionary defeatism' before the Nazi advance into Finland. Indeed, he was soon moved to sever his links with organised communism, even if he continued to be drawn towards the explanatory power of Marxism and many of its ideals.[41] The patriotism that had been evident in certain passages of *The Coming Struggle for Power* and *The Theory and Practice of Socialism* – particularly in his praise for English poetry and the English countryside – now overwhelmed him, as it did in the case of Harry Pollitt, forced to resign as General Secretary of the Communist Party of Great Britain in the wake of the Nazi–Soviet pact.[42] Even in 1938, Strachey had remarked to a correspondent that the forces of the left should make contact with 'the oldest and deepest theme in British public life', 'the freedom and independence of Britain from a foreign tyrant'.[43] Whig liberalism may have been at a low ebb in the 1930s; however, when Britain came under the threat of external invasion, its leading intellectuals returned to patriotic type, and – with the aid of Whiggism – began to count their national blessings once more. George Orwell's celebrated attack on the divorce in Britain between 'patriotism and intelligence' in *The Lion and the Unicorn* of 1941 did not do justice to the conflicting loyalties and influences on the intellectual left at this time.[44] Strachey's roots in the intellectual aristocracy of Victorian Britain became abundantly clear in his plea to the left to heed the call of patriotism. Similarly, the ethic of public service which Rowse imbibed at All Souls, for all his humble origins as the son of a Cornish tin miner, put paid to his youthful Marxism when the survival of Britain as an independent nation appeared doubtful. But the revival of Whiggism is to anticipate the subject of a later chapter, in which Rowse plays a major role.

Notes

1 P. Ironside, *The Social and Political Thought of Bertrand Russell: The Development of an Aristocratic Liberalism* (Cambridge, Cambridge University Press, 1996), p. 157.
2 S. Hastings, *Evelyn Waugh: A Biography* (London, Sinclair-Stevenson, 1994), pp. 227–8.
3 Quoted in J. Callaghan, *Rajani Palme Dutt: A Study in British Stalinism* (London, Lawrence & Wishart, 1993), p. 168.
4 H. J. Laski, *Communism* (London, Thornton Butterworth, 1927), pp. 246, 249.
5 K. Asher, *T. S. Eliot and Ideology* (Cambridge, Cambridge University Press, 1995), p. 64.
6 On Christian communism, see N. Wood, *Communism and British Intellectuals* (London, Gollancz, 1959), pp. 64–9; and E. A. Roberts, *The Anglo-Marxists: A Study in Ideology and Culture* (Lanham, Ma, Rowman & Littlefield, 1997), ch. 4.
7 N. Thompson, *John Strachey: An Intellectual Biography* (London, Macmillan, 1993), pp. 105–9.
8 J. Morley, *On Compromise*, ed. J. Powell (Edinburgh, Keele University Press, [1874] 1997), p. 98.
9 S. Cripps, 'Parliamentary institutions and the transition to socialism', in G. Bernard Shaw *et al.*, *Where Stands Socialism To-day?* (London, Rich & Cowan, 1933), pp. 52–3.

10 Strachey, contribution to *I Believe* (London, Allen & Unwin, 1940), p. 132.

11 Thompson, *John Strachey*, pp. 76, 106.

12 H. Thomas, *John Strachey* (London, Eyre Methuen, 1973), p. 123.

13 Thomas, *John Strachey*, p. 53.

14 Thomas, *John Strachey*, p. 130.

15 Thomas, *John Strachey*, p. 160.

16 Thompson, *John Strachey*, p. 67.

17 D. Mirsky, *The Intelligentsia of Great Britain* (1935), quoted in Thomas, *John Strachey*, p. 111.

18 J. Strachey, *The Coming Struggle for Power* (London, Victor Gollancz, [1932] 1934), p. 358.

19 Strachey, *The Coming Struggle for Power*, p. 21.

20 Strachey, *The Coming Struggle for Power*, pp. 156–7.

21 Strachey, *The Coming Struggle for Power*, pp. 216–17.

22 Strachey, *The Coming Struggle for Power*, p. 217.

23 Strachey, *The Coming Struggle for Power*, p. 221.

24 Strachey, *The Coming Struggle for Power*, p. 223.

25 Strachey, *The Coming Struggle for Power*, p. 203.

26 John Strachey, *The Theory and Practice of Socialism* (London, Victor Gollancz, 1936), ch. 23.

27 Strachey, *The Coming Struggle for Power*, p. 18.

28 Strachey, *The Coming Struggle for Power*, pp. 256–60.

29 Strachey, *The Theory and Practice of Socialism*, pp. 220, 223.

30 See Douglas Hyde, *I Believed: The Autobiography of a former British Communist* (London, William Heinemann, 1951), pp. 185, 213, 225. Drawn to communism in the early 1930s, in violent reaction against what he perceived to be the bankruptcy of liberalism, Malcolm Muggeridge's illusions were shattered by a visit to Moscow in 1933. Although he did not become a Catholic until 1982, his biographer notes that his conversion was a 'logical conclusion' to anyone who had followed the course of his career. Not least, his interest in religion had been revived immediately after his experience in Stalin's Soviet Union, and under the influence of the literary critic Hugh Kingsmill, a man whose religious instincts ran deep and who coined the term 'Dawnism' in response to attempts by his contemporaries to realise paradise on Earth. Muggeridge's own religiosity was much aided by the influence of Dr Johnson, whose strengths in this respect Kingsmill taught him to see. R. Ingrams, *Muggeridge: The Biography* (London, Harper Collins, 1995), pp. 234, 100–6; see also M. Muggeridge, *Chronicles of Wasted Time*, 2 vols, II, *The Infernal Grove* (London, Collins, 1973), pp. 64–71.

31 Strachey, *The Coming Struggle for Power*, p. 161.

32 E. Barker, 'Rival faiths?', in H. Wilson Harris (ed.), *Christianity and Communism* (Oxford, Basil Blackwell, 1937), pp. 4–5.

33 J. Strachey, 'The strangled cry' (1960), in *The Strangled Cry and Other Unparliamentary Papers* (London, Bodley Head, 1962), pp. 30, 32, 76.

34 Strachey, 'The strangled cry', p. 77.

35 R. Ollard, *A Man of Contradictions: A Life of A. L. Rowse* (London, Allen Lane, 1999), pp. 91–5.

36 A. L. Rowse, *Politics and the Younger Generation* (London, Faber & Faber, 1931), p. 227.

37   Rowse, *Politics and the Younger Generation*, p. 196.
38   A. L. Rowse, 'Marx and Russian communism' (1939), review of I. Berlin's *Karl Marx*, in *The End of an Epoch* (London, Macmillan, 1948), p. 255.
39   Ollard argues that Rowse 'never retracted his early admiration for Karl Marx . . . It was from Marx that he learned, and continued to believe, that at the base of human history lay its economic facts'; *A Man of Contradictions*, p. 3. Against this I have argued that Rowse's Marxism was so attenuated in his historical studies and so over-shadowed by other concerns as to be of neglible influence. See my review of Ollard's biography in *Reviews in History*, no. 101 (March 2000).
40   A. L. Rowse, *The Use of History* (London, Hodder & Stoughton, 1946), p. 138.
41   Thompson, *John Strachey*, pp. 181–2.
42   Kevin Morgan draws out well the conflict in 1939 between Harry Pollitt's British loy-alties and Rajani Palme Dutt's internationalism, which masked Soviet interests. He writes, 'It might disturb our cruder notions of both Englishness and Communism, but how very English a phenomenon was Stalinism in the shape that Pollitt gave it'; Morgan, *Harry Pollitt* (Manchester, Manchester University Press, 1993), pp. 111, 128.
43   Thompson, *John Strachey*, p. 173.
44   G. Orwell, *The Lion and the Unicorn: Socialism and the English Genius* (London, Penguin, [1941] 1982), pp. 64–5.

5

Alfred Zimmern and
the world 'citizen-scholar'

I

The previous two chapters have explored the ways in which the ideal of public scholarship in the field of political thought enjoyed a considerable revival in Britain in the wake of the multiple crises of the interwar period. They have particularly highlighted the way in which the resurgence of Christianity and the growth of Marxism in the intellectual culture of Britain both fuelled, and were themselves fuelled by, this development. These two currents pitched their responses to what their adherents regarded as a fundamental malaise of human consciousness at the most general social level, that of modern civilisation. A conviction that no less universal a unit of analysis would serve the intellectual and political needs of contemporary society after 1918 also characterised the founders of the discipline of international relations. This chapter will conclude the analysis of the themes of the public scholar, the 'civilisational' perspective, and Christian influences on political thought in the interwar period through examining the work of one such founder: Alfred Eckhard Zimmern. However, before turning to this period, it will be necessary to pick up the threads of Zimmern's early career. This well illustrates the transition in some quarters from the 'civic' perspective of Edwardian political thought to that of the 'international' after 1918 – a transition which was nonetheless much influenced by paradigms of Englishness.

II

Zimmern exemplifies the permeability of Britain's intellectual elite in the early decades of this century and also its deep grounding in classical culture. He was born of prosperous German–Jewish roots, his parents having fled to England in 1848. He attended first Winchester School and then New College Oxford, where he subsequently became a Fellow and Tutor in Classics. It will be recalled from Chapter 2 that Zimmern became notable as the author of *The Greek Commonwealth* (1911),[1] a study of the politics and society of Athens in its

Golden Age and which he dedicated to 'the two St. Mary Winton Colleges'. But he quickly yearned for a wider influence and audience than it was possible for a university teacher to achieve. He found, also, that he could no longer confine his expansive intellectual interests within the four square corners of a single culture. These characteristics became obvious in the years immediately preceding and following the First World War.

After a brief period of (unpaid) lecturing in Sociology at the London School of Economics, Zimmern's first point of retreat from an Oxford whose 'dead-weight of academic inertia'[2] he had come to loathe was the Board of Education. In 1912, he became an inspector of adult education.[3] He had been much involved at Oxford in extending the resources of higher education to the working classes, a project which he pursued with almost missionary zeal because of the prospect of England's 'redemption' – and, indeed, that of the industrialised western world – it appeared to hold out.[4] His Germanic background had impressed upon him the low premium that was set upon 'intellect' in Britain, in deference to a zest for life that appeared to give its inhabitants a 'much stronger hold on essential qualities, such as common sense, judgement, knowledge of men' than those of Germany. He recounted in a letter to Chaim Weizmann – who was also exercised by this 'problem' of the English – in 1915 his own experience of school in England, in which he took literally his teachers' admonishment to work hard. Hence he regularly came top of the class, whereas his peers realised the 'sham' of such harangues, and 'spent on cricket the brains they might have spent on Greek irregular verbs'. Similarly, his sojourn in Berlin after taking his degree at Oxford was 'such as going from a school to a University'. He took it upon himself to help enrich his adopted homeland in this respect, and to bring a greater awareness to it of the connection between 'knowledge and life'. But he ventured to suggest that Weizmann's straightforward teutonic solution of training the individual intellect was not the answer; rather, education in England had to take place at the level of 'corporate life – group study'. This evidently explained Zimmern's keen interest in organisations such as the Worker's Education Association which were admirably well equipped to meet the challenge of modern industrial work, fundamentally based as it was upon 'team-work'.[5]

At the Board of Education, Zimmern's specific brief was to inspect classes in liberal subjects run for working-class men and women. It was a post whose rich opportunities for social observation inspired him with the hope that one day he might write 'a book [about England] at once vivid and philosophical on the lines of my Greek one'. This aspiration was confided to Oliver Wendell Holmes, to whom he had been introduced in the course of a visit to America which he made just before he took up his appointment.[6] Once again, in communicating his impressions of America to Holmes, the influence of his classical background and achievements in shaping them is clearly in evidence, as is the 'civilising', educative function he – along with other members of the intellectual elite in the years before 1914 – accorded to the state. 'It is not the business of governments', he was moved to write, to regulate peoples [*sic.*] lives and incomes, but I think it will be to concern itself with the spiritual atmosphere in which they live and to interfere when, in the old Greek phrase, it is 'diseased'. That is what made me feel so sad about the second generation of the newer immigrants. They seem to be starving and yet no statesmen seemed to be concerned about it – only a few seers such as Miss Addams. I don't know that we are much better yet in Europe; but then our problems in this respect are less acute and we have not the same chaos'.[7]

His experience of America emphasised to him the importance of 'nationality' as a spiritual buffer against the mechanical and standardising forces of industrialism, especially in societies – such as the United States – in which the ideal of 'assimilation' seemed to strip the immigrant of all sense of self. The consequences were alarming to behold. As Zimmern remarked to R. W. Seton-Watson, 'The only thing that can save the second generation of the immigrants (who are one of the great problems of American life) is to preserve their European roots. Let the young Croatian forget Croatia and he becomes a hooligan'.[8] On the other hand, Zimmern shrank from the political doctrine of nationalism, having observed the havoc it had wreaked in the Balkans in 1910 when he was writing *The Greek Commonwealth* in the British School at Athens.[9]

When the First World War broke out, Zimmern's eyesight prevented him from joining the armed forces. His German ancestry and hence 'alien' status militated against the role in administering the war machine that he would have liked instead.[10] Whether or not as a direct reaction to this exclusion, his sense of 'English' identity was greatly challenged. He professed in the midst of a lengthy correspondence with J. A. Hobson in 1916 that 'this war has made me feel far less "Anglo-Saxon" and far more cosmopolitan even than I was before. To me it is a real *civil war*, and I go to visit enemy aliens regularly just for the pleasure of talking German'.[11] He made a similar point to Walter Lippmann, only framed in the Actonian theory of nationality that was forming the basis of his emergent theory of world federation: 'If your people understood what nationality was you would not be so alarmed at the US Germans . . . the old Emperor's portrait still hangs in our house at home, and Goethe and Schiller still adorn our shelves'.[12] Yet Zimmern was quick to defend his fellow Anglo-Germans against the suspicions of collusion and treachery which had resulted in, and was further exacerbated by, the highly repressive Aliens Restriction Act and Defence of the Realm Acts of 1914.[13] He himself had not experienced any such animosity – indeed, in 1918, he at last moved to a far more central and sensitive government position in the Political Intelligence Department of the Foreign Office, and was employed especially on economic problems.[14] But he wished that he had, instead of the 'poor innocent, frightened hairdressers and waiters'.[15] To Violet Carruthers – a well-connected public servant and prominent fellow Liberal – he intimated that suspect national loyalty was far more likely to be found on the left in Britain, in figures such as Robert Smillie, Philip Snowden and G. D. H Cole. (A conviction of the intellectual left's growing sympathy with 'Bolshevism' – which he regarded as 'Prussianism upside-down' – from the end of the First World War was not the least impetus in Zimmern's move to become a 'citizen-scholar', and in opposition to the category of 'intellectual' in the interwar period. Certainly, in 1918 he declared himself 'very much out of patience with intellectuals just now'.[16]) The result of the present action, and talk of 'internment' and 'repatriation', could only be 'to convert hundreds, perhaps thousands, of people who loved and honoured England into a bitter Irish spirit of enmity which is just what the Germans want'.[17]

Excluded from war work for most of the duration of the War, Zimmern remained at the Board of Education until mid 1915. Then, having grown tired of the briefs on primary and secondary education he was increasingly asked to prepare, he resigned.[18] The following year, he joined the newly formed Reconstruction Committee, working with the Conservative MP Arthur Steel-Maitland on the problem of industrial supplies. He welcomed the efforts of his friend Vaughan Nash, Joint Secretary with G. M. Young, in changing the terms of the sub-committee of which he was the Secretary from the needs of British manufacturers to 'the whole world-situation'. He also welcomed Nash's success in changing the composition of the committee in favour of 'idealists' at the expense of businessmen. Zimmern himself aimed to seize all the opportunities afforded by his position as Secretary of the committee to 'shovel in new ideas'.[19] He believed it was possible to effect the same 'silent revolution' in the social and industrial fabric of the country – indeed, he believed it was already underway – that had marked all the great changes in English history. The key factor in such transformations was that of 'mind'. Whether it be through the influence of Wyclif and the Lollards on the Reformation, or the Puritans on the Revolution, or the Evangelicals on the slave trade and the Factory Acts, or the philosophic Radicals on colonial self-government, or Thomas Arnold on the Indian Civil Service, or 'the forty years [of] devoted labour of the elementary teacher [on] Kitchener's army', the way of English/British life had changed perceptibly for the better. Such transformations of the national spirit generally passed unnoticed, for to acknowledge them would 'stir the depths' to which the Englishman remained constitutionally adverse. But – always endeavouring to keep his finger pressed firmly on the cultural pulse of the nation – he stressed that the readiness of the English people to embrace far-reaching change in terms of a lessening of social and political tensions, and to benefit from the investment in education that would help to effect such a change, was now obvious.[20]

Zimmern's new appointment, in combination with the one he had left the previous year, signified the concentration of his mind at several, interrelated levels in the course of the War: industrial relations, internationalism and intellectual leadership. For example, to Violet Markham Zimmern stressed that 'Reconstruction is a huge subject'. He had requested a talk from her in early 1918 on one of the many themes which the label embraced: the 'capital and labour problem'. He had become an easy convert to Whitleyism, the view that organised conciliation through Industrial Councils was the best route to avoiding the strikes that had done so much financial and moral damage in British industry since the Trades Disputes Act of 1906. He set forth his own, very similar outlook on the question of employer–employee relations in his letter when talking of the need to 'steer boldly between the reactionaries on the one hand and the class war-ites on the other'. The upshot would be the reconciliation of industrialism with 'ethical – indeed Christian – principle. "Industry in the spirit of public service", "the Surplus product to the State", and the taking of the workers into equal part-nership seem to me the guiding principles'. In conscious opposition to socialism, Zimmern maintained that if the 'incentive' to production were 'Christianised', it would be possible to introduce higher taxation 'without killing the goose'. He was much influenced in this respect by Lionel Hichens, Chairman of Cammell Laird from 1910 to 1940, and an activist in industrial peace movements such as the Industrial Christian Fellowship.[21] Hichens, like Zimmern, was also a stalwart member of the Round Table, and in early 1918 had delivered an extremely influential lecture on industrial relations and the relationship between industry and the state.[22]

Zimmern certainly believed that the efforts of enlightened liberal thinkers such as himself could effect this change in industry. In 1916 he was still consid-ering writing his book on England, on the basis of his 'firsthand knowledge' of the different sides of its life, working back from the present to the past in the same manner as he had worked back from the Greece of the fifth century to its beginnings in tribal life. This would reinforce his work for the Round Table organisation in liaising with working-class organisations such as the Workers' Education Association, bringing knowledge of foreign affairs, particularly the empire, before them, and becoming the Round Table's expert on industrial affairs in turn.[23] Such endeavour held great potential for 'interpret[ing] the think-ing sections of the rich and poor to one another' and for working out an 'indus-trial philosophy'. Using Fredrich Naumann's book[24] as his starting point, this industrial philosophy would emphasise, in particular, how German ideals of industrial organisation conflicted with English traditions, and were far inferior as a result.[25] Certainly, there was much potential in modelling such contempo-rary industrial movements for greater worker participation as the Guilds on 'dis-cussions and standpoints which are essentially English – the practical problems of constitutionalism, of the organisation of political bodies, of the relation between the legislature (i.e. the general meeting) and the executive, of the psychology and the workings of group life'. This was painstakingly outlined to G. D. H. Cole, in a long letter which was written in response to an invitation to a Guild Socialist conference in 1915. He was trying to steer Guild Socialism away from the 'continental influences' in which he evidently suspected it was becom-ing ensnared. If Guild Socialism were put in such terms as he had outlined, it would appeal to 'tens of thousands of men, Trade Unionists, non-Unionists and middle classes, workers and newspaper readers who have never been interested in what seems to most Englishmen the vague theories of Socialism or the repul-sive tidiness of Collectivism'.[26] At the same time, it would supply a vital correc-tive to the corruption of British industry by the 'iron law of wages', which in turn had become a model for Prussian militarism. In 1914, Zimmern had argued that the Germans were merely 'apt disciples' of this English law:

> 'business is business' can be no less odious a watchword than 'war is war'. Treitschke and Nietzsche may have furnished Prussian ambitions with congenial ammunition; but Bentham with his purely selfish interpretation of human nature and Marx with his doctrine of the class struggle – the high priest of Individualism and high priest of Socialism – cannot be acquitted of a similar charge.[27]

Zimmern's Anglophilia – for all that his national identity had been thrown into confusion by the War and despite his contempt for English 'gradgrindism' – can also be seen in his steadfast upholding of the British Commonwealth. This is signified most obviously in his membership of the Round Table's inner circle, the 'Moot' from 1914. He was one among several younger Round Table members who followed Lionel Curtis beyond the Unionist, autarkic goals for South Africa pursued by the group's founders towards a 'principle of the commonwealth'. Through the 'organic' federation of the British Empire with a world state, it was thought that this could provide a lasting force for international stability and order. Ambitiously, the project was premissed upon the belief that the true mission of empire could only be fulfilled by drawing dominions and dependencies alike into a single political unit in the settlement of whose affairs there would be equal participation; it was not a matter of spreading the ideas, institutions and citizens of the metropole abroad in order to fashion self-governing and independent states. The cause of imperial federation had been given a new fillip by the War, which laid bare the contradiction between the dominions' independence with regard to internal affairs and their dependence on Britain for the security of their wider, and in Curtis's eyes – more vital – imperial identity. Influenced in his youth by Hegel and T. H. Green, and then Lord Milner in South Africa, Curtis held passionately to the view that nothing less than imperial federation could satisfy the high moral bond of mutual obligation between the various peoples of the world which it was England's destiny to promote.[28]

On the one hand, Zimmern invoked the 'commonwealth' ideal against those whom he regarded as 'syndicalists'. These ranged from Harold Laski in England to Lippmann in America. They were characterised for him by a denial of the absolute allegiance owed to the democratic states by their citizens,[29] the shining example of which was Pericles' Athens. His antagonists were quick to reply in terms of the failure of the state to treat all of its citizens on an equal footing, and therefore prove itself worthy of such allegiance. Responding to an article on 'The Labour movement' in Zimmern's book *Nationality and Government*, Laski observed that

> You criticise the Welsh Miner; but why don't you ask what leads to his lawlessness? Why doesn't your [English] state treat Carson as it treated Jim Conolly, or Northcliffe's papers as it treated the Nation and the Herald? I agree that the Oxford I knew (and worshipped) didn't die for Bolshevism, but neither did it die to make Northcliffe and Rothermere and Beaverbrook the masters of England; or Curzon and Milner for that matter.[30]

On the other hand, Zimmern invoked the 'commonwealth' ideal against those thinkers who adhered to an abstract vision of internationalism – which they opposed to the *imperial* state, at least – such as J. A. Hobson. Hobson had critically reviewed Lionel Curtis's, *The Problem of the Commonwealth* (1916) in the *Manchester Guardian*, and he and Zimmern took each other to task in a lengthy correspondence which ensued. Zimmern proceeded to summarise their differences, and settle them in his favour thus:

> I assent to your statement of the international ideal and you to mine, at least as a *pis-aller* – of the ideal of the Commonwealth. But you are as pessimistic about the prospects of the latter as I am about the former. The two are not inconsistent: indeed they are complementary: for an Imperialism which denied international obligation, internal and external, would be the negation of all I care for.[31]

This imperial route to the expansion of national horizons would be reinforced by breaking up such autocratic empires as Austro-Hungary and encouraging their successor states to grant full cultural rights to the minorities within. This approach to nationhood Zimmern pressed with much ardour when at last he assumed a role in government intelligence at the end of the War. His work for the Foreign Office involved joint responsibility with Lord Eustace Percy for preparing the British government's submission for a League of Nations' Covenant to the Paris Peace Conference of 1919. The League of Nations, he argued, should exercise an advisory role (and supervisory role, in cases such as the Balkans) in ensuring policies of toleration in states which were culturally diverse.[32] For Zimmern, national consciousness and the cultivation of original languages among immigrants and national minorities alike were essential complements of the 'single World-State' towards which mankind was evolving as 'commerce and intercourse' gradually caused the world to shrink.[33] Cultural nationalism in this form was a force for harmony among the peoples of the world; political nationalism, by contrast, could only lead to strife, both internally and externally. Such views Zimmern propagated in the periodical *The New Europe* – founded by R. W. Seton-Watson in October 1916 – under the highly appropriate pseudonym, 'Atticus'.

Indeed, so convinced was Zimmern of the merits of this combined route of (British) imperialism plus cultural nationalism to world federation that he dissociated himself completely from attempts to show that the source of human unity lay elsewhere. In 1915 Zimmern declined F. S. Marvin's invitation to participate in the 'Unity' lectures delivered at the Woodbrooke Settlement near Birmingham, which trained social workers in a 'religious spirit'. The lectures were inspired by the belief that, while Britain's cause and that of her allies in the First World War was just, 'it is not inopportune to reflect on those common and ineradicable elements in the civilization of the West which tend to form a real commonwealth of nations and will survive even the most shattering of conflicts'.[34] Zimmern wrote to Marvin that his focus on the *polis* and the meaning of citizenship would be at odds with this main theme. 'The fact is', he wrote, 'that in my political philosophy the bond between London and Nigeria is closer than the bond between London and Dusseldorf.'[35] These remarks occasioned much sadness in Ernest Barker, to whom they were communicated by Marvin, eliciting his deep expression of regret that 'so good a man' as Zimmern had become 'such a definite nationalist'. He added, poignantly, 'if that is what the city-state means I am glad it perished'.[36] But Zimmern's views were typical of the Round Table circle, the influence of which was amplified by the support of Waldorf and Nancy Astor and the rich political linkages opened up to it at Cliveden, their country seat at Taplow.[37]

Finally, Zimmern was much moved by Zionist arguments in this period, a question to which again he applied English ideals and achievements – this time of nationality. Despite his Jewish descent, it was not until he became an undergraduate at Balliol in the company of Leon Simon and Harry Sacher that Zimmern first came into contact with Zionist ideas. He was converted to the cause of Jewish nationalism not long after, when he attended the World Zionist Congress at Basle in 1905.[38] His Zionism was much inspired by the Hebrew philosopher Achad Ha-Am (Asher Ginzburg), who argued that the establishment of a Jewish state would not in itself fulfil the Jews' biblical destiny. Rather, return to the Palestinian homeland would be a 'psychologically' and 'spiritually' significant act, providing a conscious and vital symbol of Jewish nationhood to the remaining communities of the Diaspora. It would also offer the Jews a means of gaining greater respect among other nations.[39] Zimmern also drew on another source in elaborating his Zionist ideal: that of the ancient Greeks. He was much struck by the potential of the Jews in Palestine for re-creating the ancient Greek spirit of citizenship in the modern world. It was a belief he shared with notable American Zionists such as Justice Louis Brandeis, whose Zionism was greatly shaped by the vision of a society – at once free, just and democratic – which cohered around the bonds of citizenship that Zimmern had set out in his *The Greek Commonwealth*.[40] But there was a further, English dimension to Zimmern's Zionism. He maintained at the time of the Balfour Declaration that the English and the Jews were the only peoples who understood the true nature of nationalism: the English were tremendously proud as a nation but that pride was not expressed politically; and while the Jews invested all their national hopes in the *land* of Palestine, this was a far cry from investing their hopes in a Jewish *state*. Zimmern's commitment to Zionism soon weakened, however. He certainly welcomed the establishment of the Palestinian homeland in 1917 as a focus of Jewish identity.[41] But he was dismayed on visiting it in July 1919 with Brandeis to discover a replica of the 'Ghetto atmosphere of the *Judenfrage*, when you are expecting to find a community as rooted to the soil as that of Stratford-on-Avon was in Shakespeare's time and is today'.[42]

III

Zimmern had resigned from his post at the Foreign Office in May 1919, to become the first holder of the Wilson Chair of International Relations at

Aberystwyth. Greek analogies came to him with remarkable ease, and he described his professorial study in the National Library of Wales as situated on 'a sort of Acropolis, overlooking the blue waters of Cardigan Bay'.[43] Perpetually restless as he was, he remained there for only two years. Evidently, he found even the Chair of International Relations at Aberystwyth – with its generous provision, at Zimmern's insistence, of one term off in three for travel abroad[44] – too much of a constraint upon his aspiration to shape the course of human destiny.

Nevertheless, it was with the study of international relations that Zimmern's academic associations lay for the rest of his career.[45] Both he and his second wife Lucie – an ardent French patriot whom he had met at Aberystwyth – were greatly excited by the establishment of the League of Nations. After extensive travel in Europe and America in the early 1920s,[46] they sought to influence the officials serving the League's various institutions in the course of the next decade.[47] It was Zimmern's view that the League should not be confined to the fulfilment of a diplomatic role once a dispute had broken out; rather its Council and Assembly held great potential for attending to the 'health and wellbeing' of all the citizens of its constituent states, and hence acting as an agent of international solidarity.[48] Again, there are strong echoes here of the *polis* in its golden, Periclean age – the Athens of Solon, based as it was upon 'a firm foundation of order and social solidarity'.[49] The vision was also supported by Zimmern's perception of the success of the British Commonwealth in bringing mutually well-disposed powers into regular contact and hence a relationship of 'civility, consideration, and neighbourly feeling'. He had tried to embody such a vision in the British submission for a framework for the Covenant: as the League developed, he had to rest content with its more partial realisation in the spirit of the Washington Treaties.[50]

Notwithstanding defeat on this question and anxious to do everything in his power to achieve his internationalist vision, Zimmern and his wife established the International School of Studies at Geneva in 1924, an institution which he described as 'a human laboratory for the study of contemporary world affairs'. The School offered lectures by leading intellectuals, politicians and administrators on a wide variety of subjects relating to the social and intellectual life of the twentieth century. Not surprisingly, the inspiration behind the School was a belief, 'growing out of the study of ancient Greece', that specialist knowledge alone would not solve human problems, but only in combination with 'a constant sense of the variety and complexity of the modern world'.[51] Believing ancient Greek society to be 'the most intellectual community of which history bears record',[52] Zimmern looked forward to its replication at an international level. This would be assisted by the School at Geneva and also the International Institute of Intellectual Co-operation organised by the League of Nations at Paris, of which he was Deputy Director. He apologised to Holmes for the 'prig[ish]' sound of such an organisation, but he reassured the octagenarian – whose pessimistic views on human nature were diametrically opposed to Zimmern's[53] – that 'we are not an asylum of prigs: [merely] that we have not yet found an unpriggish English translation for "co-operation intellectuelle"'.[54] Zimmern was evidently still marvelling at the low intellectual base line of English life, and hoping to raise it by such ventures. But at the heart of the idea of 'intellectual co-operation' was the belief that war was neither the product of insecurity nor power ambitions among states, but simply the clash of ideas and national outlooks, a clash that could be rectified by greater international contact and understanding between the various levels of different societies, not least the level of the intellectual elite. Central to this process of engendering world harmony was the rejuvenation of Christian values in political life.

From the middle of the 1930s onwards, especially, Zimmern dwelt perpetually on the need for political pratitioners and analysts – particularly of world affairs – to abide by Christian ideals and standards. As we have seen, he had been much concerned about the weak spiritual condition of contemporary societies from the outset of his career. In the 1930s, like A. D. Lindsay, he increasingly saw this problem as soluble only through the medium of Christian influences. Like Lindsay, too, he regarded as imperative the closure of the gap between the public and private realm which kept Lutherans, in particular, from recognising the scope for Christianising the former. In a lecture forming part of a series delivered in 1939 he took to task the admiration expressed by Friedrich Naumann for Bismarck in the Schleswig-Holstein War. Naumann had emphasised the irrelevance of such actions to Christianity, taking refuge instead in a conception of two kingdoms: that of the state and that of Christ. The lectures are significant on a number of accounts. First, they were delivered to theology students at Oxford. Second, his account of Naumann was drawn from a book written by the Modernist Catholic theologian who lived in England, Baron Von Hügel, during the First World War entitled *The German Soul in its Attitude towards Ethics and Christianity*. It is likely that he had come across the book when it was first published: as we have seen, he was certainly interested in Naumann in 1916. But there was evidently little place for it in his political analysis before the 1930s. The same is true of a further reference which Zimmern made to Von Hügel in the lecture, recalling a powerful response he had heard him make in the course of a conversation with a self-satisfied industrialist on factory reforms during the First World War. Third, Zimmern appealed directly to Burke in transcending this problem of the 'double morality' as practised by Lutherans. He quoted Burke's conception of the duty 'to bring the dispositions that are lovely in private life into the service and conduct of the Commonwealth: so to be patriots as not to forget that we are gentlemen'. Like Burke, Zimmern had no difficulty in emphasising the 'spiritual' basis of the latter status. The gentleman, he maintained, conformed with certain standards. It was important to recognise, however, that

> social standards do not come into existence automatically, by a spontaneous process of social evolution, whatever some of our materialistically minded social thinkers may say. They are the result of spiritual effort – the effort of individual human souls – in the past, the effort of men who tried so to be gentlemen as not to forget spiritual values.[55]

This affirmation of the close relationship between political conduct and religious belief marked a clear shift in the basis of Zimmern's thought.[56] In Chapter 2 it was seen that, as a pupil of Wallas, he had – in his earlier writings – made much play with a psychological-cum-evolutionary approach to the study of Politics, one which sat rather oddly with his Christian convictions. In the 1920s, he was still extolling the Greeks for succeeding in avoiding the 'English fallacy that "institutions are not made but grow"'.[57] As late as his inaugural lecture at Oxford in 1931, as the first holder of the Montague Burton Chair in International Relations, he was insisting on the importance of the divorce of politics from theology. This had 'set free men's minds to study first government and then society without prejudice or prepossession and thus made possible the application to them of methods akin to those already worked out in the realm of natural sciences'.[58] In his 1939 lectures, however, this preference is reversed through the suggestion that the doctrinaire adherence to principle in politics, which rationalism and dogmatic religion alike often produce, is best counteracted by the religiously inspired pragmatism of Cromwell and Burke.[59] By contrast, Wallas – just before his death – remained an unreconstructed rationalist, celebrating the lives of fellow reformers in Australia such as Justice Henry Bournes Higgins: for Wallas, the latter exemplified the lesson which 'we and our sons have learned that social progress can only be secured, and disaster avoided, by human thought and will'.[60]

However, it is clear from Zimmern's writings during the First World War that he was not an uncritical admirer of the English or, indeed, of English forms of religion. The English 'caste system' was central to his ambivalence, even though he baulked at the socialist commitment which seemed the natural corollary.[61] He was the equal of leading socialist moralists such as R. H. Tawney in castigating the sharp divisions of class which inhibited the ease of social intercourse achieved in other European countries. For Zimmern, however, the roots of class in England were as much religious as economic, and so embedded had hierarchical attitudes become in the culture that they had lately found a new, international expression. The seventeenth-century hierarchy in which the Anglican parson was firmly subordinated to the country gentleman gave way subsequently to a new one in which the former occupied a position of superiority over the Nonconformist minister. The gulf between Church and Chapel was itself superseded by new relations of social superiority and inferiority – between the white colonial race and the non-white subjects of the empire. This problem especially exercised Zimmern as a scholar of international relations, as did the 'dislike' which the English seemed habitually to meet in international circles. Although he recognised the basis of the latter response in English 'reserve',[62] nonetheless he regarded this trait as reflecting badly on the national character, emanating, as it did, from an inveterate sense of superiority wrought by unparalleled success, particularly in the field of politics and literature. Above all, it was 'none too creditable to our Christianity'.[63]

Zimmern felt moved to assert the need to realign international relations with Christian doctrines of humility and equality because of the deep-felt sense he shared with other thinkers in the 1930s that the increasingly ascendant ideal of scientific detachment militated against the role of scholars as critics of culture and public policy. Defending Acton against Bury over the place of moral censure in historical science, Zimmern again sought to close the gap between public and private realms of conduct, in the interests of 'educating opinion'.[64] Church leaders, by themselves, were inadequately placed to shoulder this task. Recent experience showed, for example, that they were too much prone to 'wishful thinking' about the League of Nations, too much prone to envisaging it as a servant of their nation's interest alone and negligent in exposing gross political improprieties. Almost all had failed, for example, to criticise Lloyd George's reneging on the modest reparations clause of the Armistice agreement in favour of a far more demanding one, within a few weeks of its signing.[65] He implied that the Christian scholar, by contrast, was equipped with the right combination of political expertise, moral sensibility and detachment from all personal and national, although not human, interests to guide public opinion through the quagmire of world events.[66]

Zimmern had several models in mind in sketching out this role of 'citizen-scholar'. One was George Louis Beer – an American historian whom Zimmern had met at the Paris Peace Conference in 1919. Another was Thucydides, to whom Zimmern compared Beer.[67] Others were Acton, Lord Bryce and Tamas Masaryk, all of whom engaged in 'a species of modern humanism, with a rich background of culture nurtured by philosophic reflection and the prolonged observation of men and cities'.[68] But how credible did Zimmern seem in this role of 'citizen-scholar' himself? He certainly failed to convince his American friends, who expressed increasing concern in the 1920s that Zimmern was spreading his energies too widely, and squandering his intellectual gifts in the process. A row erupted in a correspondence with Felix Frankfurter, a leading American jurist, in 1925. The immediate cause of discord was a difference of interpretation over the Geneva Protocol. Zimmern took the view that this document represented 'a bold extension of the realm of law: the acceptance by the Great Powers of the peaceful settlement of all disputes, whether justiciable or non-justiciable'.[69] However, Frankfurter was much more cautious, adhering to the view of M. Politis (author of the interpretive report accompanying the Protocol) that boundaries set by existing treaty rights, and therefore subject to *judicial* arbitration, lay outside the remit of the instrument. The Geneva Protocol, to Frankfurter's mind, applied only to the prevention of future disputes by *political* means, and was therefore far more precarious. It was important to Zimmern that the Protocol be interpreted generously so that burning frontier disputes such as the Polish corridor should be regarded as no less insoluble than the boundary separating Alaska from Maine. But Zimmern's readiness to merge these two classes of dispute brought forth the following expression of candour from Frankfurter:

The new edition of your [Greek] Commonwealth brings back with an intensified sense how much stimulation of Geist I owe to you through the printed page and how much my indebtedness was reinforced through personal contact. Apart from the sweet personal gifts which you signify, you were always for me a disinterested searcher for the truth, however doubtful or unknown its destination. Therefore I must say to your face, what a number of friends have said with sadness to one another, that more recently the disinterested searcher for truth, the guide to understanding, has been subordinated to the propagandist for panaceas. The cause which absorbs you is, to be sure, nothing less than civilisation. But so far as that great end is concerned I do not believe that some of the rest of us are one jot or tittle less eager than are you for the peace which means civilisation. But I do not believe that great end can be won on terms less rigorous and objective than those on which nature reveals her mysteries to the devotees of science.[70]

In his reply, Zimmern compared Frankfurter's role in promoting world peace unfavourably with his own. 'You have sat apart in the ivory tower of a Law School, nursing your disillusion, and emerging only to support a Wisconsin leader who is even more of a back number as regards European affairs than you are yourself'. He went on to identify two sources of influence – one ancient and culturally distant and one modern and local – which underlay his sense of responsibility as a public intellectual: 'As regards the second part of your letter, if you mean that you would rather I studied the past than the present, I can only say that Thucydides has always been my master and that I owe it to my pupils who gave their lives for a better world to continue their work under the same inspiration'.[71]

Clearly for Zimmern the world 'citizen-scholar' was pitted against not only the sectarian intellectual of the left, but also the detached intellectual, and was heavily inspired by the sacrifices of a talented younger generation of the British officer class. The world 'citizen-scholar' was also highly distinct from intellectuals who were wedded to some specious conception of the national interest that militated against the prior needs of international co-operation. It was on such grounds that he condemned H. A. L. Fisher for not lending his wholehearted support to Lord Cecil's proposals for a combined treaty of disarmament and mutual guarantee in 1923. Fisher had voiced scepticism of the proposal on the ground that it would endanger the unity of the British Empire, which could not reasonably be expected to act in concert in protecting territorial integrity throughout the world. For Zimmern, 'if our present imperial arrangements are an obstacle to the "opening of a new chapter in human relations" then the sooner they are altered the better'.[72]

Zimmern never wavered in his commitment to the world 'citizen-scholar', and continued to feel constrained by all narrowly academic initiatives. In 1934, for example, when approached by another old Zionist friend, Horace Kallen, to lend support to a British branch of the International League for Academic Freedom which Kallen was trying to organise, Zimmern declined. He pointed out that the PEN. club 'had woken up and is raising the banner of freedom for writers'. In addition, thought Zimmern, 'the assassins who rule Germany have shown their hand too plainly, and I feel in my bones that the wake of dictatorship has broken'. He went on, however, to dispel any 'negative' tone in his reply, indicating instead his

> belief in the broad highway. The other day, I was sent to represent Oxford at the centenary of the University of Berne and had the chance of making a speech in German on academic freedom, [which was] broadcast. This was much better, and more representative, than an ad hoc demonstration.[73]

But while Zimmern found institutional life somewhat suffocating, he never ceased to believe in the importance of the universities, both to the study of international relations and to international relations themselves. In his inaugural lecture at Oxford in 1931, he emphasised the model which *literae humaniores*, in particular, represented to the nascent field of international relations. The study of international relations in close proximity to that school of studies would impart 'the steady vision, the sensitive edge, the philosophical reflectiveness, the refinement of appreciation, with humour ever peeping round the corner'.[74] International contacts had multiplied, he maintained, throughout the nineteenth century. But they had first been forged by traders, then by governments. Universities had only lately realised their potential for systematic reflection on this contact. In this way, 'internationalism ha[d] been inaugurated at the wrong end'. [75] At the same time, however, that interaction had increased vastly between countries, national differences had intensified.[76] It was therefore incumbent upon the student of international relations to embrace 'Sociology in its widest extent'.[77] Only in this way could the insight of the Greeks into the 'altogetherness of the public affairs . . . the problem of the One in the Many, the Many in the One'[78] be reflected in the discipline. Hence, in the Examination Statutes up until 1941, international relations was said to comprise 'the study of the relations between governments and between peoples, and the principles underlying their development'.[79]

IV

By the 1940s, however, this conception of the nature of international relations, and the theoretical assumptions about international society on which it was based, had come under heavy fire. The 'idealist' school of international relations of which Zimmern was a leading representative had been exposed to the merciless criticism of E. H. Carr in *The Twenty Years' Crisis*: wars were not to be construed as aberrations in a world order marked by an essential harmony of interest and preventable through reason and education, but as the consequence of conflicting national interests which had not proved amenable to the application of 'pragmatic realism'.[80]

It appears that Zimmern did not respond to Carr. Neither were his beliefs and activities deflected from their previous course. He retired from the Oxford Chair in 1944, but he remained active as Deputy Director (under his one-time pupil, Arnold Toynbee) of the Foreign Office Research Department until 1945. From 1947 until his death a decade later, he lived and worked in the United States, fully supporting that country in its bid to lead the United Nations to world peace.[81] His conception of the heavy burden of responsibility of the world citizen-scholar to educate his political leaders and fellow citizens alike continued to disturb any peace of mind he may have occasionally allowed himself the luxury of enjoying. He sent an extraordinary letter to Toynbee in 1950, castigating several lamentable instances of *la traison des clercs* in the last two decades, not in Benda's sense of answering the call of citizenship but in deserting it. He lamented bitterly that in his last few months at the Foreign Office he did not push Toynbee more strongly in the way of communicating his misgivings about the Soviet Union to British representatives on the Armistice Commissions. 'I ought to have taken a sterner line, even to the point of endangering our friendship', he wrote. He believed that he and other intellectuals could have done more since 1947 to alert British public opinion to the Soviet annexations in Eastern Europe. He also reproached severely Chatham House (the Royal Society for International Affairs) for not having done more to 'prepare British public opinion for the Second World War, still less to avert it'. The unfortunate Toynbee was also subjected to Zimmern's expression of regret that 'mistaken loyalty' had perhaps prevented him from speaking out publicly against *A Study of History*.[82] He implied that the concept of civilisation had become much less the powerful tool of the responsible, public intellectual of the interwar period and more 'an opiate sending people into a dreamland of fanciful speculation about the rise and downfall of civilizations – including the downfall of our own – when they should have been bracing themselves for a great new constructive work'. He continued, 'I think your book, conceived in and for a different age from that in which we are now living, will take its place in the literary record, but in these grim days it is, alas!, a diversion – almost a *divertissment*'.[83]

But to Zimmern's successors at Oxford after his retirement in the United States in 1944, his syllabus – and no doubt his conception of his professional duty too – appeared 'too large and too pretentious'.[84] The new Montague Burton Professor, E. L. Woodward, and the two University Lecturers in International Relations – A. J. P. Taylor and A. Headlam-Morley – simplified the entry in the Examination Statutes to read as follows: 'The subject comprises the study of international relations from 1919–1939 with special reference to the policies of the Great Powers.'[85] The revolt did not represent an entirely clear-cut break with the past, as Taylor – at least – went on to outrival Zimmern in his bid to educate public opinion in the ways of politicians and diplomats. There was no attempt, however, on Taylor's part to articulate and disseminate a set of public values which would guide the beliefs, attitudes and conduct of his fellow-countrymen – no attempt to broach large historical and spiritual questions in the process of addressing contemporary events. In the Preface to his volume of essays, *Englishmen and Others* (1956), he wrote: 'I am not a philosophic historian. I have no system, no moral interpretation. I write to clear my mind, to discover how things happened and how men behaved.'[86] Although, in turn, much maligned by his contemporaries for his unscholarly activities,[87] nevertheless he remained a consummate but strict narrator of events.

Notes

1   A. Zimmern *The Greek Commonwealth: Politics and Economics in Fifth-Century Athens* (Oxford, Clarendon Press, [1911], 1924).

2   Zimmern to Violet Carruthers, 26 May 1919; Markham MSS, 25/92, British Library of Political and Economic Science (BLPES). Zimmern's efforts to reform Oxford in the early years of the twentieth century – particularly in relation to the provision of adult education and 'modern' studies – are illustrated by his article 'Oxford in the new century', *Independent Review*, III (1906), 95–104.

3   He announced his appointment to Justice Holmes, whom he had recently met in America, in a letter of 14 August 1912. The Papers of Oliver Wendell Holmes, Harvard Law School Library, Box 52, Folder 6.

4   A. Zimmern, 'The evolution of the citizen', in Oliver Stanley (ed.), *The Way Out: Essays on the Meaning and Purpose of Adult Education* (London, Oxford University Press, 1923), p. 37.

5   Zimmern to Weizmann, 9 July 1915; File 315, Weizmann Archives, Rehovot, Israel.

6   Zimmern to Oliver Wendell Holmes, 28 March 1913; The Papers of Oliver Wendell Holmes, Box 52, Folder 6.

7   Zimmern to Oliver Wendell Holmes, 7 September 1912; The Papers of Oliver Wendell Holmes, Box 52, Folder 6.

8   Zimmern to R. W. Seton-Watson, April 1912; Seton-Watson MSS, School of Slavonic and East European Studies, University of London, SEW/17/31/4.

9   Zimmern, 'True and false nationalism' (1915), in *Nationality and Government: With Other War-Time Essays* (London, Chatto & Windus, 1918), pp. 66–8.

10 Zimmern to Oliver Wendell Holmes, 25 October 1916; The Papers of Oliver Wendell Holmes, Box 52, Folder 6.

11 Zimmern to J. A. Hobson, 29 September 1916; Round Table MSS, Bodleian Library, Oxford, MS Eng. Hist. C817 (156).

12 Zimmern to Walter Lippmann, 23 June 1915; Walter Lippmann Papers, Manuscripts and Archives, Yale University Library, Box 35, Folder 1323. Zimmern elaborated on this conception of nationality in 'Nationality and government' (1915), reprinted in *Nationality and Government*, pp. 32–61.

13 On these Acts, and the background to them, see A. Dummett and A. Nicol, *Subjects, Citizens, Aliens and Others: Nationality and Immigration Law* (London, Weidenfeld & Nicolson, 1990), pp. 104–9.

14 Zimmern to Felix Frankfurter, 8 May 1918; Felix Frankfurter MSS, Library of Congress, Washington, DC, Container 113 (Microfilm 69).

15 Zimmern to Violet Carruthers, 20 July 1918, Markham *MSS*, 25/92.

16 Zimmern to Violet Carruthers, 17 January 1918; Markham MSS, 25/92.

17 Zimmern to Violet Carruthers, 20 July 1918; Markham MSS, 25/92.

18 Zimmern gave notice of his intention to leave the Board of Education for this reason

in a letter to Arnold Toynbee of 17 July 1914. MS Arnold J. Toynbee, Bodleian Library, 'Individuals' Series, Box Z. His letter of resignation is in the Zimmern Papers, Bodleian Library, Box 13 Folder, 185.

19 Zimmern to Graham Wallas, 4 November 1917; Wallas MSS, BLPES, 1/53/61–2.

20 Zimmern, 'Reconstruction', *The Round Table*, (September 1916), reprinted in *Nationality and Government*, pp. 243–4.

21 Zimmern to Violet Carruthers, 26 January 1918; Markham MSS, 25/92.

22 E. W. M. Grigg's entry for Hichens in the *Dictionary of National Biography, 1931–1940* (London, Oxford University Press, 1949), pp. 426–7; W. L. Hichens, *Some Problems of Modern Industry: The Watt Anniversary Lecture* (London, Nisbet & Co., 1918). The spirit of the lecture is well captured in the following passage (p. 27): 'Unless industry is really recognised as primarily a national service, in which each individual is fulfilling his function to the best of his ability for the sake of the community, in which private gain is subordinated to public good, in which, in a word, we carry out our duty towards our neighbour – unless we build on this foundation, there is no hope of creating the House Beautiful'.

23 See the letter from E. W. M. Grigg to Zimmern, 14 February 1914; MS. Round Table, Eng. Hist. c817, fols 14–15. The idea that the working class needed educating in foreign affairs provided the impetus behind a book which Zimmern wrote with fellow members of the Round Table – Lord Eustace Percy, Arthur Greenwood, J. Dover Wilson and R. W. Seton-Watson – at the outbreak of the First World War, entitled *The War and Democracy* (London, Macmillan, 1914). The book was dedicated to the Worker's Education Association.

24 Probably his *Briefe über Religion* (1906). Extracts of this book appeared in Baron Von Hügel's *The German Soul in its Attitude towards Ethics and Christianity, the State and War* (London, J. M. Dent, 1916), pp. 51–8, a work which Zimmern made reference to in 1939 (see p. 100 below). Von Hügel castigated the Darwinism which came to overlay Naumann's Lutheranism and resulted in the belief of the ex-pastor turned 'national socialist' leader that the Christian ethics of the Gospels applied only to the Galilean community in which they were formulated: they were irrelevant to an international environment characterised by intense economic and strategic competition. Christianity, according to Naumann, had to be reconciled to a world in which 'power and right' possessed their own imperatives.

25 Zimmern to Wallas, 14 April 1916; Wallas MSS, BLPES, 1/53, 36–7.

26 Zimmern to G. D. H. Cole, 14 April 1915; MS. Round Table, MS Eng. Hist. c817, Folder 82.

27 Zimmern, Introduction to *The War and Democracy*, p. 13.

28 Lionel Curtis has recently become the subject of a wide-ranging and perceptive study by Deborah Lavin, *From Empire to International Commonwealth: A Biography of Lionel Curtis* (Oxford, Clarendon Press, 1995), from which the above paragraph is drawn. See pp. 112, 124, 129, 330.

29 A. Zimmern, 'Supremacy of the state', *The New Republic* (15 September 1917), 191–2.

30 Laski to Zimmern, 20 September 1918; Zimmern MSS, Box 15, Bodleian Library, Oxford.

31 Zimmern to J. A. Hobson, 29 September 1916; MS Round Table, MS Eng. Hist, c. 517 Folder 155. For Lippmann's response, see his editorial note at the end of Zimmern's article, 'Supremacy of the state'.

32 Percy–Zimmern Memoranda on The League of Nations for the Peace Conference,

1919, FO 371.4353 (150), PID: Peace Conference Series. Zimmern reproduced his memorandum in his book *The League of Nations and the Rule of Law* (London, Macmillan, [1936] 1939), although he did not disclose his identity as its author. In elaborating upon the aspirations for, and model of, the League in that book, he invoked (p. 191) the British Imperial Conference. See note 48 below.

33 A. Zimmern, 'The meaning of nationality', *The New Republic* (1 January 1916), 215–17. Zimmern was highly critical of H. A. L. Fisher's suggestion in 1924 that vernacular languages should be 'squeezed out' on the grounds that 'a nation is handicapped by the possession of a subordinate language'. The temperature of the ensuing debate ran high – as was usual with Zimmern – with personal experience providing the latter's touchstone. Zimmern defended the richness of Welsh life as a result of the Welsh language, and also hinted that Fisher did not know the full half of Zimmern's complicated national descent which was not the least ground for his taking issue with the erstwhile Minister of Education. Zimmern, 'Studies in citizenship', *The Nation & the Athenaeum* (15 March 1924), 840–1. For Fisher's response see *The Nation & the Athenaeum* (29 March 1924), 917. Zimmern replied in *The Nation & the Athenaeum* (5 April 1924), 12–13.

34 F. S. Marvin (ed.), *The Unity of Western Civilization* (London, Oxford University Press, 1915), p. 3.

35 Zimmern to F. S. Marvin, 9 April 1915; MS Marvin, Eng.Lett.d.263, Folder 50, Bodleian Library, Oxford.

36 Barker to Marvin, 18 April 1915; MS Marvin, Eng. Lett.d.263, fol. 52.

37 N. Rose, *The Cliveden Set: Portrait of an Exclusive Fraternity* (London, Jonathan Cape, 2000). For other examples of English insularity among the group, see 45, 57.

38 Zimmern, Introduction to Leon Simon, *Studies in Jewish Nationalism* (London, Longman, 1920).

39 See L. Simon (ed.), *Ahad Ha-Am: Essays, Letters, Memoirs* (Oxford, East and West Library, 1946). Ahad Ha-Am's conflict with Theodor Herzl, author of *The Jewish State: An Attempt at a Modern Solution to the Jewish Question,* transl. S. D'Avigdor (1896), is illuminated in Y. Hazony, *The Jewish State: The Struggle for Israel's Soul* (New York, Basic Books, 2000).

40 P. Strum, *Louis D. Brandeis: Justice for the People* (Cambridge, Ma., Harvard University Press, 1984), pp. 237–43. Strum contends that Brandeis and Zimmern had not met before their trip to Palestine in 1919, and that the year in which Brandeis's attention was drawn to *The Greek Commonwealth* is unclear. Their coincidence of views, however – not just on Palestine but the 'progressive' values in terms of which Zimmern had painted ancient Greece and in terms of which Brandeis was engaged in reforming labour law under President Wilson between 1912 and 1914 – may have emerged in the course of Zimmern's visit to the United States in 1912. Certainly, Zimmern possessed a letter of introduction to Brandeis written by Horace Kallen, stating that 'Mr. Zimmern is deeply interested in "social engineering" and particularly in your proposals for adjudicating differences between industrial classes'; 18 April 1912, Zimmern MSS, Box 13.

41 Zimmern, 'The passing of nationality' (1917), in *Nationality and Government*, p. 97.

42 Zimmern, address to the Zionist Organisation (London Bureau), 19 August 1919; Central Zionist Archives, Jerusalem, Z4/5071, p. 10.

43 Zimmern to Lippmann, 23 May 1919; Lippmann MSS, Box 35, 1323.

44 B. Porter, *The Aberystwyth Papers: International Politics, 1919–1969* (London, Oxford University Press, 1972), p. 361.

45 Zimmern's work has been reviewed critically in the light of the intellectual assumptions of the modern discipline of international relations by D. J. Markwell, 'Sir Alfred Zimmern revisited', *Review of International Studies*, 12 (1986), 279–92.

46 Their European and American travels, encounters and impressions are documented in letters to R. W. Seton-Watson of 29 May 1921, 2 August 1921, 9 August 1922 and 10 March 1923. Seton-Watson MSS, SEW/17/31/4.

47 Entry for Zimmern in the *Dictionary of National Biography* (1951–60), by Sir Arthur Salter. Zimmern's first marriage in 1912 to a well-connected American was disastrous. See his letters to Holmes of 14 December 1912 and 28 March 1913; The Papers of Oliver Wendell Holmes, Box 52, Folder 6. Zimmern's second marriage – to the wife of another professor – caused something of a scandal at Aberystwyth. See Porter, *The Aberystwyth Papers*, p. 362.

48 A. Zimmern, 'The League in being', *The New Europe*, 11 (8 May 1919), 83.

49 Zimmern, *The League of Nations*, p. 193.

50 Zimmern, *The League of Nations*, pp. 367–8.

51 Zimmern, Introduction to the 'Geneva Series' of books, which included Salvador de Madariaga's *Englishmen, Frenchmen, Spaniards: An Essay in Comparative Psychology* (London, Oxford University Press, 1928), p. vii.

52 A. Zimmern, *Learning and Leadership* (London, Oxford University Press, 1928), p. 27.

53 Oliver Wendell Holmes to Zimmern, 2 January 1915; The Papers of Oliver Wendell Holmes, Box 52, Folder 6.

54 Zimmern to Oliver Wendell Holmes, 25 April 1927; The Papers of Oliver Wendell Holmes, Box 52, Folder 6.

55 A. Zimmern, *Spiritual Values and World Affairs* (Oxford, Clarendon Press, 1939), pp. 18–23.

56 The enhanced influence of Christianity on Zimmern's thought is mirrored in the intellectual development of Arnold Toynbee, whom he taught at Oxford in the early years of the twentieth century. On the abandonment of Toynbee's 'paganism' derived from his education in Classics and his rejoining of the Anglican communion in 1940, see C. Navari, 'Arnold Toynbee (1889–1975): prophecy and civilization', *Review of International Studies*, 26 (2000), 289–301.

57 A. Zimmern, 'Political thought', in R. W. Livingstone (ed.), *The Legacy of Greece* (Oxford, Clarendon Press, 1921), p. 333.

58 A. Zimmern, *The Study of International Relations* (Oxford, Clarendon Press, 1931), p. 13.

59 Zimmern, *Spiritual Values and World Affairs*, pp. 50–1.

60 G. Wallas, Preface to N. Palmer, *Henry Bournes Higgins* (London, George G. Harrap, 1931), p. vi.

61 Zimmern had rejoiced in the defeat of the Labour Party in the 1922 General Election, declaring that it would achieve nothing until it had 'cleansed itself of the Marxist poison which had been fed to it by Hyndman, the Webbs, MacDonald, Snowden, Cole and successive intellectuals since 1880'; Zimmern to Horace Kallen, 18 November 1922; Horace Meyer Kallen Papers, File 889, YIVO Institute for Jewish Research, New York. But just two years later, he stood as the Labour candidate against Lloyd George in Caernavon, although more on the grounds of MacDonald's

foreign policy towards Russia – his attempt to bring the Soviet Union into the disarmament conference – than any new warmth towards socialism. He was interviewed for *Stend's Review*, 15 December 1924; MS Zimmern, Box 178.

62 Zimmern's characterisation of English inscrutability in international circles was depicted more comically through the Scottish eyes of Donald Cameron in A. G. MacDonell's novel *England their England* (London, Macmillan, 1933). 'Donald went out [from his interview with Foreign Office experts at Geneva], feeling that he had gained some sort of insight, at first hand, into the subtle diplomacy which had spread the Union Jack upon all the potential aerodromes of the world. He could see that the genius was there, though he could not have explained for the life of him how it worked. But, of course, that was the genius of it' (p. 159).

63 Zimmern, *Spiritual Values and World Affairs*, pp. 137–42.

64 Zimmern, *Spiritual Values and World Affairs*, p. 76.

65 Zimmern had attacked Lloyd George's action in 'The economic provisions of the peace treaty', *The New Europe*, 11 (22 May 1919), 124–7. Not long afterwards, he had also criticised Lloyd George's 'secret agreement' with the French government to give priority in the allocation of the raw materials of the empire to the allied powers, thereby impeding the economic recovery of Europe as a whole on which lasting peace – to Zimmern's mind – depended. A. Zimmern, 'Another secret agreement?', *The New Europe*, 13 (25 December 1919), 326–9.

66 Zimmern, *Spiritual Values and World Affairs*, pp. 88–94.

67 Zimmern, 'The scholar in politics' (1921), reprinted in A. Zimmern, *The Prospects of Democracy* (London, Chatto & Windus, 1932), p. 7.

68 Zimmern, Introductory Report to the discussions in 1935, in A. Zimmern (ed.), *The University Teaching of International Relations*, a record of the eleventh session of the International Studies Conference in Prague (Paris, International Institute of Intellectual Co-operation, League of Nations, 1939), p. 10.

69 A. Zimmern, 'Europe and the Geneva Protocol', *The New Republic* (4 February 1925), reprinted in *The Prospects of Democracy*, p. 259.

70 Felix Frankfurter to Zimmern, 7 April 1925; Frankfurter MSS, container 113 (microfilm 69).

71 Zimmern to Frankfurter, 27 April 1925; Frankfurter MSS, container 113 (microfilm 69).

72 Zimmern, 'Studies in citizenship', p. 342.

73 Zimmern to H. Kallen, 8 July 1934; Horace Meyer Kallen MSS, File 889.

74 Zimmern, *The Study of International Relations*, pp. 20–1.

75 Zimmern, *The Study of International Relations*, p. 25.

76 Zimmern, *The Study of International Relations*, p. 17.

77 Zimmern (ed.), *University Teaching*, p. 7.

78 Zimmern (ed.), *University Teaching*, p. 11.

79 *Examination Statutes* (Oxford, Clarendon Press, 1940). In his *The League of Nations and the Rule of Law*, Zimmern argued that the relations between states was only a small part of the field of international relations. While his analysis was necessarily confined to methods of co-operation between states, this was not history itself, but merely 'an episode against the background of history – unintelligible without a knowledge of the larger issues of policy involved and of the still larger problems of the relations between *peoples* and of the interaction of the cultures, traditions, attitudes, ingrained ways of thinking and feeling, which constitute the raw

material of policy . . . Descartes, Burke and Jefferson were not members of the committee that drafted the Covenant of the League of Nations: but their ghosts were an active influence throughout its proceedings'; pp. 6–7.

80 E. H. Carr, *The Twenty Years Crisis, 1919–1939: An Introduction to the Study of International Relations* (London, Macmillan, 1939). On the complexities of Carr's position, see C. Jones, *E. H. Carr and International Relations: A Duty to Lie* (Cambridge, Cambridge University Press, 1998).

81 Markwell, 'Sir Alfred Zimmern revisited', pp. 281–2, 288.

82 A. Toynbee, *A Study of History*, 12 vols (London, Oxford University Press, 1934–61).

83 Zimmern to Toynbee, 13 July 1950; MS Toynbee, 'Individuals' Corr., Box Z. On Toynbee's *A Study of History* see C. Navari, 'Arnold Toynbee', and James Joll, 'Two prophets of the twentieth century: Spengler and Toynbee', *Review of International Studies*, 11 (1986), 91–104.

84 Memorandum from E. L. Woodward, A. J. P. Taylor and A. Headlam-Morley to the University Registry, 23 November 1945; Reports of the Board of the Faculty of Social Studies, FA4/18/2/6, p. 73, Oxford University Archives, Bodleian Library.

85 *Examination Statutes* (Oxford, Clarendon Press, 1945).

86 Quoted in A. Sisman, *A. J. P. Taylor: A Biography* (London, Sinclair-Stevenson, 1994), p. 237.

87 Sisman, *A. J. P. Taylor*, p. 213.

Part III

Political thought and public values, 1930–70: English perspectives

The last three chapters considered attempts on the part of leading political and literary intellectuals in the interwar period to close an increasingly obvious gap between public and intellectual opinion after the First World War. The key figures of these chapters showed concern for the increasing exclusiveness of philosophical and cultural knowledge and its adverse effect upon no less a universal ideal than civilisation itself. However, another set of writers were equally prominent in the 1930s, and they – and their values and beliefs – continued to make their mark in the postwar decades. Like those considered previously, they stressed the importance of public education in the widest sense. But in their view that education had to be focused at a prominent level within a national framework of 'Englishness', a cultural ensign that stood out in sharp relief against the tyranny which was perceived to have surfaced regularly over much of the European continent.[1]

Central to this conception of English exceptionalism was an opposition to the 'abstract', intellectualist values which were often deemed responsible for the political travails abroad. But while its advocates inveighed against intellectuals, their antipathy was levelled against a certain type of intellectual only, as often as not one whose political allegiances lay securely on the left, or whose opinions on social and moral questions were unconventional, or whose arguments were perceived to be grounded in a form of rationality that was divorced from, and often actively opposed to, everyday – particularly English national – experience. The latter, it was felt, had been forced on to the defensive as a result. For a new generation of conservative thinkers and historians, one seminal way of invigorating national life was through intelligence itself, replacing instinctive (and reactionary) conservatism with one that was well informed by history and theory – albeit firmly rooted in the experience of the previous century.[2] The quality and value of intellect *per se* were not in question: deeply suspicious of modern intellectuals though he was, A. L. Rowse could praise William Plomer – along with T. S. Eliot – as a 'witty, an *intellectual*, poet. And that is rare among the English, at least since the seventeenth century'.[3] Nor was the importance of the intellectual vocation itself ever doubted by such champions of England and Englishness, particularly in a democracy which they saw themselves as continuing to play a key role in educating. But not being 'antagonistic' to the existing grain of national life, unlike many of their counterparts on the left, they failed to take on the characteristics of the classic, alienated intelligentsia to be found abroad. Neither, however, did their deep sense of affinity with England lead them to collude with the state as a vehicle for achieving their cultural and political ends, in the manner of the nationalist, intellectual 'mandarins' of Germany in the interwar period.[4] The typical 'non-intellectual' intellectual in Britain in the 1930s and subsequent decades continued to remain wary of officialdom and to cherish his autonomy, despite the opportunities which government work – particularly in the Second World War – offered for gaining influence. This is well illustrated in a letter which Ernest Barker wrote to Herbert Butterfield in 1949. Sympathising with a lecture which Butterfield had delivered in 1949 on the importance of maintaining the utmost rigour in the writing of history, particularly those academic historians who were engaged in writing the official histories of the War, Barker confessed that:

> I have suffered myself – though in a small way, and only in regard to a pamphlet – from the attention of Government Departments. Mind you, the members of the Department were most extraordinarily decent; they showed their hand without reservation; and I understood why they made their points. But the little experience which I had – only last week – taught me that my freedom was the dearest thing I had.[5]

The political beliefs of the thinkers and writers who feature in the following two chapters were broadly situated on both sides of the boundary that separated conservatism from liberalism, one which became more indefinite as its significance increased. While not as successful in influencing political opinion in the 1930s in the organised way of their counterparts on the left, nevertheless their central category of English/British 'national character' was to play a pivotal role in the civilian War effort of the Second World War. Subsequently, it flowed into a cultural stream which rallied middlebrow opinion in postwar Britain to the cause of national revival out of the embers of decline, and which an inverted form of Whiggism was in the process of charting.[6] This later development – associated primarily with Arthur Bryant and John Betjeman – will form the subject of Chapter 8. Those whose work in the 1930s and 1940s will be considered in Chapters 6 and 7 include Bryant, G. M. Trevelyan, Ernest Barker, A. L. Rowse, E. M. Forster and Francis Brett Young. While most of these figures were primarily historians or writers – Barker was the only professional political theorist among them – nevertheless the political world, the role of intellectuals in it and its basis in the national culture, engaged them all.

It is not suggested that the animosity of this set of writers towards the modern intellectual was directed at all, or indeed any one, of the figures considered in the previous chapters. On the contrary, Barker, for example, remained on the most cordial terms with Lindsay and Zimmern throughout this period. Similarly, overlapping concerns are evident for example, in the importance which the subjects of this chapter, along with Collingwood, attached to the countryside in combatting totalitarianism. Nor was there ever a complete harmony of outlook between those who defended English character and traditions against 'intellectual' attempts to subvert them: the issue of appeasement was particularly divisive in this respect. Nevertheless, the classification of intellectuals in accordance with loyalties and sympathies that were broadly internationalist, on the one hand, and English/British, on the other, highlights an important but neglected aspect of intellectual life during the 1930s – one in which intellectualism itself proved a major bone of contention with clear political and cultural implications.

Notes

1   This theme of England's cultural distance from Europe in the writings of G. M. Trevelyan, Arthur Bryant and H. A. L. Fisher has been explored by Philip Bell in 'A

historical cast of mind: some eminent English historians and attitudes to continental Europe in the middle of the twentieth century', *Journal of European Integration*, 2 (1996), 5–19; and A.Varsori, 'Is Britain part of Europe? The myth of British "difference"', in C. Buffet and B. Heuser (eds), *Haunted by History* (Providence, Rhode Island, Berghahn Books, 1998), pp. 134–56.

2　See R. N. Soffer, 'The long nineteenth century of conservative thought', in G. K. Behlmer and F. M. Leventhal (eds), *Singular Continuities: Tradition, Nostalgia, and Identity in Modern British Culture* (Stanford, Stanford Univeristy Press, 2000), pp. 143–62.

3　Rowse to Plomer, 23 August 1971; William Plomer MSS, Folder 187 (4), Durham University Library.

4　F. K. Ringer, *The Decline of the German Mandarins: The German Academic Community, 1890–1933* (Cambridge, Ma., Harvard University Press, 1969).

5　Barker to Butterfield, 27 July 1949; Butterfield Papers, 130/4, Cambridge University Library.

6　Whig history's transmutation into a story of English decline in the mid twentieth century has been emphasised by Victor Feske in *From Belloc to Churchill: Private Scholars, Public Culture, 1900–1939* (Chapel Hill, University of North Carolina Press, 1996), pp. 238–9.

6

The recovery of Englishness and the flight from intellectualism in the 1930s and 1940s

I

The common identity that existed between the figures who form the subject of this section is apparent in a letter which G. M. Trevelyan – who has been called 'the last Whig historian'[1] – wrote to Bryant in 1944. He was responding enthusiastically to the publication of the second volume of Bryant's study of the Napoleonic Wars,[2] a timely reminder to the British public that once before they had stood their ground against a continental tyrant and triumphed over him. He remarked that

> You and I, and [Milton] Waldman and Rowse, together make a group (I will not say a 'school') of historians of somewhat the same kind, with somewhat the same view of history and how it should be written. We are of course not all agreeing on all points in the past, though all are in love with England which is the essential. I am glad of this. For when I started life I was very much alone, or leaning backwards to my father. Now I lean forwards . . . and do not feel alone. I cannot tell you how much this pleases me.[3]

The ties that bound these figures together are evident in several book dedications of the 1930s and 1940s: Bryant's *Macaulay* of 1932 was dedicated to Trevelyan as 'master of my craft'. Rowse followed suit in 1944, dedicating his book *The English Spirit* to Trevelyan as 'admirable exemplar of the English spirit'. Bryant dedicated the first volume of his study of Britain during the Napoleonic Wars – his *The Years of Endurance* (1942) – to Rowse, 'in common devotion to the English past'. Rowse was clearly delighted by the dedication in *The Years of Endurance*,[4] and reciprocated with *The Early Churchills* (1956). Finally, Bryant acknowledged the assistance of Milton Waldman – Editor at Collins – in the Preface to *The Years of Endurance*. It is significant, too, that Trevelyan, Rowse and Bryant – together with Rowse's student Veronica Wedgewood – all became Presidents of the English Association in the late 1940s and 1950s. This was in recognition of their shared belief that historical writing at its best was inseparable from the literary imagination, notwithstanding the broad appeal that such scholarship would inevitably make.[5]

This circle of writers who sensed a mutual affinity extended to other senior figures in British academic life whom Bryant courted in the 1930s; for example, Ernest Barker. Barker responded warmly to Bryant's openings. He had been a close friend of Bryant's father – Sir Francis Morgan Bryant, George V's Sergeant-at-Arms – in the elite dining association known as the Confrères formed during the previous decade.[6] Barker had then been Principal of King's College London, and the circle was drawn from leading figures in the key military, business, administrative and academic institutions of the capital. He also lectured at the Bonar Law Memorial College at Ashridge in Hertfordshire, both early in the 1930s and again in 1937.[7] The College was established in 1929 on the basis of donations by Urban Broughton, Sir Edward Brotherton, Lord Inchcape and another anonymous donor. An endowment fund was formed which was entitled the Bonar Law Memorial Trust. The College was set up specifically to promote adult education in areas such as the British Constitution and British Empire which were of special concern to Conservatives. Indeed, the money was raised by John Davidson as Conservative Party Chairman, capitalising on a new and highly effective drive to educate citizens in the principles of Conservatism during the 1920s.[8] Although it was primarily used to train Conservative Party agents and speakers, its classes on citizenship were levelled at a wide spectrum of British political society.[9] Bryant was the College's Educational Adviser, and was appointed to the Governing Body in 1936.

In a similar fashion to Trevelyan, Barker wrote to Bryant in the late 1930s, expressing the increasing closeness of his political views to Bryant's self-styled Toryism.[10] This rapport had been precipitated by a long period of alienation from Liberal politics in Britain, prompting him to confide his anxiety concerning the

> abstract intellectualism of those with whom I used to associate, and by the conventional lip service to phrases in my old party – the Liberal Party. I admire more and more the practical wisdom of the good ordinary Englishman, facing the facts and 'feeling' the right way through them – as a good Englishman feels his way through a new countryside.[11]

This was a significant statement as hitherto Barker had associated intellectualism with the rarified world of German thought. For example, when approached by H. A. L. Fisher in 1933 to write the book on Marx for the Home University Library which was eventually undertaken by Isaiah Berlin, he declined on the grounds that the '*lehre* or system' in Marx would exceed his patience. He continued, 'I have a general dislike for German *lehre* at the moment. I am just finishing a biggish volume on Gierke's Political Theories of the Modern Age . . ., and 2 years spent among German theorists have almost destroyed me'.[12] Towards the end of the 1930s, however, he was clearly sensing, and becoming alarmed by, if hardly identical then in some ways analogous trends in British thought, and in the Liberal Party of all places. Like Trevelyan, Barker was tempted to give up on liberalism, not least in view of its increasing alliance with 'progressivism' (although Liberal opposition to the government's foreign policy was also an instrumental factor in his disillusion, as will be seen in the following chapter). While he signed the cross-party manifesto, *The Next Five Years: An Essay in Political Agreement*[13] – whose principal forces were the Conservative progressive Harold Macmillan and the ex-Independent Labour Party leader, now National Labour politician, Clifford Allen – this was more out of the spirit of consensus which lay behind the document than any sympathy with the ambitious goals of state planning and social justice it set out. Certainly, in his *Reflections on Government* published in 1942 and based on university lectures delivered in the previous decade, he expressed severe reservations about the compatibility of planning with democracy on anything other than a limited scale and, further, in a lecture of 1949, with the historic liberties of the British people.[14] His animus against 'abstract intellectualism' and conception of its opposition to the essentially pragmatic English temper is significant in this context. For he clearly sensed a change in the basis of both political and intellectual culture in Britain – a move away from the statesmanlike model of the scholar-politician-educationalist provided by such heroes of his youth as James Bryce, and towards that of the social engineer, who had turned his back upon all established cultural and political traditions and the political insights afforded by classical learning.[15]

In his antipathy to contemporary intellectuals Barker was joined by A. L. Rowse and Trevelyan, as well as Bryant. All four men used the term 'intellectual' in a negative, derogatory sense. For Trevelyan, the archetypal intellectual was a member of Bloomsbury, holding disagreeable and dangerous views on private morality.[16] It was in this vein that he wrote to Bryant in 1936, approving the King's abdication. It was fitting, he commented, not just because Edward VIII was 'unsuited' to monarchy, but because

> a stand has been made against the view that sexual license is a natural right of man, a doctrine which half our literary and intellectual leaders have been preaching for the last 40 years. I feared they might have converted the country, but clearly they haven't.[17]

Barker professed total ignorance of Bloomsbury, despite passing most of the 1920s in close geographical proximity.[18] This was a mark not only of the exclusiveness of that literary set but also its inability to make any appreciable impact upon some of the survivors of Victorian intellectual culture with which it was so much in conflict. For Barker, like Trevelyan, Edward's position had become indefensible.[19]

For Rowse and Bryant the term 'intellectual' referred primarily to a thinker on the left. The two men struck up a regular and warm correspondence during the Second World War, by which time Rowse's patience with the Labour Party, whose Cornish supporters he had actively sought to represent in the 1930s, had run out. We saw, at the end of Chapter 4, that Rowse's Marxism was selective in the extreme. Lacking the essential ingredient of the dialectic, it did not take long before it was defeated by its rival, patriotism, for his intellectual and emotional convictions. Rowse's increasing disdain for the 'idiot people', to whom, in his eyes, he had rendered faithful service as a Labour candidate, was matched only by a disdain for the 'Left orthodoxy' and the dangerous play they had made with their home culture. The views of the latter, he claimed, had been moulded indiscriminately by

> Wells and Shaw and Russell, by Lytton Strachey, the Woolfs and Bloomsbury. All these people belonged to an older generation, an easier world in which it was possible to make a great reputation by calling in question accepted ideas and institutions, pouring cheap ridicule on traditional values and standards – without understanding their inner rationale – denigrating the achievements of the past.

In between these two battalions of the people, on the one hand, and intellectuals, on the other, stood the 'sensible Trade Unionists and Labour men of good sober judgement and experience', [20] a leading example of which – to Rowse's mind – was Ernest Bevin. One of Rowse's post-mortems on the 1930s – a collection of essays entitled *The End of an Epoch* – was dedicated to Bevin, 'fellow west countryman and a great Englishman'.

Like Trevelyan and Barker, Rowse began to discern in Bryant a greater ally than many in his own party, although his continued adherence to Labour was strongly anchored in his gratitude for the foreign policy of rearmament and anti-appeasement it had pursued in the 1930s – against the 'lunacy' of its pacifist fringe.[21] As we shall see in the following chapter, Bryant's outlook on these matters was diametrically opposed to that of Rowse. But, oblivious to the extent of Bryant's appeasement activities in the late 1930s, Rowse listed in a letter of 1942 what he regarded as the two most vital overlapping concerns between himself and Bryant:

> (1) A deep devotion to the historic past of our country and one both inspired by its glories and achievements.

> (2) We both loathe the abstract intellectualism of Left intellectuals, whether Liberal or Socialist – the mentality of the *New Statesman* par excellence – what more appalling?[22]

A great admirer of Churchill (although he had publicly supported Halifax for Prime Minister in May 1940[23]), Rowse was incandescent at the kind of criticism which thinkers such as Bevan and Laski had levelled at the wartime leader.[24] This led him to reflect that there was something 'unhealthy and unsound about the character and general line of contemporary "intellectual" life'.[25] It mirrored – he noted in *The English Spirit* – the 'bitter', 'sour' note which Carlyle had introduced into Victorian letters, his extravagance and worship of force being totally antithetical to the more authentic, 'merry' tone of England characterised by Belloc and Chesterton: 'the England of maypoles and church-ales and dancing on the village green, of harvest-homes and Twelfth Night'.[26]

The English Spirit is notable on several accounts. First, it was launched with an astonishing print-run of 10,000 copies, thereby emphasising Rowse's growing authority as an interpreter of English culture and history.[27] Second, Rowse claimed in the Preface that its central theme – 'something more than pride in, a deep love for English things' – was evident in some of the pieces which were written well before the outbreak of War, and was not, therefore, the product of a hasty patriotic conversion. Third, it reflected the clear inspiration of George Santayana, whose *Soliloquies in England*, published in 1922, exercised a profound influence on a generation of non-Marxist intellectuals and public figures who wrote in the interwar period: Barker, W. R. Inge, G. M. Trevelyan and Stanley Baldwin.[28] Fourth, the heroes of the book reflected Rowse's antipathy towards the masses, on the one hand, and the intellectual elite, on the other. He emphasised, again in the Preface, that 'This may be the century of the Common Man – it certainly is of the common *cliché* – but I prefer to look for the uncommon man, the man of genius or ability.'[29] Those whom he singled out for attention in this way included Churchill, Drake, Sarah Churchill, Horace Walpole and Macaulay, all selected for their outstanding contribution to the English nation's well-being, and presented as a foil to the carping Left intellectuals.

Another writer who shared these pro-English and anti-intellectual views was Francis Brett Young. A physician who had trained at the University of Birmingham, Brett Young had joined the Royal Medical Army Corps in the First World War and served in Smuts's East Africa campaign. Out of this experience he had written his first novel, *Marching on Tanga* (1917).[30] Suffering considerable ill-health after the African venture, Young continued to write in his native Worcestershire, his last work being the epic poem *The Island*, which was published in 1944. The work was hardly noticed in the press but considerable approval was communicated to its author in private correspondence by Bryant, Gilbert Murray, G. M. Trevelyan and Barker.[31]

Brett Young had begun writing *The Island* four years earlier, one reason being his frustration with the failure of the Ministry of Information to harness the skills and patriotic loyalty of imaginative writers such as himself to further the War effort.[32] In the early months of 1940 he wrote a series of letters to the extremely well networked Lionel Curtis (with whom he shared South African connections), bemoaning the fact that 'not a single imaginative writer of standing . . . has as yet been asked to help the Ministry [of Information] in the one task which their experience and reputation qualif[y] them to perform'. He went on, in a subsequent letter, to draw a contrast with the First World War when 'Buchan and Arnold Bennett and Wells were all contributing their imagination'.[33] Curtis promised to look into the matter, but all that transpired – for Brett Young, at least – was a local speaking engagement to which his talents were not given.[34] This was after the sluggish, early incarnation of the MOI had been shaken up in July 1940 by the arrival of Duff Cooper as its third Minister in less than a year. Nevertheless, the Ministry continued to remain aloof from ordinary citizens. Its personnel proved incapable of the great feats of mass communication centred upon British national qualities associated with Churchill, on the one hand, and J. B. Priestley, on the other. The employment of Priestley as a BBC speaker on behalf of the Ministry was the latter's only venture down the road of popular, plain speaking, and his success with listeners in forcing a 'reconstructionist' front in wartime propaganda was a fiasco in the eyes of officials.[35] Both Priestley and Churchill believed in the inherent strengths of the people whom they sought to move; the officials who staffed the Ministry did not.[36]

Brett Young persevered with *The Island* despite failing health, and such was the effort required that – once the book was finished – he was under strict medical orders not to write another word again.[37] As Barker wrote to Brett Young's wife in 1944, 'It is the result of this war that it galvanises the spirits of us older men into activity which the body can hardly rise to'.[38] The poem was a chronicle of England/Britain's good fortune since Caesar's invasion, but its celebratory tone changed perceptibly when it came to the interwar period. There, decline had set in, with a country that had yielded to selfishness, cynicism and a derisive view of the past. Brett Young reserved his most caustic words for the intellectuals – philosophers, dramatists, writers and poets (for whom poetry had become 'propaganda', 'with spite for satire, vitriol for wit'). Not least in Brett Young's list of condemned intellectuals were the

> frigid, half-alive
> Highbrows of Bloomsbury, who with eyes of stone
> Stiffly disdain all talents but their own;
> Strict snobs of letters, chary to admit
> There's such a thing as wisdom, style or wit
> Beyond the boundaries their pundits keep alive. . . .
> Such are are seers and prophets! Can you wonder,
> Led by such guides, our race is going under,
> Sinking in treacherous quicksands none can sound?[39]

Another writer outside of the realm of historical study with whom Bryant also sensed a common effort to break the stranglehold of British intellectuals on the cultural life of the country was H. J. Massingham, chronicler of rural decay in the manner of his hero, William Cobbett. Bryant had become acquainted with Massingham – son of the radical journalist H. W. Massingham – in the 1940s. He shared fully Massingham's conception of the countryside as the crucible of England and his wider concerns for the wholesomeness of a life lived in close contact with Nature and God. In a tribute to Massingham in the *Sunday Times* when the latter died in 1952, Bryant compared his friend very favourably with such overrated luminaries as 'Bertrand Russell, or, on a far lower level, . . . that of the magnificent writer and brilliant but facile popularizer, H. G. Wells'.[40] Bryant's admiration was returned in the form of the dedication of Massingham's *The Wisdom of the Fields* to him in 1945.[41]

II

An aversion to the urban bias of mainstream intellectual culture was typical of this circle of writers who were worried about the growth of an intelligentsia of the left in Britain. Trevelyan was active in the National Trust and keenly extolled the countryside over towns and cities. It was, moreover, no backward-looking 'nostalgia' for pre-industrial forms of life that inspired him but, on the contrary, a sense that the basis and values of the countryside – particularly the English countryside – were vital in combatting the totalitarian threat. The countryside, he maintained, should not be regarded as simply an occasional or even regular tonic for the inhabitants of the compressed spaces of the towns (a view he shared with R. G. Collingwood[42]), but as a powerful reminder of the transient and shallow nature of most new ideas. The weight of this association between the countryside and stability against the backdrop of growing political extremism in the 1930s is evident in the quintessentially liberal tone of scepticism which Trevelyan sounded at the end of a lecture in 1931:

> The appeal of natural beauty is more commonly or at least more consciously felt to-day than ever before, just because it is no new argument, no new dogma, no doctrine, no change of fashion, but something far older yet far more fresh, fresh as when the shepherd on the plains of Shinar first noted the stern beauty of the patient stars.[43]

Trevelyan continued by invoking the characteristically consensual note of his liberalism, suggesting that natural beauty – and natural beauty alone – constituted the 'highest common denominator in the spiritual life of to-day'. Significantly, it was a basis for consensus that was markedly lacking in any overt party-political content, suggesting that Trevelyan – contrary to the 'progressive' movements of his age – did not see scope for political or any other divisions being bridged on their own plane, but requiring instead a far higher, 'spiritual' dissolvent.[44] It is certainly the case that the strong consensual forces which Trevelyan perceived in English history were rooted in the dominance of the land in the lives of most before the Industrial Revolution. Furthermore, this common environment by no means signified uniformity but – as Baldwin had emphasised – infinite diversity, as reflected in 'the great variety of life in different counties and regions, on different estates and farms'.[45] The new, shared experience of urban life was devoid of any such characteristic, giving rise, instead, to the mass mind on which totalitarianism easily preyed. It was not, therefore, a 'mindless' and 'ignorant' nostalgia which informed Trevelyan's histories,[46] but a determination to make explicit the values on which a fading rural world once rested. These values were integral to the inextricable tie between Englishness and liberalism that had provided the key to political stability in the past. The preservation of rural England – for which Trevelyan worked tirelessly – constituted an essential counterbalance to the volatility of intellectual and political life in the present.

While not an active conservationist, Barker was equally wary of urban life, which he saw as a denial of the most fundamental condition of the liberal state: the autonomous individual. The spectacle of 'crowds' had a deeply unsettling effect upon him, one which became central to his understanding of totalitarianism as an essentially 'group'-based phenomenon. He voiced his concerns about modern urban life in an address he delivered to a society promoting adult education in 1936. There he reflected sadly that 'perhaps the urban aggregations in which men now live make them unhappy unless they are crowding together to some common game or spectacle'.[47] Suburban life fared no better in his estimation. In 1944 he confessed to Arthur Bryant – an old Harrovian – his dislike of the physical surroundings of Harrow which he had experienced on a recent visit. 'Looking out from our bedroom at night from the hill, we saw what seemed millions of lights in little suburban dwellings all huddled round the hill. There almost seemed something wrong [with] it – that vast crowded mass below and the quiet secluded hill above'. Harrow, he thought, should move out of town.[48] Dedicated to a Victorian ideal of improvement which was centred upon the individual and which drew upon Aristotle's distinction between the noble pursuits of 'leisure' and the mere play activities of 'recreation', Barker stressed that 'education' for the former offered the only effective antidote to the urban predicament he had outlined.[49] It was an ideal of cultivated individuality that he shared with his fellow confrère, John Reith.[50] Like Trevelyan and like E. M. Forster (who will be discussed presently), Barker drew a rigid distinction between the political and the spiritual realm – the only true realm of individuality, freedom, originality and choice. Like them, too, he was painfully aware of how easily the latter was elided in the modern search for the material betterment of mankind.

Peter Mandler has shown that such anti-urban sentiments were a minority view in the period between the wars – that the new enthusiasm of the masses for country life was built precisely on that search for recreation and exploration of which Trevelyan and others who stressed a deeper, more spiritual and mystical, nexus despaired. He argues that the countryside made its greatest cultural impact in these years as a modernising force, rendering rural life part of the townscape through the creation of new opportunities for 'tourism'.[51] Yet although it would seem that exponents of a purer rural vision were fighting a losing battle in this respect, this sensibility was not without considerable ideological force. In the ways suggested above, it formed a significant political and cultural motif in the liberal-conservative resistance to totalitarianism. It was also central to the hostility towards intellectuals which this group of writers typically cultivated, and also their patriotism. As Philip Williamson has noted in relation to Baldwin's use of country themes, to lose sight of local attachments expressed above all in the countryside was to desert the wider nation which had historically evolved from such attachments, and for tyrannical political creeds which were mere figments of the intellectual imagination rather than liberal outgrowths of native soil.[52]

This conjunction of forces – anti-intellectual, patriotic and rural – is equally evident in the writings of E. M. Forster. In 1932, for example, he sought to explain why the bicentenary of William Cowper had passed largely without notice. It was because 'England is perishing, and he was English'. The steadiness of vision through which Cowper had captured the more humble and characteristic elements of the English landscape had been superseded by a more dramatic one. Forster continued:

The country Cowper loved is precisely what is going to disappear. The grander scenery of England will probably be saved, owing to its importance in the tourist industry, but it will pay no one to preserve a stray elm, puddles full of ranunculus, or mole hills covered with thyme; and they, not the grandeur, are England. They will be swept aside by pylons and arterial roads, just as Cowper himself is being trodden underfoot by the gangs of modern writers who have been produced by universal education. Excellent writers, many of them. Writers of genuius, some of them. But they leave no room for poor Cowper. He has no further part in our destinies. He belongs to the unadvertised, the unorganised, the unscheduled.[53]

That this was a protest against the new, urban intelligentsia is evident in Forster's broadsides against the left in the late 1930s and 1940s. The modernist visions of the intelligentsia were stunted precisely because the latter had ceased to breathe the pure free air of the countryside. In turn, the intelligentsia was bent on destroying English rural life through an enthusiasm for 'planning' which was rooted in an alien, cosmopolitan commitment to socialism and communism. In 1946, for example, Forster attacked the communist scientist, J. D. Bernal. He was participating in a series of radio broadcasts on 'The challenge of our times' to which Bernal had also contributed. Forster stressed Bernal's confident belief in applying 'objective' scientific wisdom to human affairs, which left little scope for assessing the ensuing 'moral' loss as well as material gain from such a hard-headed response to 'the challenge of our time'. Mourning the defacement of rural Hertfordshire – where he had grown up – after the War, in efforts to improve the dilapidated housing stock of North London, Forster emphasised the inescapable conflict of values which had resulted. On the one had, it had enabled some families to enjoy a far superior standard of housing. But on the other, 'something irreplaceable has been destroyed, and . . . a little piece of England has died as surely as if a bomb had hit it. I wonder what compensation there is in the world of the spirit for the destruction of life here, the life of tradition'.[54] It was a rhetorical question: for Forster there was no 'spiritual' compensation for the creation of 'meteorite towns' such as Stevenage, from which the organic, spontaneously formed relationships of the communities it replaced was wholly absent. Here again, we see the yoking together of countryside, mankind's 'spiritual' life and freedom – associations which are also evident in his eulogy of Cowper. It was a synergy to which the left in Britain during its postwar heyday was regarded by Forster as wholly insensitive. Forster, like Trevelyan and Barker, identified the realm of freedom as essentially spiritual rather than political: politics might create the optimal conditions of that realm, but it was mere casuistry to try and conflate the two spheres, as communists writers such as Caudwell did in their anticipation of the perfect social state.[55]

It is significant that Forster did not distance himself from the identity of the 'intellectual', in the manner of some of those who shared his rural perspective. Rather, he fully embraced the term as a writer and artist who considered himself 'more in touch with humanity than is the confident scientist, who patronizes the past, over-simplifies the present, and envisages a future where his leadership will be accepted'.[56] This appropriation of the term 'intellectual' in reaction to political progressivism was readily thrown back negatively on the literary community in the war of the 'two cultures' which C. P. Snow – an admirer of Bernal – launched in his Rede Lecture of 1959.[57] Not surprisingly, however, Snow made no mention of the communist literary figures of the interwar years – Caudwell, Spender and Auden – who had dug their political trenches in close proximity to his own.

Notes

1 J. M. Hernon, Jr, 'The last Whig historian and consensus history: George Macaulay Trevelyan, 1876–1962', *American Historical Review*, 81:1 (1976), 66–97.

2 A. Bryant, *Years of Victory, 1802–1812* (London, Collins, 1944).

3 Trevelyan to Bryant, 30 November 1944; Bryant Papers, Liddell Hart Centre for Military Archives, King's College London, Box E3.

4 Rowse to Bryant, 7 August 1942; Bryant Papers, E4.

5 A. Bryant, *The Art of Writing History*, (London, English Association, 1946); G. M. Trevelyan, *English Literature and its Readers* (London, English Association, 1951); A. L. Rowse, *A New Elizabethan Age?* (London, English Association, 1952); and G. V. Wedgewood, *Literature and the Historian* (London, English Association, 1956). All were Presidential Addresses to the English Association.

6 E. Barker, *Age and Youth: Memories of Three Universities and Father of the Man* (London, Oxford University Press, 1953), p. 152. His memorial notice for Bryant's father appeared in *The Times*, 2 September 1938.

7 Barker thanked Bryant for sending his book, *Macaulay*, in 1932 and with which Bryant had also sent greetings from Major-General Sir Reginald Hoskins, the College Principal. Barker referred to 'those days at Ashridge . . . *candida creta notute* [made bright by memory]'; Barker to Bryant, 31 October 1932; Bryant Papers, E1. Barker is listed as a Lecturer at the College in 1937 in Box C53.

8 On the establishment of the college at Ashridge, see J. Ramsden, *A History of the Conservative Party*, Vol. 3, *The Age of Balfour and Baldwin, 1902–1940* (New York, Longman, 1978), pp. 221, 224, 236, 239; and R. Rhodes James (ed.), *Memoirs of a Conservative: J. C. C. Davidson's Memoirs and Papers, 1910–37* (London, Weidenfeld & Nicolson, 1969), pp. 290–2.

9 The Conservative Party's heightened interest in education and propaganda in the 1920s has been well documented by N. R. McCrillis, *The British Conservative Party in the Age of Universal Suffrage: Popular Conservatism, 1918–1929* (Columbus, Ohio State University Press, 1999), ch. 5.

10 For an example of such self-styling, see Bryant to Lord 'Jack' Lawson, 11 June 1945; Lawson Papers, Second Deposit, Durham University Library. Much of this paragraph is taken from my article, 'Resisting the centre at the extremes: "English" liberalism in the political thought of interwar Britain', *British Journal of Politics and International Relations*, 1:3 (1999), 270–92.

11 Barker to Bryant, 7 October 1938; Bryant Papers, Box E1.

12 Barker to H. A. L. Fisher, 30 July 1933; MS Gilbert Murray, Bodleian Library, Oxford, 408, fol. 165.

13 L. Abercrombie *et al.*, *The Next Five Years: An Essay in Political Agreement* (London, Macmillan, 1935).

14 E. Barker, *Reflections on Government* (London, Oxford University Press, 1942), pp. 248–9, 259; and *Change and Continuity*, The Ramsay Muir Memorial Lecture (London, Gollancz, 1949), p. 14.

15 See his memorial notice for Bryce in the *English Historical Review*, April 1922; reprinted in E. Barker, *Church, State, and Study* (London, Methuen, 1930), pp. 273–80.

16 D. Cannadine, *G. M. Trevelyan: A Life in History* (London, Harper Collins, 1992), pp. 38–45.

17 Trevelyan to Bryant, 7 December 1936; Bryant Papers, E3.

18 Barker, *Age and Youth*, p. 151.

19 He wrote to Geoffrey Dawson, offering deep gratitude and admiration for the *Times* editorial of 3 December 1936, which called for an end to the embarrassing silence surrounding the King's affair. Barker to Dawson, 3 December 1936; Dawson Papers, Bodleian Library Oxford.

20 A. L. Rowse, *The End of an Epoch: Reflections on Contemporary History* (London, Macmillan, 1947), pp. 6–7.

21 The surprisingly high degree of support for appeasement on the Labour left in September 1938, due to pacifist figures such as George Lansbury and Arthur Ponsonby, and many ex-Independent Labour Party members, is emphasised by M. Cowling, *The Impact of Hitler, 1920–1924: The Beginnings of Modern British Politics* (Cambridge, Cambridge University Press, 1971), p. 267.

22 Rowse to Bryant, 7 August 1942; Bryant Papers, E4.

23 A. L. Rowse, Letter to *The Times*, 9 May 1940. On Halifax's role in shifting Chamberlain away from the extremes of appeasement in 1939 and the beginning of 1940, and his greater ability than Churchill at this time at uniting all shades of political opinion on high spiritual ground against Nazism, see Philip Williamson, 'Christian conservatives and the totalitarian challenge, 1933–1940', *English Historical Review*, 115:462 (2000), 607–42.

24 On the outbreak of the Second World War Bevan had responded angrily to Churchill's contention that the country was fighting 'in defence of the values of traditional England'. Such a presumption triggered a blistering attack in *Tribune* upon all things British and a hearty defence of the Soviet Union. It concluded with Bevan's assurance that the latter country 'will re-establish her connections with the main democratic inspirations of the twentieth century'. Bevan's outrage typically followed from his belief that 'Political toleration is a by-product of the complacency of the ruling class. When that complacency is disturbed there never was a more bloody-minded set of thugs than the British ruling class'. M. Foot, *Aneurin Bevan: A Biography*, 2 vols, I, 1897–1945 (London, MacGibbon & Kee, 1962), p. 348. Although initially warm towards Churchill as 'national' prime minister, Laski quickly turned against him – in *Tribune*, the *New Statesman* and the *New Republic* in July and August of 1942 – when it became clear that Churchill's priority was victory, not the transformation of British society in the process. I. Kramnick and B. Sherman, *Harold Laski: A Life on the Left* (London, Hamish Hamilton, 1993), pp. 436–7.

25 Rowse to Bryant, 1 October 1944; Bryant Papers, E4.

26 A. L. Rowse, *The English Spirit: Essays in History and Literature* (London, Macmillan, 1945), p. 37.

27 R. Ollard, *A Man of Contradictions: A Life of A. L. Rowse* (London, Allen Lane, 1999), p. 179.

28   Rowse, *The English Spirit*, pp. 36–8; G Santayana, *Soliloquies in England and Later Soliloquies* (London, Constable, 1922). Rowse also drew on Santayana's *Egotism in German Philosophy* (London, J. M. Dent, 1916) in 'Germany: the problem of Europe' (1941), reprinted in *The End of an Epoch*, p. 196. For further evidence of Santayana's influence, see J. Stapleton, 'Political thought and national identity, 1850–1950', in S. Collini, R. Whatmore, and B. Young (eds), *History, Religion, and Culture: British Intellectual History, 1750–1950* (Cambridge, Cambridge University Press, 2000), p. 264, n. 103.

29   Rowse, *The English Spirit*, p. vi.

30   Francis Brett Young, *Marching on Tanga: With General Smuts in East Africa* (London, Collins, 1917); see also A. Gyde, 'Francis Brett Young', *Dictionary of National Biography (1951–60)* (London, Oxford University Press, 1971), pp. 1090–1.

31   See Francis Brett Young Papers, Birmingham University Library, 1992 (Bryant), 3179 (Murray), 2544–5 (Barker), 3384 (Trevelyan).

32   F. A. Hayek remarked on the shortcomings of British propaganda during the Second World War in *The Road to Serfdom* (London, Routledge, 1944, 1986). See Chapter 9.

33   The correspondence is in the Francis Brett Young MSS, Birmingham University Library, 2657–62. These, and many other popular writers, were recruited to an active propaganda campaign in the first month of the First World War by Charles Masterman and centred on 'Wellington House', headquarters of the National Insurance Commission. See S. Wallace, *War and the Image of Germany: British Academics, 1914–1918* (Edinburgh, John Donald, 1988), pp. 171–4.

34   Brett Young to Nora St John Ervine, 2 September 1940; Francis Brett Young MSS, 2700.

35   S. Nicholas, '"Sly demagogues" and wartime radio: J. B. Priestley and the BBC', *Twentieth Century British History*, 6:3 (1995), 247–66.

36   I. McLaine, *Ministry of Morale: Home Front Morale and the Ministry of Information in World War II* (London, George Allen & Unwin, 1979), pp. 98–9.

37   Brett Young to Edwin Cerio, 14 July 1947; Francis Brett Young MSS, 2620.

38   Barker to Brett Young, 27 December 1944; Francis Brett Young MSS, 2545.

39   Francis Brett Young, *The Island* (London, Heinemann, 1944), pp. 437–8.

40   The tribute is reprinted in E. Abelson (ed.), *A Mirror of England: An Anthology of the Writings of H. J. Massingham* (Bideford, Green Books, 1985), pp. xiv–xvii.

41   H. J. Massingham, *The Wisdom of the Fields* (London, Collins, 1945).

42   In an unpublished paper entitled 'Man goes mad', Collingwood had written, 'Instinctively we turn to the country when we seek for a renewal of emotional power, as Antaeus in the fable derived fresh strength from touching the earth: in walking and camping and field sports we try not so much to exercise our bodies as to refresh our minds. But these are only drugs for a jaded civilization'; Dep. Collingwood 24/4, Folder 37, Bodleian Library, Oxford.

43   G. M. Trevelyan, 'The calls and claims of natural beauty', the Rickman Godlee Lecture for 1931, reprinted in *An Autobiography and Other Essays* (London, Longmans, 1949), pp. 105–6.

44   On the search of 'progressives' for political consensus in the interwar period, see David Blaazer, *The Popular Front and the Progressive Tradition: Socialists, Liberals, and the Quest for Unity, 1884–1939* (Cambridge, Cambridge University Press, 1992); on the fissures in the 'planning' movement which was central to the progressives'

initiatives, see D. Ritschel, *The Politics of Planning: The debate on Economic Planning in Britain in the 1930s* (Oxford, Clarendon Press, 1997). The claim that the 1930s constituted a 'decade of agreement' was made by Arthur Marwick, 'Middle opinion in the thirties: planning, progress and political "agreement"', *The English Historical Review*, 79:311 (1964), 285–98.

45   G. M. Trevelyan, *Illustrated English Social History* (Harmondsworth, Penguin, [1942] 1964), 4 vols, IV, pp. 30–1; for Baldwin's projection of the diverse nature of the English countryside – certainly before it was possible to transport building materials out of their natural habitat – in which buildings and landscape constituted a perfect harmony, see 'The love of country things' (1931), reprinted in *This Torch of Freedom* (London, Hodder & Stoughton, 1935), p. 121.

46   Cannadine, *G. M. Trevelyan*, p. 174.

47   E. Barker, *The Uses of Leisure* (London, World Association for Adult Education, 1936), p. 7.

48   Barker to Bryant, 21 January 1944; Bryant Papers, E1.

49   Barker, *The Uses of Leisure*, pp. 6–11.

50   See D. L. LeMahieu, 'John Reith (1899–1971): entrepreneur of collectivism', in S. Pederson and P. Mandler (eds), *After the Victorians: Private Conscience and Public Duty in Modern Britain, Essays in Memory of John Clive* (London, Routledge, 1994), pp. 189–208.

51   P. Mandler, *The Fall and Rise of the Stately Home* (New Haven, Yale University Press, 1997), p. 232.

52   P. Williamson, *Stanley Baldwin: Conservative Leadership and National Values* (Cambridge, Cambridge University Press, 1999), pp. 249–52, 325.

53   E. M. Forster, 'William Cowper, an Englishman', review of Lord David Cecil's *The Stricken Deer, The Spectator*, 16 January 1932, reprinted in *The Prince's Tale and other Uncollected Writings*, ed. P. N. Furbank, (London, Andre Deutsche, 1998), pp. 112–13.

54   E. M. Forster, 'The challenge of our time' (1946), reprinted in *Two Cheers for Democracy* (Harmondsworth, Penguin, [1951] 1965), p. 68.

55   E. M. Forster, 'The long run', review of Caudwell's *Studies in a Dying Culture*, reviewed in *New Statesman and Nation*, 10 December 1938, reprinted in *The Prince's Tale*, pp. 291–5.

56   Forster, 'The challenge of our time', p. 69.

57   On Snow's highly selective examples of 'intellectuals' (Yeats, Pound, Eliot and Wyndham Lewis) to demonstrate the reactionary, 'luddite' nature of the genre, see Stefan Collini's Introduction to *The Two Cultures* (Cambridge, Cambridge University Press, [1959] 1994), pp. li–lii.

7

English liberty, appeasement and the National Book Association

It is clear that Forster shared Barker's sense of the inevitable and irreconcilable clash between social justice and individual liberty. Although both men recognised a place for the former in public policy, their chief concern was the maintenance of the largest possible sphere for the latter. The sense of this dichotomy marked them off from the one instinctively Tory member of that group of writers and thinkers in the 1930s whose public philosophy was anchored in the triple poles of nation, countryside and distrust of intellectuals: Arthur Bryant.

In various works of the 1930s, 1940s and 1950s, Bryant assumed an organic relationship between English liberty and paternalistic social policy, the linchpin of which was rural life. He was an arch-critic of the individualist policies of *laissez-faire* which, he claimed in his account of English decline in the last one hundred years – his *English Saga* of 1940 – grew up under the respectable shelter of Benthamism. Instead, he looked back to an era in which, for him, liberty was associated with strength of character and flourished under a regime of rights matched by a stern sense of social duty – a legacy of the medieval Church which was carried over into the national state at the time of the Reformation.[1] This was a uniquely English formula, he implied, and one which continued to find expression in the last Whig ministry – Palmerston's – between 1855 and 1865. It was an ethic that was rooted squarely in the countryside and had been translated into public policy by a succession of wise statesmen. English dynamism, stability and social concern were held up for admiration by visiting foreigners, claimed Bryant, qualities that were captured in the

> Miltonian landscape, the prosperity of its rose and ivy-covered cottages, the strength and assurance of its thriving farms and lordly parks . . . wonderful oaks and green lawns, the sleek, lowing cattle, the smoke curling up from cottage chimneys in a mysterious and blended sea of tender verdure, the strong, kindly men and women who were so at home among its familiar scenes.[2]

No wonder that Bryant – reverting to a close rival for the *locus classicus* of Englishness, the sea – could quote Conrad's metaphorical allusion to England as 'the great flagship of the race' at the Victorian high-noon.

But the tide of liberalism could not be held back, and when Palmerston died – the efforts of the 'half-alien patriot', Disraeli, notwithstanding[3] – Gladstone ensured that the 'march on [Bentham's] utopia' resumed.[4] Liberalism, maintained Bryant, was driven above all by the urban and educated middle classes;[5] presumably, for Bryant, the seed-ground of the modern intelligentsia who were so much out of tune with England and English character. Its mission was to strip away all the restraints inherited from a tradition-bound society without putting new protections in their place. It was as doctrinaire and 'determinist' as he found contemporary socialism, deeply rooted as the latter was (or so it seemed to him) in Marxism. Indeed, while Bryant assumed the mantle of the Tory democrat against liberalism in its most rationalistic guise, he exchanged it with ease for that of the liberal when confronted with the reorganising zeal of intellectual socialism. Denouncing Orwell's torrid and insensitive (to the inhabitants) account of Wigan in the *Illustrated London News* of 1937, he attempted a spirited defence of the mechanism of spontaneous change. 'By all means', he asserted,

> let us try and improve the conditions under which men live and labour . . . But do not let us fall into the fallacy of believing that we can cure them by destroying the very mainspring of human benevolence and virtuous activity – that freedom of choice and thought that makes a man the imperfect image of God rather than a meaningless machine.[6]

Nevertheless, for all Bryant's denunciation of bureaucratic socialism, his liberal sympathisers could not go all the ideological way towards his Toryism: to them it was insufficiently differentiated from the socialist view of English history which was then gaining considerable ground. Acknowledging a copy of Bryant's *Pepys*, Volume III, in November 1938, Barker was moved to reflect on how Bryant's stress on the 'inglorious' side of the Glorious Revolution – the 'unleashing of the aristocracy' and the 'bad social consequences' it brought in the age of the Industrial Revolution – led him to join forces with socialists such as R. H. Tawney. It was not a view which Barker himself could share, and he defended the old Whig history that Tawney and others were attempting to revise:

> I remember Tawney arguing that the Stuart Kings (James I and Charles I) had a better social policy than the Parliamentary opposition. Of course there is truth in the argument. But it could be applied, in many ways, to the defence of Hitlerism and Italian Fascism. I think I shall always cherish myself, however my opinions change, the idea that political liberty is worth a big and heavy price. It is fair to emphasise the price paid; but I feel that the value of the commodity bought has not been too much emphasised by the old school of historians. I cannot feel that England under a continuing Stuart Dynasty (James III, Charles IV, etc) would have been a good England. I should like to write, some day, a history of England if the Revolution had not occurred – an imaginary history of England under James III, Charles IV.[7]

Yet, when set against the increasing lack of deference towards country among modern intellectuals, the ideological differences between Barker and Bryant paled into insignificance, and in any case there was a side to Bryant which saw great virtues in the English aristocracy before 1840 – its vigour yet cultivation, humanity, self-possession and forthright expression.[8] By contrast, for Tawney, there were few, if any, redeeming features to speak of. For example, in indicting the Church for condoning the new moral climate of acquisition following the Glorious Revolution, he maintained that it

> reproduced the temper of an aristocratic society, as it reproduced its class organ-
> ization and economic inequalities, and was disposed too often to idealize as a
> virtue that habit of mean subservience to wealth and social position which, after
> more than half a century of political democracy, is still the characteristic and
> odious vice of Englishmen.[9]

Moreover, while Bryant attempted to keep his Toryism and a more full-blooded socialist interventionism at arm's length, thereby creating the basis of significant common ground with his liberal allies, the latter in turn moved closer to his Conservative outlook on the front of foreign policy in the mid 1930s. The policy of appeasement which Bryant staunchly upheld was shared fully by such notable liberal figures as Trevelyan and Barker. All three men felt genuinely ill at ease with the crippling burden of debt which their country had helped to impose on Germany by the Versailles settlement. They supported appeasement on this basis, together with further arguments which they drew from their analysis of English character and history. The strength of Bryant's convictions in this regard led him to sail in dangerous political waters on the right, a tendency which is also evident in his endeavour to rival the Left Book Club's success in educating public opinion in the principles of communism and socialism. However, caution is nec-essary in labelling Bryant a political extremist.[10] On the basis of existing evi-dence, his worst sins were those of naivity and lack of judgement, failings which were not uncommon in Europe at the time:[11] his overriding concern, like that of his contemporaries just across the liberal border with Conservatism, was the preservation of England/Britain. In his case, this was to be achieved through endeavouring to reason with Hitler, on the one hand, and through the creation of a national intelligentsia of the right, on the other. This chapter highlights further the increasingly indeterminate, although ultimately distinctive, nature of that ideological border territory towards the end of the 1930s as the combined pressure of foreign affairs and the growth of communism induced some consid-erable shifting towards the right of the high liberal ground that British intellec-tuals had characteristically occupied since the middle of the nineteenth century.

II

Barker detested conflict in any form, let alone the armed conflict for which he believed Britain was fundamentally unprepared towards the end of the 1930s. He had welcomed – in a letter to *The Times* of October 1938 following the Munich agreement – what he saw as 'the substitution of discussion and the force of argument for the play of force and the arbitrament of war' in European history. But he felt that it was sheer revulsion for war rather than the existence of the League of Nations which had made the greatest impact upon recent developments. The League, he believed, had been built without 'common spiritual foundations'. In the light of recent events, he rather optimistically believed, it could well be rebuilt 'into a house where there are neither victors nor vanquished and which rests on a genuine common horror of the bestiality of war'. Barker's praise for the Munich agreement was also qualified by an emphasis on Britain's responsibility for bringing Czechoslovakia's current fate to pass through having turned a deaf ear to 'the protests against its composition until presented in their direct form by Germany'.[12] He was no lover of Nazism, which he perceptively analysed from its early emergence. He considered it as simply one of three forms of totalitarianism in contemporary Europe – Soviet communism and Italian fascism constituting the others – which were rooted in a pathological 'eruption of the group' and 'eruption of the personal' in modern politics.[13] But the events of 1938 to 1939 considerably challenged his liberal loyalties, already under strain from the progressive tendencies of the Liberal Party in a domestic context. The result was, not the abandonment of his liberalism but its reformulation in a conservative direction.

This became clear in the course of Barker's contribution to a debate in *The Times* in March 1939, initiated by Gilbert Murray's exasperated attack on Chamberlain and his nostalgia for the 'national' character of Baldwin's government. Murray had written:

> There must be some way in which the Government can convince us that it has some moral basis, that it is not always ready to side with the strong against the weak and to radiate satisfaction over the calamities of the innocent. Lord Baldwin once admitted frankly that events in Abyssinia were to him 'a bitter humiliation', and that one phrase took the sting out of the opposition criticism. His sympathies were on the right side, and that made all the difference.[14]

Chamberlain did take note of this criticism, or at least did so at the prompting of Bryant, who was in the process of preparing an edition of Chamberlain's speeches for the National Book Association (NBA). He urged Chamberlain to make the book seem more the result of Chamberlain's own efforts rather than Bryant's, by agreeing to the title of *My Policy* and by writing a Foreword. In doing so, Bryant wrote, Chamberlain would 'provide a complete answer to the point of view expressed in Gilbert Murray's letters to *The Times*'.[15]

Barker's contribution to this debate was prompted as much by the government's recognition of Franco at the end of the previous month as the failings or otherwise of the policy of appeasement. Like Murray, he considered himself an '"old"-Liberal, who is still a Liberal', and like Murray, too, he considered the primacy of the moral perspective as the essence of liberalism: in friendly private correspondence following their clash in *The Times*, Murray had identified liberalism as a 'sort of Gladstonian or perhaps Aristotelian view, that politics are really ethics on a grand scale'.[16] Barker agreed but, unlike Murray, he associated the moral nature of liberalism with the 'realism' which he believed Chamberlain had skilfully practised in the conduct of foreign affairs. 'We are prone', he asserted, of the English nation,

> to an easy idealism which, in the view of those who are not our friends, is just a Machiavellian mantle under which we conceal, perhaps even from ourselves, interested designs. But the danger to us of that easy idealism is less hypocrisy, as I see the matter, than a Johnny Head-in-the-air attitude which fails to look at honest facts and forgets the need of material resources to back and nerve ideals . . . My Liberalism will be the better . . . for an operation that was done on it at the end of February 1939. I am bound to confess that I have learned a great deal in the last twelve months.[17]

As for Baldwin, while it was true that Chamberlain was 'less of the English type' than his predecessor, this was all to the good in the current climate of world affairs. 'He [Chamberlain] stands for the name and ideal of peace all over the Continent – effective peace, achieved by hard work and sweat, and not the mere name of peace'.[18] This did not mean, however, that there was no further need of a Liberal Party. As Barker explained to Murray, he merely disagreed with 'that side, or element of the Party which entirely devalues the Government's foreign policy and looks to alliance with Cripps'. What was needed was a Liberal Party that was 'independent of, but not necessarily hostile to, the Government', and so long as J. A. Spender – another supporter of Chamberlain[19] – was content to remain within the Party, so Barker felt that there was room for him also.[20] Significantly, the correspondence that ensued between Barker and Murray dwelt on the increasingly conservative nature of both men's liberalism – for all their opposing attitudes towards Chamberlain – not on Hitler's occupation of Prague which had taken place just a few days earlier, on 15 March. Murray, like Barker, had found himself gravitating from liberalism to conservatism in recent years – although not the Conservative Party – on account of appreciating

> the truth that the anthropologists teach us emphatically, that every savage tribe, or indeed every human community, is held together and supported by an immense network of custom, traditions, and beliefs, and is apt to fall to bits if you remove them too rapidly or violently. It is the network of normal expectations that holds society together, and if once you begin not to know what to expect, things are dangerous.[21]

Barker could not have agreed more: 'The life expectable', he wrote; 'It is a thought very much on my mind. Some security of expectation is the basis of manners, morals, and politics'.[22]

But Barker had not simply turned a blind eye to events in Europe, nor was he under any illusion about the nature of the Nazi regime. Reviewing a complete

English translation of *Mein Kampf* at the end of March 1939, he paused to comment on Hitler's conception of race,

> which is shot through and through with golden historic memories of the Reich: the Race and the Reich are two threads, not altogether of the same texture, and what cannot be done in the name of the one must be done (as it was actually done, only last week) in the name of the other. Race leads to unity as well as purity; and because the tradition of unity is the tradition of the Reich, it leads to the renovation of the Reich.

Barker was also concerned in this review to resist any suggestion of significant analogies between Britain and Germany. Patriotism, he argued, was perfectly possible in Britain, but on an altogether more 'natural' and 'quieter' basis than in Germany. Moreover, 'the things which we are bound, by our tradition and our belief to remember are things which are deeper than the natural piety of blood – a piety which, uncensored and uncontrolled, may turn to impiety'.[23]

Rowse, on the other hand, was a vehement opponent of appeasement, although he – like Murray and Barker – called in British traditions, this time of the central role the country had played in ensuring European security for centuries through a system of alliances, in support of the policy.[24] Yet he was prepared to overlook Bryant's defence of appeasement, even though he found it inexplicable in so strong-minded a patriot.[25] It is true that he was not aware of Bryant's visit to Germany in July 1939, in which he had met a senior Nazi official – Walter Hewel – and assured him of Britain's peaceful intent towards Germany.[26] When he was informed of this visit by the historian and critic of Bryant, Andrew Roberts, after Bryant's death in 1985, he was shaken, and commented that Bryant 'never dared to mention that enterprise to me – if I had known, it would have ended our friendship'.[27] There is certainly no evidence for the basis of Rowse's later hostility – that Bryant gave the impression that 'Hitler could go ahead' with the invasion of Poland.[28] In Roberts's account itself, Bryant stated to Hewel that 'he could not help feeling that an affray between Poles and Germans . . . must bring Britain in on the side of Poland'.[29]

Also, Rowse would surely have known of Bryant's *Unfinished Victory*.[30] This was an account of events between the two World Wars which was published in January 1940, although written before the Second World War and planned as part of a larger work which presumably would have argued for the policy of appeasement had war not intervened. Given the continuance of their friendship, there are no grounds for believing that Rowse passed as severe a judgement on the book as Roberts, who maintains that 'it displayed a depravity that far exceeds mere poverty of judgement'.[31] On the contrary, *Unfinished Victory* was grounded in a widely held view that Nazism originated in the heavy penalties imposed on Germany by the Versailles settlement and which had made another war inevitable, a view which is intimated in Barker's remark about the League of Nations above, and which is echoed in Trevelyan's argument in 1937 that

> Germany and England must learn to 'tolerate' . . . each other's form of government. Dictatorship and democracy must live side by side in peace, or civilization is doomed. For this end I believe Englishmen would do well to remember that the Nazi form of government is in large measure the outcome of Allied and British injustice at Versailles in 1919.[32]

Not surprisingly, Trevelyan was very receptive to the book. Acknowledging *Unfinished Victory*, together with the argument for British economic independence which Bryant had made concurrently with a former Conservative MP, Henry Drummond-Wolff[33] – under the pen name 'Junius' – in the pamphlet *Britain Awake!*,[34] Trevelyan professed to have read both 'with great interest and much agreement'. *Britain Awake!* was interpreted by Trevelyan not as an anti-Semitic pamphlet but as a lament for the neglect of empire, shipping and agriculture by successive governments – not least Liberal governments – in Britain since the late nineteenth century.[35]

Bryant also dispatched a copy of *Unfinished Victory* to his friend, the poet Edmund Blunden, who described it as 'clear and humane'. Blunden agreed with the emphasis of the book on the fact that 'Germany, Germans suffer, and are even entitled to fair play'. He voiced his despair of his fellow countrymen, so many of whom that he had met

> are still possessed with furious visions of Huns, against whom any malice is a virtue. For any other race, apparently (even the Italians are beginning to count as human!) we have vast reservoirs of justice and sympathy ready to be tapped at the first yarn from the first Ancient Mariner in the office.[36]

Barker wrote to Bryant at the end of January 1940, stating that he had extracted his correspondent's book from Viola Garvin (Literary Editor of *The Observer*) for review.[37] This review did not appear, although a fellow *Observer* reviewer, Ivor Brown, wrote favourably of *Britain Awake!*.[38]

It is undoubtedly true that Bryant sympathised with Nazi arguments against the Jews as a corrupt, degenerate influence on the German nation. He stressed, however, that the profligacy and moral degradation which had come to characterise the culture of the German capital in the interwar period could be associated with the migrant Jew only (although it is difficult to imagine that the *ostjuden* were in a position to influence German capital): the long-established Jewish settlers 'had learnt to live and think as Germans and . . . had often conferred, especially in the realms of learning, science and medicine, the greatest distinction on their adopted country'.[39] He reported that 'there were many Germans who believed . . . that th[e] organised orgy of vice . . . was part of a planned international campaign to overthrow the existing order by undermining the traditional standards of morality'.[40] However, he did not in any way endorse this belief. He was by no means blind to Nazi persecution of the Jews, which he portrayed as 'revolting and sickening'.[41] He also emphasised the debt which modern civilisation owed to its Semitic half – the 'diviner' half, moreover, than its Aryan Greek and Roman equivalent. And against Hitler's notion of Marxism as a 'Jewish' doctrine which rejected the 'aristocratic principle in nature' in favour of the 'mass and dead weight of numbers', Bryant responded that 'This may possibly be true of Marxism: it is profoundly untrue of the historical philosophy of the Jewish race'.[42] There were other passages in which Bryant denounced the Nazi regime in the most unambiguous terms, while recognising Hitler's obvious appeal. He could thus write of Hitler that 'His racial theory may be repulsive gibberish, his ambitions barbarous and ridiculous, his motives cruel and sadistic, but only a man deliberately shutting his eyes to realities can deny his astonishing genius for leadership'.[43] Nor was he completely taken in by the greater unity among Germans that the Nazis seemed to have created during his visit in the summer of 1939, 'knowing what the plain German did not know of the blind impatient and arrogant resolve of his rulers . . . [to effect] the crucifixion of Europe'.[44] Most fervently of all, Bryant wanted his compatriots to refrain from suing for another punitive peace at the end of the Second World War, carried, as they had been in the 'khaki' election of 1919, on a wave of 'imperceptible but unavoidable mental deterioration'. He thought that an account of the consequences in Germany of the settlement then would help prevent a Third World War rising out of the ashes of the Second. It was important to give such an account at the beginning rather than the end of the War since, 'with the tragic example of 1919 before us, we cannot afford to wait until the public has become too embittered even to try to think objectively'.[45]

III

Bryant's efforts on behalf of the NBA, like those he made on behalf of appeasement, have also proved controversial. They are certainly revealing of perceptions on the right of the main, leftward thrust of intellectual and political opinion in Britain during the later half of the 1930s, although their extremist associations once again should not be exaggerated. In its origins, the NBA represented nothing more sinister than an attempt to articulate, and hence strengthen, a hitherto muted but widely held form of political conservatism. The Association was set up to counter the influence over the public that had been gained by Victor Gollancz's Left Book Club (LBC). The latter had been launched in May 1936, and had attracted an instant membership of 11,500.[46] The idea of the NBA had been formed on a very tentative basis in April 1936, and an agreement made with Hutchinson's publishing house. Bryant warned – in a letter to Stanley Baldwin, who was to become the Association's President on his retirement in 1937 – that there was as yet no ready-made right-wing reading public, and that much 'quiet effort' was required prior to a gradual 'inva[sion] [of] both the educational and general reading market through encouraging the work of young writers'.[47] But the rapid success of the LBC – and the threat of pre-emption by the establishment of rival right-wing book clubs – forced the hand of those who became the core NBA organisers: Bryant, Sir Geoffrey Ellis, Walter Hutchinson and Sir John Davidson (who has been described as Baldwin's 'principal lieutenant'[48]). By

February 1937, it was agreed that production should be hastened, although even at that date the plan was merely to publish books in a series entitled the 'Defence of Freedom'. A month later, when Bryant returned from abroad, where he had been recovering from ill-health, he was presented with a *fait accompli*: the formation of the NBA – committed to the monthly production of books for members – with his name given as General Editor in promotional material appearing in the press. Byrant was not best pleased, as his account of recent events to the publisher's Editor, Frederick Heath, who had forced the pace along in response to the establishment of Foyle's Right Book Club, in April 1937 conveys.[49] However, his commitment to the wider educational project triumphed over annoyance at his failure to be consulted, his deep reservations about the capacity of the organisation to meet such a schedule, and also his dismay at the burden of work that would fall largely upon him. The Association was to be neither 'left' nor 'right' but aimed at defending 'the English ideal of individual freedom against all who believe in coercion, physical or moral'.[50] It would also reinforce the work which Bryant had carried out at Ashridge – that of 'preserv[ing] what sanity there is in democracy and . . . extend[ing] that sanity'.[51]

Bryant was particularly anxious to avoid any public partnership between the NBA and the Conservative Party, although he acknowledged the discreet 'moral backing' of Conservative Central Office. It is possible that the anonymous donation which was made to the Association in the spring of 1938 came from the same source, or at the very least one of Lord Davidson's rich associates in the Party.[52] Lord Davidson himself emphasised the Party's 'full approval and backing' of the NBA when urging, successfully as it turned out, Sir Reginald Hoskins – Principal of the college at Ashridge – to resign from the selection committee of the Right Book Club.[53] Ashridge itself may have been the channel for funds – either those donated by the Party or individual Party members. Nevertheless, despite obvious Conservative Party links, Bryant's primary aim in launching the NBA was to educate and mobilise what he perceived to be the predominantly conservative and Christian cast of public opinion in Britain against the – to him – alarming inroads made by socialist and communist thought on British life.

The latter had concerned Bryant for several years. In April 1934, for example, he had urged a notable Cambridge historian – and soon to become Cambridge's Conservative MP – Kenneth Pickthorn,[54] and also Sir John Davidson to complain to the BBC about the 'crudest perversion of truth' in a *Radio Times* caption advertising a talk on the origins of trade unionism in Britain. Worried that his Toryism might prejudice his case, he wrote to John Reith himself but evidently never dispatched the letter, although it began, revealingly, 'Sometime ago you asked me to communicate with you if ever I felt that undue left-wing propaganda was being introduced into BBC programmes and publications'.[55] A few months later, he had cause to express his outrage at the refusal of the Oxford Delegacy for Extra-mural Studies to support Ashridge's application for a University Extension Class in the adult education movement to be held at the College. Bias against Conservatism seemed the obvious explanation for the refusal where no actual explanation was given, although Bryant could not see that there was any reason why, when the Delegacy supported classes held in Labour Party and Trade Union premises, there should be any objection to the much looser tie between Ashridge and Conservatism. He implored Sir Geoffrey Ellis – a member of the Executive Committee of the National Union – to remonstrate:

> If we allow this to pass without a real fight, we shall allow the whole case of adult education to go by default. Everyone with whom I have discussed this, at the Universities and in the world of adult education, agrees that the situation is an exceedingly serious one; a comparatively small group of Socialist intellectuals are obtaining a monopoly of the machine of adult education . . . in order to propagate a philosophy of life which has a political implication from start to finish. Believing us to be stupid and weak, they are determined to prevent the slightest attempt on the part of conservatively minded people to interfere with the machine.[56]

Against this background, the NBA project was pressing, as is clear from several of the memoranda which Bryant wrote on the project. He emphasised in one that the whole tenor of educated opinion in Britain had changed in the course of the previous three decades. Instead of the typically 'traditionalist and Christian' tone of the 'old national monthlies [and] of the review columns of the greater newspapers' of the early twentieth century, the 'highbrow' press was now 'almost entirely left-wing. No one but a man of Left-wing views can hope for an opening in papers like the *New Statesman, Time and Tide, Spectator, Manchester Guardian,* and *News Chronicle*'.[57] (There was clearly some exaggeration here, particularly in Bryant's description of the learned press earlier in the century as 'traditionalist and Christian': even the *Spectator* on the accession of John St Loe Strachey as Editor, a periodical whose core readers, the country gentlemen, could not have been more conservative, was associated with 'Independent Liberalism' by its friendly rival, the *Daily Mail*.[58]) More interestingly, he emphasised in another memorandum the need for the NBA to be free of party control, pointing to the way in which, 'in the early days of the Socialist [Labour] Party Shaw, Wells and other popular Fabian writers were allowed to expound Socialism in their own individual and unorthodox way'. This was 'an important contributory cause to the later success of that Party at the polls'.[59] Clearly, he felt that for too long the Fabian Society and similar organisations on the left had monopolised the work of political education in Britain. Here, there was more substance to his assertion. His views were consciously formulated to appeal to 'national' political figures such as Stanley Baldwin, and also to a number of eminent figures in the academic and literary world whose moderate but non-partisan views would enhance the credence of the project. Chief among those names were Trevelyan and Barker, together with Charles Morgan (Literary Editor of *The Times*). These were representative, for Bryant, of 'the intelligent centre and Liberal opinion we're out to capture', and whose views would thus be aligned with the conservative, national and moderate strain of political opinion which Baldwin's association with the scheme would be sure to rally.[60] Baldwin became the President of the NBA on his retirement in May 1937, having made it a condition of his taking up the post that support be gained not just among Conservative, but also Liberal National, National Labour and Liberal politicians 'of the first rank'.[61] Other figures whom Bryant duly set out to court included Wells, John Buchan, Albert Mansbridge, Bertrand Russell, E. D. Simon, Arthur Salter, H. A. L. Fisher, Dean Inge and Francis Yeats-Brown.[62]

It is unclear how many of these figures were approached or, indeed, lent their support. A letter from Bryant to Trevelyan in May 1937, soliciting his support, was abandoned, although it painted a vivid picture of the need to enter battle against the flourishing left-wing book market. 'For years past', wrote Bryant, 'a rootless intelligentsia (to use, as S[tanley] B[aldwin] once said, a very ugly word for a very ugly thing) have been undermining the English tradition, which for some reason they loathe; in adult education, in the provincial universities, above all in the printed word'.[63] Lord Davidson also informed Bryant that he had heard, through Ernest Simon, that Barker was 'quite prepared to write a History of British Democracy . . . on greatly expanded . . . lines than his Life of Cromwell,[64] showing how democracy grew by free discussion in the Chapels and the pubs, etc'.[65]

However, these leads were not pursued. There are a number of plausible reasons why such figures as Trevelyan and Barker may have preferred to keep their distance from Bryant. Certainly, the NBA lacked solid intellectual foundations, Bryant increasingly favouring a more populist and ideological fare than these writers either could or would produce. Its list was primarily constituted by unknown writers, and was quickly found to be unsatisfactory as a result, as the large numbers of subscriptions that were hastily withdrawn give evidence. It also lacked the professionalism of Gollancz's LBC, a shortcoming of which Bryant visibly despaired in his response to Hutchinson's bizarre ideas for following the LBC's example in launching a magazine: Hutchinson proposed emphasising leisure activities and 'chat' rather than serious politial discussion.[66] The enterprise was dogged, almost from the start, by editorial rivalry between Heath and Hutchinson.[67] The Association hence struggled to maintain a membership of 3,500 after its first year, the bulk of its 'star' members being Conservative MPs and peers.[68] In 1938, by contrast, the LBC had acquired 50,000 members and Foyle's Right Book Club, 25,000.[69] The NBA only managed the higher circulation figure of 5,000 in the first half of 1939 when it issued *Mein Kampf* as its June issue.[70] At this point it lost the prestigious support of its President, Lord Baldwin, who resigned in July 1939 – ostensibly on the grounds of an excess of commitments – but almost certainly in response, too, to growing allegations that the NBA was a pro-fascist organisation.[71] But at about this time, in any case, Bryant had received a cheque from Lord Davidson with which to pay off the NBA's debts and wind it up.[72]

The issuing of *Mein Kampf* certainly emphasised the increasing association of the NBA with right-wing extremism and Bryant's heightened sympathy with the Nazi regime. If he was honest enough to inform his readers in an introductory note that the edition before them was 'incomplete and expurgated', the

parallels he attempted to draw between Nazism and Toryism were wild to say
the least. For example, he extolled Hitler's commitment to social reform, comparing it with 'the old idea of historic English Toryism'. He also upheld Hitler's
'Disraelian' view that 'It is not the highest aim of man's existence to maintain a
State or a government but rather to conserve its national character'. It has to be
said that Bryant's editorial note to *Mein Kampf* stopped short of unconditional
praise. In underlining, for example, the Disraelian parallel of Hitler's view that
'race is everything', he added that in Hitler's case it was preached 'with an intolerance against one race that mars the force of his thought and alienates sympathy'.[73] It is unlikely, however, that given Bryant's evident attraction to Nazism, he
could have overcome the distrust of Conservatism which liberal intellectuals had
traditionally harboured, and thereby helped to forge a united intelligentsia of the
right with a clear organisational focus.

IV

To the extent that such a coterie developed, it was on a much looser, more infor-
mal basis after the War, although with Bryant as a principal figurehead. This will
be seen in the following chapter. But it should be emphasised at the close of this
discussion of Bryant's work in the late 1930s that, however sympathetic to the
Nazis he became then, and however unforgivable this seems in the retrospective
view of later decades, his patriotism is not so questionable as one historian –
Andrew Roberts – has lately suggested. Rightly or wrongly, he had always perceived communism as the greatest threat to the survival of Britain as an independent power, and Nazism – because of its 'nationalist' trappings – its greatest
guarantee. Nor was his patriotism exclusive, however disfigured by an unappeal-
ing sense of self-importance, as when he suggested to Chamberlain in August
1939 a final, last-ditch attempt to 'avert a calamity whose end no man can cal-
culate'. This was for the Crown to make an appeal to 'the head of the German
state for a pause for reason and, perhaps, if it were thought advisable, an invitation to this country for a private talk between the two, not on the political questions at issue, *but on the fate of humanity*'. He continued by explaining the
'excuse' for this initiative in his father's service to the Crown 'for half a century,
... always envisag[ing] that the carefully shepherded reserve power of the Crown
might one day be used in such an emergency'.[74]

But Bryant gave up on the idea of a negotiated peace with Hitler as soon as
war was declared with Germany, maintaining, in September 1939, that in the last
resort 'lust for power ... can only be met by force'.[75] He justified his former reluctance to do so in terms of a thinly disguised self-portrait of the Englishman who,
on numerous occasions in the past, had shown difficulty in sensing danger until
it nearly overwhelmed him. Inveterately mistrustful of government, he 'begins by
half-doubting the grounds on which his country has gone to war, and finds it
impossible to believe that his enemy is quite as bad as he is officially painted'. But
when the dark hour came, the English rose (and would always rise) magnificently

to the occasion: 'the sequel to Antwerp and Gallipoli is always victory'.[76] Clearly, for all that the Treaty of Versailles continued to rankle,[77] Bryant was supporting Britain well before his country faced ruin in northern France, and certainly well before the Battle of Britain in September 1940.

Therefore, Bryant can easily be exonerated from the charge made by Roberts of an opportunistic (re-) embrace of his country, but only after its evident new ascendancy over Germany. A speech Bryant made in 1943, which is used by Roberts to underscore his apparent abandonment of Germany in favour of Britain three years earlier, fails to bear the full weight of Roberts's assertion that 'the true reason that Bryant lost his faith in the dictators' was 'because they lost'. Bryant, according to Roberts, had remarked to his audience, that

> faced with the ruthless efficiency of Germany and the 'terrific results' totalitarianism had produced in 1940, 'most of us have had moments . . . when we felt tempted to believe' that the fascist system was superior. Yet 'it was not the rigid, ruthless totalitarian system which produced the men and machines that won the Battle of Britain.'[78]

First, whether deliberately or inadvertently, Bryant was careful in stressing the 'temptation' to believe in fascism's superiority, rather than actual belief. Second, even if he had yielded to this temptation, there are no grounds here for arguing that Bryant was impressed by victory *per se*. The quotation indicates as much an appreciation of the basis of victory as victory itself.

Third, Roberts's insistence on Bryant's 'overnight' conversion to patriotism with the end of the phoney war does not stand up to the evidence of the latter's *Illustrated London News* contributions in the first few months of 1940. Certainly, during April 1940 Bryant made reference to his attendance at a Nazi rally in the previous year, when – he recalled – 'from the highest tier of the Olympium stadium at Berlin, I looked down upon the grandiose works of a newer Pharaoh'. But the tongue-in-cheek nature of this remark is evident within the wider context of the article – a reflective meditation upon the hollow ring then sounded by George Moore's *Confessions of a Young Man* of 1886.[79] Hitler, claimed Bryant, was the incarnation of Moore's romantic hero, seized with an impulse to destroy the uniformity and mediocrity of bourgeois civilisation – based on the rule of 'the pale Galilean' – and to experience the thrill of force and grandiosity not seen since the pagan days of the pharaohs and Caesar. In no way upholding Moore's vision, Bryant concluded with a paean to English philistinism, whose merits he credited Matthew Arnold in recognising, for all the latter's exasperation with the phenomenon. Arnold, according to Bryant,

> put his finger on a principal source of his country's strength and of the balanced workaday goodness in which that strength rests. For it is the greatness of England and the mark of her fitness for this world, that she always keeps the happy mean. The pendulum swings here as in other lands, but the weight of sober common sense prevents it from swinging too far. The beliefs of the moment are never held with sufficient violence or power of obsession to blind the sober eye of ordinary Englishmen to realities.[80]

This was not a single instance of Bryant's expression of patriotic support for Britain against German tyranny in the early months of 1940. In February of that year, he referred to 'the urgent business of winning the war' and of the war's 'cruel necessity'.[81] He wrote, also, of Britain's assurance of victory, if she was sufficiently determined to win, only pausing to add – not unreasonably – that 'one only prays that in the process it will not be necessary, as it proved before, to reduce half Europe to a bankrupt shambles before that victory can be won'.[82] Nor could it be said of Bryant, either in the early or the later months of 1940, that he stood firm in his belief in 'the central tenets of national socialism, . . . and his desire to replace the profit motive and free market with a form of political economy which harnessed all for the state'.[83] It was true – as we have seen – that he felt that the aristocracy had reneged on the social and political obligations attached to property ownership, thereby opening the flood-gates to socialist attempts to redistribute wealth. He acknowledged the higher standards of living and 'greater intelligence of the masses' which such socialist steps had brought about. However, he regretted the high price in terms of personal liberty which they had exacted. Writing in the *Illustrated London News* again in 1940, he declared that

> the moment a man's right of ownership ceases to be regarded as sacrosanct and is placed at the unbridled disposal of others, whether those others be his employers, his elected politicians, or the paid officials of the State to which he belongs, the decline of liberty begins . . . Because wealth has long been divorced from responsibility it has been assumed, and in all insincerity, that the individual ownership of property was antisocial. Those who made that assumption . . . unconsciously assumed that the individual possession of liberty was anti-social too.[84]

Inevitably, Bryant defended this stance in terms of 'the great ideal – [individual liberty] – which lies at the very heart of the British polity'.[85] If his patriotism was sometimes misplaced, it was anything but rotten to the core.

Notes

1 A. Bryant, *English Saga (1840–1940)* (London, Fontana, [1940] 1953), p. 31.
2 Bryant, *English Saga*, p. 175.
3 Bryant, *English Saga*, p. 117.
4 Bryant, *English Saga*, p. 199.
5 Bryant, *English Saga*, p. 198.
6 A. Bryant, 'The road to Wigan Pier', *Illustrated London News*, 17 April 1937, reprinted in *Humanity in Politics* (London, Hutchinson for The National Book Association, 1937), p. 283.
7 Barker to Bryant, 13 November 1938; Bryant Papers, Liddell Hart Centre for Military Archives, King's College London, E1.
8 Bryant, *English Saga*, pp. 24–5, 29.
9 R. H. Tawney, *Religion and the Rise of Capitalism* (Harmondsworth, Penguin, [1922] 1977), p. 193.

10   Bryant is accused of extremism – and worse – by Andrew Roberts, in *Eminent Churchillians* (London, Phoenix, [1994] 1995), in a chapter entitled '"Patriotism": the last refuge of Sir Arthur Bryant'. While critical of Roberts's use of sources, Reba Soffer does not contest his portrayal of Bryant as 'traveling much farther with Hitler than the other appeasers and changing direction only when faced with arrest in 1940'; 'The long nineteenth century of conservative thought', in G. K. Behlmer and F. M. Leventhal (eds), *Singular Continuities: Tradition, Nostalgia, and Indentity in Modern British Culture* (Stanford, Stanford University Press, 2000), p. 159. The claim that Bryant 'faced arrest' in 1940 (Roberts, *Eminent Churchillians*, p. 315), requires much stronger evidence than Roberts brings to bear.

11   Leon Blum, for example, told Schacht, 'I am a Marxist and a Jew', adding, 'we cannot achieve anything if we treat ideological barriers as insurmountable'. Quoted in A. P. Adamthwaite, *Grandeur and Misery: France's Bid for Power in Europe, 1914–1940* (London, Edward Arnold, 1995), p. 210.

12   E. Barker, letter to *The Times*, 4 October 1938, p. 10.

13   Barker, *Reflections on Government* (London, Oxford University Press, 1942), chs. 4 and 5.

14   G. Murray, letters to *The Times*, 4 March 1939; see also his letter of 9 March 1939.

15   Bryant to N. Chamberlain, 10 March 1939; Neville Chamberlain MSS, 10/4/50, Birmingham University Library. The volume appeared as *The Struggle for Peace* (London, Hutchinson, 1939).

16   Murray to Barker, 18 March 1939; Murray MSS, Box 86 (142), Bodleian Library, Oxford.

17   E. Barker, letter to *The Times*, 6 March 1939. These remarks were analogous to Keynes's strictures in the *New Statesman* and in private correspondence with the Editor, Kingsley Martin, two years previously against the left's call for the government to abandon its policy of non-intervention in Spain; see R. Skidelsky, *John Maynard Keynes*, Vol. 3, *Fighting for Britain, 1937–1946* (London, Macmillan, 2000), pp. 32–4. Barker's support for appeasement and opposition to intervention in Spain also found echoes in the stance of the revisionist socialist Evan Durbin. For the latter's implied attack on fellow socialists for waging new 'wars of religion' in Spain, see his *The Politics of Democratic Socialism: An Essay on Social Policy*, Foreword by Hugh Gaitskell (London, Routledge, [1940] 1954), p. 329. Gaitskell refers to Durbin's support for appeasement in his Foreword.

18   Barker, letter to *The Times*, 6 March 1939. Chamberlain's confidence that he could handle the problem of Hitler single-handedly is well illustrated in E. Goldstein, 'Neville Chamberlain, the British official mind and the Munich crisis', in I. Lukes and E. Goldstein (eds), *The Munich Crisis, 1938: Prelude to World War Two* (London, Frank Cass, 1999), pp. 276–92.

19   Spender had written to *The Times* in much the same vein as Barker. His letter was also published on 6 March 1939.

20   Barker to Murray, 13 March 1939; Murray MSS, Box 86 (133).

21   Murray to Barker, 18 March 1939; Murray MSS, Box 86 (142).

22   Barker to Murray, 20 March 1939; Murray MSS, Box 86 (144).

23   E. Barker, 'Hitler's Bible', *The Observer*, 26 March 1939, p. 4.

24   A. L. Rowse, letter to *The Times*, 20 August 1937, reprinted in *The End of an Epoch: Reflections on Contemporary History* (London, Macmillan, 1947), p. 27.

25   Rowse to Bryant, 7 August 1942; Bryant Papers, E4.

26 Roberts, *Eminent Churchillians*, pp. 303–5.
27 A. L. Rowse, *Historians I have Known* (London, Duckworth, 1995), p. 33.
28 Rowse, *Historians I have Known*, p. 33.
29 Roberts, *Eminent Churchillians*, p. 305.
30 A Bryant, *Unfinished Victory* (London, Macmillan, 1940).
31 Roberts, *Eminent Churchillians*, p. 311.
32 G. M. Trevelyan, letter to *The Times*, 10 August 1937, quoted in D. Cannadine, *G. M. Trevelyan: A Life in History* (London, Harper Collins, 1992), p. 93.
33 Roberts, *Eminent Churchillians*, pp. 300, 311.
34 Junius, *Britain Awake!* (London, Collins, 1940).
35 Trevelyan to Bryant, 12 January 1940; Bryant Papers, E3. See p. 29.
36 Edmund Blunden to Bryant, 18 February 1940; Bryant Papers, E10.
37 Barker to Bryant, 21 January 1940; Bryant Papers, E1.
38 I. Brown, 'The alarum bell', *The Observer*, 21 April 1940, p. 4.
39 Bryant, *Unfinished Victory*, pp. 142–3.
40 Bryant, *Unfinished Victory*, p. 145.
41 Bryant, *Unfinished Victory*, p. xxix.
42 Bryant, *Unfinished Victory*, pp. 203–4.
43 Bryant, *Unfinished Victory*, p. 237.
44 Bryant, *Unfinished Victory*, p. xxxv.
45 Bryant, *Unfinished Victory*, pp. xi–xii.
46 H. Thomas, *John Strachey* (London, Eyre/Methuen, 1973), p. 154.
47 Bryant to S. Baldwin, 2 April 1937, Bryant Papers, C/39, file 2.
48 P. Williamson, *Stanley Baldwin: Conservative Leadership and National Values* (Cambridge, Cambridge University Press, 1999), p. 71.
49 Bryant to Frederick Heath, 22 April 1937; Bryant Papers, C/39, file 2.
50 Bryant to Heath, 2 April 1937; Bryant Papers, C/39, file 2.
51 Bryant to Sir John (Viscount) Davidson, 7 April 1937; Bryant Papers, C/41, p. 2.
52 In a memorandum on the NBA dated 20 December 1938, Bryant mentions a 'generous don[ation] at the instance of Lord Baldwin and myself' which would continue for two further years. Bryant, Memorandum on The National Book Association, 20 December 1938; Bryant Papers, C/41. In the minutes of a meeting of the provisional committee of the NBA on 3 March 1938, mention is made of a fund known as the 'X Trust Fund' of which Bryant and Sir Geoffrey Ellis – Conservative MP and member of the Directing Board of the NBA – were joint trustees; Bryant Papers, C/48.
53 Sir John Davidson to Hoskins, 24 March 1937; Davidson Papers, House of Lords Record Office, HLRO DAV/230.
54 On Pickthorn see M. Cowling, *Religion and Public Doctrine in Modern England* (Cambridge, Cambridge University Press, 1980), pp. 48–60.
55 Bryant to Davidson, 22 April 1934; Bryant to Pickthorn, 23 April 1934; Bryant to Reith, 23 April 1934; all Bryant Papers, E63.
56 Bryant, 'Report on proposed course of University Extension Lectures, 1934'; Bryant to Geoffrey Ellis, 8 August 1934; Bryant Papers, C52.
57 Bryant, 'Preliminary memorandum for Lord Baldwin, first draft', n. d.; Bryant Papers, C/48.
58 A. Strachey, *St. Loe Strachey: His Life and his Paper* (London, Gollancz, 1930), p. 92.
59 Bryant, 'Memorandum on the means of combatting left-wing and communistic propaganda in literature and in the universities', 22 April 1937; Bryant Papers, C/40.

60 Bryant to Hutchinson, 24 June 1937; Bryant Papers, C/40.
61 Davidson to Bryant, 7 May 1937; Davidson Papers, HLRO DAV/230.
62 Bryant to Davidson, 11 May 1937; Davidson Papers, HLRO DAV/230.
63 Bryant to Trevelyan, 1 May 1937; Bryant Papers, C/41.
64 E. Barker, *Oliver Cromwell and the English People* (Cambridge, Cambridge University Press, 1937).
65 Davidson to Bryant, 5 October 1937; Bryant Papers, C/41.
66 Bryant to Hutchinson, 1 December 1938; Bryant Papers, C/39, file 1.
67 See, for example, the letter from Heath to Bryant, 4 April 1937; Bryant Papers, C/41.
68 Heath to Bryant, 17 May 1938; Bryant Papers, C/39, file 1; a list of the names of the 'great and good' who became members of the NBA at an early date are given in advertising material; Bryant Papers, C/48.
69 Item entitled 'Book club news' from unnamed periodical in Bryant MSS, C/39, file1.
70 Hutchinson to Bryant, 15 May 1939; Bryant Papers, C/40.
71 Williamson, *Stanley Baldwin*, pp. 323–4.
72 Roberts, *Eminent Churchillians*, pp. 305–6.
73 Bryant, Draft Introduction to *Mein Kampf*; Bryant Papers, C/44.
74 Bryant to Chamberlain, 22 August 1939; Chamberlain MSS, 7/11/32/29. My italics.
75 A. Bryant, 'Our notebook', *Illustrated London News* (hereafter, *ILN*), 16 September 1939, p. 442.
76 *ILN*, 11 May 1940, p. 612.
77 *ILN*, 28 October 1939, p. 634.
78 Roberts, *Eminent Churchillians*, p. 317.
79 G. Moore, *Confessions of a Young Man* (London, Sonnenschein & Lowrey, 1888). Moore has recently been the subject of a fascinating biography; A. Frazier, *George Moore, 1852–1933* (New Haven, Yale University Press, 2000).
80 *ILN*, 13 April 1940, p. 472.
81 *ILN*, 10 February 1940, p. 162.
82 *ILN*, 3 February 1940, p. 134.
83 Roberts, *Eminent Churchillians*, p. 316.
84 *ILN*, 17 February 1940, p. 194.
85 *ILN*, 17 February 1940, p. 194.

8

Cultural conservatism and the nation in postwar Britain

I

It is understandable that Bryant – eliciting the involvement of Stanley Baldwin – should have also sought the support of Ernest Barker and G. M. Trevelyan for his National Book Association (NBA). Both men helped to sustain well into the twentieth century an essentially Victorian conception of the intellectual as public – although not civil – servant. Their moral and political ideas were rooted in what they believed to be the lived ideals of a supremely practical English nation. Their work assumed a 'best national self' underlying all the activities of the English people and a responsibility on the part of the educated classes for bringing that self to greater public recognition, and hence the activities to greater perfection. The elevation of the masses – in this mould – was central to Victorian liberalism. However, the knowledge which its adherents envisaged as appropriate to this task was neither insular nor to be imparted in the manner of 'drill'. Awareness of the dangers of too narrow a civic training – such as that which was emerging in the totalitarian regimes of continental Europe – led Barker to warn against

> treating the young as means – means to a greater and finer England: chosen instruments for the setting of Jerusalem in this land. Well, it is their duty to do what they can for that consummation; but the fact remains, the ultimate fact, that they are ends – ends in themselves. We educate them to be that; and therefore we educate each of them to be a whole man – not *miles pro patria* [soldiers for the fatherland], nor even *civis pro civitate* [citizens for the state], but a whole man.[1]

In its Idealist reference to the 'whole' man this understanding of the duty of the public intellectual would certainly have appealed to the NBA's President, Stanley Baldwin and other leading public figures who, similarly inspired by Idealism, spoke the language of 'national' community in the 1930s as the fulfilment rather than negation of individual liberty.[2]

The notion of the intellectual as public servant, concerned with articulating the sources of national identity as a vital component of the self-knowledge of citizens, continued to animate the successors of Barker and Trevelyan from the 1950s until the 1980s. Two major figures who fulfilled this role were Bryant himself and the poet and writer, John Betjeman. They were separated from Barker and Trevelyan by a generation. This was sufficient to ensure considerable continuity of cultural concern as values and beliefs moved rapidly away in the twentieth century from the late Victorian age in which all four men were anchored. At the same time, however, there are discernible differences of outlook between the two sets of British intellectuals. As we saw in Chapter 6 both Trevelyan and Barker were distrustful of mass politics and urban culture as inimical to the fostering of individuality that was central to their liberalism. By contrast, Bryant and Betjeman came to perceive the 'essential' English char-acter as far more widely spread throughout British society. It was not simply concentrated in the rural heartland of England. This is not to argue, however, that they may be seen as protagonists of the 'Britishness' which, some historians have recently maintained, defined the culture and politics of the postwar decades.[3] As will become clear, their conception of national life was strongly anglo-centric, forming a bridge between the English nationalism of the interwar period and its resurgence in the late 1960s under the influence of Enoch Powell. Not least, they reacted strongly against the welfarism that was driving the new concept of Britishness and British citizenship. Nevertheless, the experience of the Second World War was pivotal in their more socially expanded concept of Englishness, as it was for those who framed a more multinational ideal of Britain.

    For example, Bryant found that his previous disdain for London was shamed in the face of the indomitable Cockney spirit. As if to distance himself from the model of German nationalism which he had held up for emulation just before the outbreak of the War, he wrote that this spirit represented 'something that was older and stronger and more communal than all the *Volk* pride and strident unity of the Reich'.[4] Betjeman, too, was led to revise his previously derogatory view of suburbs, especially since petrol rationing had forced many cars off the roads which provided their lifeline to the cities. Just months before the outbreak of War – at Whittington station in Shropshire – he had been converted to John Piper's aesthetic acceptance of the ordinary in architecture from the high-Modernism of the *Architectural Review*. The way had been prepared still earlier in 1933, when the puritan, Georgian standards of 'good taste' he was anxiously attempting to cultivate against his better Victorian instincts yielded fully to the charm of Leeds's provincial architectural offerings and the attachment they clearly spawned among its inhabitants.[5] In a BBC broadcast of July 1940, he spoke vividly of the positive impressions left upon him after bicycling recently in the suburbs of a 'great city', contemplating 'those houses' with 'their sham Tudor beams'. 'I mean', he exclaimed, 'there they are . . . They are part of England; I've got to put up with them. Then I will try to see the best in every-thing, even in the half-baked Tudor dreams of the man who designed that deserted roadhouse'.[6] Both he and Bryant were capable of celebrating the 'ordinary' in English life – both contemporary and historical – to a far greater extent than their intellectual ancestors, albeit not always wholeheartedly. For this reason, they managed to sow the seeds of a considerable national revival in the arid soil of decline. But embedded within their cultural celebration was much sharp political critique.

II

Both Bryant and Betjeman began their careers as writers in the early 1930s, and at that time both were filled with a sense of cultural despair. It was not so much the political and economic crisis which fuelled their pessimism about English national life, but the erosion of standards and taste they found all around them. Bryant had ample opportunity to express his disdain when he inherited G. K. Chesterton's weekly column entitled 'Our note book' in the *Illustrated London News* in 1936, a column which he kept up until just before his death in 1985. He described his contributions in 1969 as a 'contemporary, if rambling commentary on our times', and added – in terms which emphasise the entirely unofficial status of Britain's intellectuals – that the column reflected 'the personal and political philosophy of an onlooker, holding no office or public responsibility except of a purely voluntary kind'.[7] Much of his journalism – both in this newspaper and others, such as the *Observer* – painted a deeply unflattering picture of contemporary Britain. He wrote, in 1937, of a passing world in which the 'oldness' and 'ordinariness' of objects, landscapes and institutions had once been sources of reverence and love but had now become sources of contempt. It was not so much the qualities of oldness and ordinariness in themselves that Bryant praised but the steadiness of vision, membership of established social and political 'communions' rather than rootless, selfish individualism, and quality of life with which they were ineluctably associated. As we have seen, the traditionalism at the root of this critique was centred squarely upon the countryside, albeit extended to the common life of the towns during the War; and it could be evoked – Bryant believed – only in lavish sensory images to which modern antiquarians and scholars seemed impervious in their reduction of the past to a 'pale intellectualised ghost'. He accepted that the scale, pace and artefacts of modern life might, in time, generate new forms of loyalty and attachment akin to the old. But there was no denying the fact that Bryant found modern civilisation vastly inferior to the one which was dying, overseen – as the latter was – by the house clearer and the auctioneer. This is apparent in the following passage:

> To have walked across the misty fields of autumn and come out of the raw afternoon with tingling veins and a memory of sad elms and crimson and gold gleaming down the sentenced hedges, to feel the embracing warmth of the house even before one reaches the line of its latticed, lighted windows, to raise the latch and enter into one's own home – not a concrete and steel box in a skyscraper, but a solid, ancient house that had seen successive generations of children and won the love of its owners for centuries – is to enjoy great wealth.[8]

Yet Bryant was far from content to be an elegist. The theme of national decline in his work was secondary to that of expounding and celebrating the contours of England's substantial former glory, in the hope that it would stir in others as much as it had stirred in himself, new depths of patriotism and the revival of a cultural inheritance rooted squarely in tradition. His writings certainly inspired R. F. Delderfield, the best-selling novelist, in whose historical English dramas the rural backbone of England stood in the sharpest of relief. Delderfield began a correspondence with Bryant in 1950. In 1970, Delderfield wrote to Bryant as follows: 'I have re-read most of your books in the last few years, notably, 'The American Ideal' and 'English Saga', but the merit of this last one is you can dip into it and taste the landscape and tribalism that I have been trying to put on paper all my life, using you, I might add, as an inspiration'.[9] He was strongly in sympathy with Bryant's anti-Common Market stance in the 1960s,[10] and felt that he and Bryant had a mission to 'din into the ears of those who will listen the heroic theme of this island's contribution to civilization'.[11] He suggested that he, Bryant, H. E. Bates and J. B. Priestley should write a joint letter to *The Times*, 'putting forward a spirited defence of the British to offset this frightful slide into moral defeatism'.[12] The commercial success enjoyed by both authors suggests that their positive images of the English *patria* – clothed in traditionalist garb – hardly fell on deaf ears. Bryant, himself, for all his despondency, allowed himself a glimmer of hope that the English would renounce their newly acquired tendency for material prosperity to outweigh all other values, and revert to national type – a type which, at its zenith during the aftermath of the Napoleonic Wars, was characterised by energy to the point of bawdiness, but which was also resoundingly upright, Christian and patriotic.[13] That would mean, though, a retreat from the postwar obsession with wages and welfare, a bureaucracy-driven state and contentment with a diminutive world status, and the 'resump[tion], under new forms, [of] our ancient precedence of "teaching the nations how to live", becoming once more a source of strength and stability to ourselves and a beacon and guiding light to others'.[14]

As we have seen in an earlier chapter, from the start of his writing career, Bryant felt that the English intelligentsia had let the country down badly. The 'progressivism' which Bryant associated ineluctably with intellectuals had exerted a particularly adverse influence upon attitudes towards the armed forces, a sector of society against which the intelligentsia had developed a deep-seated prejudice. The pacifism of the 1930s, following on from revulsion against war after 1914, had led to the plummeting of the Services in public esteem. In 1939, Bryant wrote of the disapproval he had encountered recently in lecturing to a University Extension class on Nelson. It was thought by the organisers that such a 'militarist' subject would corrupt the minds of working men. He claimed that he was heard sympathetically by his audience, who, like their disapproving superiors he noted, 'were dependent for almost every mouthful they ate on that sea-power which Nelson had established beyond challenge on the day of his death a century and a quarter ago'.[15] He continued to bemoan the indifference of scholars and intellectuals in the following decades, emphasising, for example, the richness of regimental histories to which the British people were oblivious.[16]

Bryant's rural idyll of England, uncontaminated by the false sophistication of urban intellectual life, was accompanied by considerable admiration for the consummate skill of the country's military leaders and forces, frequently defying the folly of their political masters. This is reflected in Bryant's two-volume account of the Second World War – *The Turn of the Tide, 1939–1943* (1957) and *Triumph in the West, 1943–1946* (1959) – which was written on the basis of the diaries and autobiographical notes of General, later Lord, Alanbrooke. Brooke became Chief of Imperial General Staff in November 1941. Both before that date in commanding the two British Expeditionary Forces in France, and afterwards, Brooke constantly strove to restrain what he described at one point as Churchill's 'impetuous nature, his gambler's spirit, and his determination to follow his own selected path at all costs'.[17] Less endearingly – for Brooke and Bryant had the greatest admiration for Churchill – Bryant had also contrasted the military judgement and dedication of Pepys with the vindictiveness and petty-mindedness of the politicians of Commonwealth and Restoration England. Bryant had written Pepys's life in three volumes in the 1930s, again based upon diary extracts and correspondence. Like the Alanbrooke volumes, Bryant's stirring titles emphasise his sense of Pepys's momentousness for the English nation: *The Man in the Making* (1933), *The Years of Peril* (1935) and *The Saviour of the Navy* (1938). Bryant also published a popular work on Nelson in 1970 and on Wellesley the following year.[18] His book on Britain in the years immediately preceding the Battle of Waterloo and its seven year aftermath, *The Age of Elegance* (1950), was dedicated to 'Field Marshal Montgomery, Victor of Alamein'. All these works celebrated the military as much as the political good fortune of Britain by which its national survival had been constantly assured. Moreover, their appeal was unusually broad, drawing admirers from as far afield as the Labour Party's political front-line.

III

'Jack' – soon to become Lord – Lawson was a prominent Labour MP in the 1940s who hailed from the purest working-class stock on the Durham coalfields. He was brought up in an overcrowded house in Boldon Colliery, a large and modern pit village consisting of row upon row of miners' terraces. The contrast with rural Cumberland, which his family left when he was eight, could not have been greater, and left a deep impression upon him.[19] From childhood he developed an avid interest in books; later, he was to attend Ruskin College, and although afterwards he chose to return to the mines, he became the MP for Chester-le-Street in 1919. He initiated a warm correspondence with Bryant in the spring of 1944, thanking the latter for praising a broadcast he had made on the Home and Forces programme on 20 February in Bryant's *Illustrated London News* column.[20] Lawson, in characteristically reflective mode, had emphasised such themes as the sanctity of life, the divine spark in all mankind, and the value and valour of the mining communities in contributing proudly to no less an end than 'the well-being and happiness of mankind'.[21] Lawson's cautionary words on the importance of preventing industry and commerce from becoming ends in themselves also touched Bryant's cultural sensibilities. Bryant had heard the broadcast, if not on active service lecturing to the Home Fleet in the Middle East, then shortly after his return. He was able to reassure Lawson that the minds of servicemen were similarly receptive.[22]

There followed a number of letters in the course of the year, precipitated by the exchange of gifts of Bryant's *English Saga* and Lawson's *A Man's Life*. When Bryant sent Lawson his *Years of Victory* – to great acclaim from the recipient – following its publication in December 1944, a close literary and political friendship was sealed. It was significant not least because Lawson was to become Secretary of State for War in August of the following year – preceded by the award of the OBE in June. One of his first foreign trips was to India, and Bryant asked him to send warm greetings to Bernard Paget – Commander in Chief in the Middle East, successor to one of Bryant's many heroes of the Napoleonic Wars, Sir John Moore, and dedicatee of *Years of Victory*[23] – should Lawson stop off at Cairo en route. The commitment which Lawson gave to constructive demobilisation was strengthened by Bryant's appreciation of the importance of the British Forces for society at large. Bryant also viewed the Services as the linchpin for national recovery. He responded with enthusiasm to Lawson's suggestion that they might discuss the possibilities of continuing the 'self and community education which the Forces have so brilliantly evolved during the War', thereby ensuring that they became 'a permanent part of the structure of our democratic life'. Bryant had been much involved in the provision of this education (for which he was awarded the CBE in 1949), and he informed Lawson that while he was doing what he could, 'on a very humble level to get something moving on the civilian side through the formation of Community Centres, . . . without help from the Services it will be still-born'.[24]

A more general cultural and political empathy emerged from this friendship over the next few years. Bryant perceived in Lawson, and the men and women among whom he had been brought up and now represented, the descendants of the earthy, honest, vivacious, yet sensitive 'God's own Englishman'. Their contribution to England's 'greatness' and simultaneously their ill-deserved fate in the nineteenth century he had taken it upon himself to expose in the interests of furthering the revival of the unified nation which seemed to be emerging 'out of all the inevitable mistakes and shortcomings of the present'.[25] Bryant was much moved by the passage in Lawson's autobiography depicting a fight between two local men, confiding to its author that 'if ever I had to compile an Anthology of England it would be one of the first things I should choose'.[26] When Lawson sent him a copy of his life of *Herbert Smith*[27] – a leading Lancashire figure in the Miners' Federation of Great Britain – in 1947, Bryant took the opportunity to express his wholehearted agreement with Lawson's interpretation of the shattering effects of industrialism on rural life which had informed the book, and which he himself was in the process of depicting in *The Age of Elegance*.[28] Indeed, he made it the subject of his *Illustrated London News* column a fortnight later.[29] In the early weeks of 1948, Bryant weighed in again in the same column, denouncing the drab and dreary surroundings of the industrialised town which had replaced the green fields. On this account, Lawson was able to reassure Bryant that his friend, Sam Watson, Secretary of the Durham Miners, 'is one of your devoted admirers'.[30] For Bryant, not the least shameful part of the episode which Lawson recounted was the ignorance 'of the rulers of England of what was happening to those whose protectors they should have been'. He was sufficiently inspired by Lawson's book to write further that socialism – 'very naturally and inevitably' – had hitherto concentrated on extending the sphere of the state to satisfy man's instincts as a consumer. Indeed, in a letter of 1945 he himself had echoed the current mantra of the need to combat the threatening peace-time enemies of 'poverty, ignorance, squalor, and hunger', as well as 'greed, intolerance, and uncharitableness'.[31] But capitalism had never solved the problem of satisfying man's nature as a producer, on which all quality of life depended. Would the socialists address that problem now, Bryant asked?[32]

However, this question, to Bryant's mind, was subordinate to a more fundamental question in the choice that had to be made between rival political parties. With the approach of the 1945 election, he professed himself unconcerned 'who governs England as long as those who do so love her and seek to serve her without thought of career or vested interest'. 'Instinctive Tory' though he was, he assured Lawson that he would have voted for him, had he lived in his Chester-le-Street constituency.[33] Lawson was similarly effusive about Bryant's achievement in cultivating a spirit of common patriotism throughout all classes in Britain, and of making them count their blessings. For example, re-reading Bryant's account of the entry of the Dutch fleet into the Medway in 1667 in *Pepys: The Man in the Making* in 1946, Lawson was moved to ask Bryant 'how many Dunkirks [have] we had altogether?' He added,

> Your recitals of these periods have rendered a great service to this country. At least the students know how we have drifted into dangers that might have ended our career altogether. If one of these affairs had ended differently how would the world have suffered . . . Some day we won't get a second chance'.[34]

These remarks were echoed on the publication of Bryant's account of the fall of France from Lord Alanbrooke's diaries.[35] His comments conformed exactly to Bryant's conception of his role in trying to make 'my brave, kindly, shrewd, enduring though sometimes perhaps confused, countrymen realise the full greatness of their heritage and of all that might be built on it'. Nowhere better was that national type realised than in the portraits which Lawson had drawn of his working-class peers, Lawson having recently dispatched to Bryant his life of another Durham contemporary, *Peter Lee*.[36] Not the least appealing aspect of Lawson to Bryant was the Christian foundation of his simple and homely, yet sound, philosophy, a foundation which he expressed in a broadcast of 1954.[37] For Bryant, the substitution of a 'vulgar press' for the Bible in the reading habits of 'our people' had played a central part in the distortion of values that had been integral to the process of 'national decline'.[38] But Bryant's heart must have warmed, also, to Lawson's anti-Common Market invective and his eulogy to the Commonwealth in the early 1960s, and his pride in the 'tolerant' political culture of his country – particularly as reflected in the structure and activities of trade unions, which he counterposed sharply to the 'top-down' approach to the organisation of labour on the continent.[39]

There can be no doubt that Jack Lawson – created a Baron in 1950 – enhanced Bryant's reputation as a leading cultural figure in postwar Britain. He happily allowed extracts from his letters which had praised Bryant's books to be used – along with other commendations by those well placed in public life – in promotional material sent to 'schools, colleges and scholastic booksellers' by his publishers.[40] There can be no doubt, either, that he and Bryant concurred in the importance of taking the people whom they served at face value, only seeking to deliver them from the false promises of a shallow materialism, reinforced by an equally shallow 'rationalism'. To both men, the sophisticated, technological, postwar age exemplified in space travel was not something with which ordinary humanity could, or should be encouraged to, celebrate, detracting as it did from the elemental decencies of human conduct and the spirit of wonder and reverence once imparted by religion.[41] This spirit Bryant had made the basis of English history in his *The Story of England: Makers of the Realm*, published in 1953 to rapturous applause by Lawson and urgings to steel himself against the onslaught of criticism that a 'modern scholar' such as Bryant would inevitably suffer for arguing so.[42] Certainly, with all his – for the most part – self-acquired learning, Lawson could not have been further from the socialist intellectual whom Bryant despised.

Nevertheless, it is obvious from the two previous chapters that Bryant was, and remained very much, a political intellectual, for all his populism, his military interests and connections, and his identity with literature.[43] While his political intiatives were frequently ill-judged, as a popular writer and teacher he posed a substantial challenge to the ascendancy of the left in political debate, not just in the 1930s but during the 1960s too. For example, as a vehement critic of the Spanish Republic, Bryant argued that democracy had been destroyed, not by the fascist forces but by the parties of the Popular Front itself. When they had won power by the slimmest of margins, they had set about eliminating all the opposition.[44] While loosening his ties with the political establishment in Britain in the post-war period, he continued to write on topics such as Rhodesia, the Common Market, the Commonwealth, the free economy and immigration. His stance on all of them was determined by a conception of English/British exceptionalism – a nation given to liberty and the spread of its benefits to other 'ocean nations'. In passionately arguing this cause, Bryant himself proved a powerful intellectual ally of the right, for all that he disdained intellectuals.

IV

John Betjeman persistently regarded himself as an aesthete, and his friends described him as an 'amateur aesthete' at that, with no disrespect intended; indeed, quite the opposite given the massed ranks of putative 'professional architects, civil servants and town planners' with whom he constantly did battle in postwar Britain.[45] He certainly reeled from any identification with the world of 'intellect'. Famously, he was sent down from Oxford for failing Divinity. He also regularly teased his wife (an Indologist) about her '*ree*search' endeavours, which he nevertheless admired and to which he felt much inferior. His adherence to the status of aesthete above that of intellectual was made plain to the Secretary of the Athenaeum in 1967 when he resigned on account of the

> ugly new lighting in the entrance hall and the trivial wallpapering of the Great Room on the first floor . . . The Athenaeum is indeed a club for intellectuals, but not for aesthetes like

Yours faithfully, John Betjeman[46]

Betjeman's understanding of the intellectual and political lines which divided the intelligentsia of his day was muddled to say the least, particularly once he had become a committed Anglican. Thus, after announcing to Alan Pryce-Jones in 1937 that 'after years of sermon tasting, I am now a member of the C of E and a communicant', he added: 'I regard it as the only salvation against progress and Fascists on the one side and Marxists of Bloomsbury on the other'.[47] Indeed, his Christianity – which he was so often conscious of failing but to which he remained steadfastly committed – set him firmly apart from his intellectual friends; those, for example, like the economist Roy Harrod, whose problem-solving approach to human life left Betjeman in a state of total mystification. In a letter to Harrod – dated provocatively the '5th Sunday in Lent' 1939 – in response to Harrod's critique of theism, Betjeman invoked the Christian themes of good and evil and the spiritual life which alone made understanding of these phenomena possible:

> I feel this will shock you, you dear Liberal intellectual old thing. And for every book you can produce which disproves the existence of the spirit, I can produce one which proves it. It boils down to the alternative, materialist or Christian. For intellectuals the materialist standpoint is the obvious one and the easiest. The second is harder, but I hold that it is the most satisfactory, especially when one comes up against injustice, birth and death. But there is no argument. The intellectual is too proud to surrender to this seemingly ridiculous story when viewed from the outside.[48]

Not surprisingly, Betjeman regarded himself emphatically as a 'non-political type', a self-identity that is well borne out by his prose, poetry, documentary films and correspondence, which betray little interest in the major political issues of the day. It appears that Betjeman could hardly ever bring himself to read the newspapers.

Yet for all the distance which Betjeman put between himself and the highbrow world of the scholar and thinker, or that of the publicist, his credentials as a public intellectual are indisputable. Few contemporary writers and commentators matched his success in appealing to elite and middlebrow culture alike, even if he did not always succeed in bridging that gap outside of his unstinting work for preservation societies. For example, his friend and Editor of the *Selected Poems* of 1948, John Sparrow, soon to become Warden of All Souls, 'admired Betjeman as a gifted landscape poet . . . [but] did not admire "Miss J. Hunter Dunn" and the suburban poems of that kind'.[49] As a freelance figure, Betjeman was under no obligation to maintain the increasingly esoteric standards of academic scholarship. At the same time, he was as anxious to protect his sense of individuality – and of an elevated kind at that – *vis-à-vis* the public whom he tirelessly served, as he was to resist absorption into highbrow ranks. One of his many self-descriptions as an aesthete was triggered by concern in the 1960s that he was in danger of being 'typecast as a silly old codger who wants to keep old buildings – in fact all I care about is good buildings. I'm an aesthete who loves the variety of English landscape'.[50] But as with Bryant, the single most important key to Betjeman's high cultural profile and the deference he easily acquired lay in his emotional recharging of the concept of English nationhood, linking the values and beliefs of ordinary people to a tradition of patriotic expression that was increasingly abjured by the intellectual elite. The 'totemistic' aspect of his Anglicanism, which Bergonzi observed,[51] was equally characteristic of his broader cultural perspective. Central to that 'totemistic' aspect was a conception of Britain's social inclusiveness, for all his acute awareness of the divisive force of class[52] and however personal he made this sense of inclusiveness to himself.

We saw earlier that Betjeman's attitude towards England had changed perceptibly during the War. He was no longer quite so concerned to condemn his native land as he had been in the early 1930s, mostly on account of the poor taste of its architecture and the increasing abandonment of the custodial role over Christian culture of its pre-Reformation landed elite – at first under the Renaissance spell of pagan antiquarianism and lately under pressure from the 'democrats and the freethinkers'.[53] But absence bred endearment: spending much of the War in Ireland as the press attaché to the British Ambassador in Dublin, Betjeman's homesickness concentrated his mind on the many glories of his native land, as well as the improved social atmosphere born of comradeship in civilian arms and the downgrading of materialism. In a BBC broadcast of 1943, he talked about the impossibility of generalising about England, as if it were a 'planned ants' nest', noting instead its magnificent profusion of oddities:

> the Church of England, eccentric incumbents, oil-lit churches, Women's Institutes, modest village inns, arguments about cow parsley on the altar, the noise of mowing machines on Saturday afternoon, local newspapers, local auctions, the poetry of Tennyson, Crabbe, Hardy and Matthew Arnold, local talent, local concerts, a visit to the cinema, branch-line trains, light railways, leaning on gates and looking across fields . . .

The list was personal, but its variations were limitless, he maintained. Both this assertion, and his derogatory reference to 'living in a developed community of ants',[54] indicate well the contours of Betjeman's cultural politics, as much as the idiosyncracies of his own points of attachment to England. Indeed, the two were connected – an aversion to the uniformity and compulsion (and profligacy) of the 'slave state'[55] being the negative counterpart to a love of the ingrained spontaneity and diversity of the English character reflected in a culture and matched by a landscape marked by contrasts.

Betjeman's new-found love of England during the War was sustained into the postwar period. American films helped enormously to relieve any lingering gloom he may have felt: exposure to the latter, he maintained to a correspondent in 1946, made 'one realise how beautiful England still is, despite its wires and prefabs and tin signs and road houses and motor cars'.[56] His English enthusiasms cannot fail to have been enhanced by the writings of Bryant, with whom he became friends at around this time.[57] The two men praised and encouraged each other, Betjeman favouring Bryant and his wife with the first version of his poem 'Sunday morning, King's Cambridge', in 1947.[58] With Bryant, Betjeman worked avidly to keep alive the notion of an English *patria* in the collective consciousness of postwar Britain. This sense of cultural mission was also shared by A. L. Rowse, who dedicated his sequel to *The English Spirit* of 1945 – *The English Past* of 1951 – to Betjeman and John Piper, 'whose genius recreates something of the English past'.[59] Betjeman and Piper had just published the first Shell guidebook to appear after the War.[60] It was an appropriate dedication, given that the bulk of the essays explored the shaping of famous figures such as Milton, Swift and Buchan by their environment, and vice versa. For the basis of Betjeman's *patria* was threefold: people (particularly writers), places (particularly in southern England) and architecture (particularly churches).[61]

V

Betjeman frequently used his ample talents as a writer and broadcaster to revisit both celebrated and obscure figures from the immediate past. He did so to summon back their spirit, as an exemplar of English character. He gave this kind of attention to the prominent poet of England in its imperial heyday, Sir Henry Newbolt, in a broadcast marking the centenary of the latter's birth in 1962. He had always warmed to the author of 'Drake's drum', 'Vitaï Lampada' and other famous poems of sea and school, congratulating Walter de la Mare on his obituary notice for Newbolt in *The Times* in 1938, and adding, 'he wasn't half so bad a poet as Bloomsbury would have us think. And what a pleasant, cultivated man'.[62] In his broadcast, Betjeman emphasised the rapidly fading world of which Newbolt was an intrinsic part: he

> belonged to the professional classes at a time when England was top dog, and
> Britannia ruled the waves, and there had not even been a Boer War let alone the

Great War of 1914. His family and his wife's family were what used to be called the backbone of England. . . . He really was a member of the establishment.

Yet Betjeman was keen to stress the qualities of those like Newbolt who inhabited such gilded circles, and who celebrated the good fortune and significance of their country as a world power. 'In a sense', he maintained,

> they were privileged but they gave themselves unflinchingly to patriotic causes and they kept their word. Newbolt himself was no hearty, bluff, slap-you-on-the-back sort of man, as you might suppose from his early poems. He was a quiet scholar with a deep knowledge of Latin and Greek and English poetry – the old and the new.

The testimonial is significant in conveying the 'gentlemanly' kind of intellectual whom Betjeman most admired. As far as he was concerned, it was not only the memorable lines and skilful technique of Newbolt's poetry that would ensure his cultural survival – against all the postwar odds – but Newbolt himself, as the archetypal Englishman. For in Betjeman's account of his last meeting with the poet – 'one summer day long before the war in Netherhampton Manor House near Salisbury'- all the things which Betjeman associated with the essential landscape, lifestyle and character of England stood out.

> He was thin, clean-shaven, silver-haired; gentle and courteous. I remember him in his attic study lined with leather-bound books and looking out from the house over the flowery garden, and beyond the elm tops to the Wiltshire Downs.[63]

Among other lately deceased Victorian figures whom Betjeman sought to rescue from postwar condescension was the Victorian hymn writer, amateur archaeologist and hagiologist, Sabine Baring-Gould. He ably defended Gould against the modern professional scholars who could find in Gould's work only inaccuracies, emphasising instead its readability and the inspiration it had given to children like himself, whose love of Devon and Cornwall it had first awakened. It was much to his credit that 'his friends were his neighbours and he was unknown in any "literary" set'. This was all part of Betjeman's disassociation from intellectuals. He similarly praised another west country parson and poet of the previous century, Hawker of Morwenstow: despite an acquaintance with Tennyson, 'Hawker did not pine for literary company' and wisely kept his opinions to himself.[64] Betjeman's other target was political, holding up Baring-Gould's 'intense individualism' to an age which had rapidly grown accustomed to 'form filling' and the nosiness of the state. 'There he stood, every day, at a high desk writing his books for love of Devon and Cornwall and to make money to improve Lew Trenchard [his parish] and to educate his family.'[65] Baring-Gould's was the sort of local patriotism that so endeared Betjeman to England more generally, as was the lively parlour songs of the 1870s and 1880s of Theo Marzials, and the pastoral poetry of Edmund Blunden – for whom Betjeman sustained his admiration in the 1920s when he and his fellow undergraduates were otherwise seeking more fashionable literary icons.[66]

At another level – that of architecture – Betjeman kept up his struggle to

bring home to his compatriots the beauty of England. The importance of buildings, he once maintained, 'increases with the disappearance of rural scenery'.[67]
Poor taste lay at the heart of his ceaseless efforts to improve on the surroundings deemed appropriate by public authorities. But it was the arrogance as much
as the philistinism of the planner against which he protested, and an associated
passion for uniformity which belied the variety of England's street architecture.[68] Again, Betjeman's cultural criticism is suffused with political satire, for
all his disengagement from party politics. There could not have been a more
damning indictment of the mentality of the planner than his spoof account of
the latter's outlook on the doomed village of 'High Frecklesby' for *Punch* in
1953:

> The village itself, at the Hall gates, consists of obsolete family units built of local
> stone and of some obsolescence. They are arranged in what can only be described
> as a rural sprawl around the antiquated church. This building, though ancient, will
> have to be demolished as it is in the very centre of the area to be replanned. Though
> we may regret its departure as an historic relic, the compensatory saving of space
> and the provision of an inter-denominational meeting room at the top of High
> Frecklesby should satisfy any dissentients.[69]

Betjeman, in particular, was notorious for his love of parish churches – which he
regarded as 'even more varied than the landscape',[70] and in which could be found
'the story of England. They alone remain islands of calm in the seething roar of
civilisation'.[71] Like old leather-bound books,[72] they were a vital link with the past
– not only of immense architectural interest in themselves but a conduit to ances-
tors long dead. It was a theme pressed to more controversial political conclusions
by the politician Enoch Powell, who also attached great significance to English
village churches and the strong, intergenerational sense of kinship that was
instantly acquired from the 'traces' of themselves left in them by the 'old
English'.[73] But the Burkean undertones of Betjeman's interest in churches are
equally resonant in passages such as the following:

> of all the old houses of England, the oldest and the most interesting are the Houses
> of God – the Churches . . . Each generation has contributed to the adornment of
> an old church, and the result isn't a museum of showpieces, but a living thing, still
> in use. Old glass still diffuses the daylight on the latest hats as softly as it did on the
> wigs of the eighteenth century or the woollen hose of the people of the Middle
> Ages. Elizabethan silver is still used for the sacrament. And from the tower a bell,
> cast soon after the Wars of the Roses, lends its note to the peal that ripples over the
> meadows and threads its way under the drone of aeroplanes. The magniloquent
> epitaph and well-carved bust of some dead squire looks down in breathing marble
> from the walls, and the churchyard is a criss-cross of slanting old stones. Here lies
> the England we are all beginning to wish we knew, as the roar of the machine gets
> louder and the suburbs creep from London to Land's end.[74]

Finally, Betjeman traced the many places – beyond single architectural monu-
ments – in which he detected the survival of a more civilised and therefore quintessential England than the barbaric tube of the modern developers down which

he feared much of the country was rapidly disappearing. Counties, villages, towns and even cities featured in his account of where the national character could still be found in a geographical sense. The west country naturally dominated the landscape of Britain for Betjeman, with Bristol as the civic jewel in its crown. Before the Second World War Betjeman was impressed by the unpretentiousness of Bristol's streets, and expressed his hope that the Corporation would never pass plans for the 'vulgar villas and fake half-timber style' which had come to plague London.[75] He travelled far and wide, however, and such British outposts as the Isle of Man and the Shetland Isles captured his cultural imagination. Nevertheless, it was village scenes from home counties such as Wiltshire that defined the image of England he liked most to recur when abroad:

> Ah Highworth as a whole! Churches and chapels, doctors' houses, vicarage, walled gardens with pears and plums, railway station, inns and distant cemetery, old shops and winding streets. . . . There was a sound of tea being cleared away in a cottage just near us. And suddenly with a burst the bells of Highworth Church rang out for Evening Service. That was Sunday evening in Highworth. That was England.[76]

Betjeman was eminently capable of praising the very different settings he found in Leeds, Sheffield and Glasgow. Of the recent efforts of Sheffield City Council to relieve the overcrowding of its two-storey streets by spaced-out tower-blocks, he was complimentary. But he reserved judgement on their ultimate effects – 'the question is: will they make a house-proud horizontal people apathetic and turn them into the machine they tend?'[77] – and for all his love of Derbyshire, his interest in the north was far patchier than that of the south.

VI

The conservative opponents of intellectualism and the egalitarian, statist culture to which it was perceived to have given rise in the middle decades of the twentieth century struck their own political keynote. This was securely anchored in the emphasis within Victorian liberalism on patriotism, experimentalism, individuality, and social and cultural diversity. A markedly selective vision of Britain emerged both from this heritage and the transient culture in which it gained new momentum – a culture in which one 'motored' to places, in which every other industrial and commercial concern was called 'Imperial . . .', and in which Sunday had its own, highly distinctive rituals. But for all its selectivity and increasing remoteness, its roots in the national psyche of England/Britain have proved difficult to shift. The churches, landscapes, writers, beliefs and people whom Bryant and Betjeman celebrated as quintessentially 'English' – indeed Bryant and Betjeman themselves – continue to find a response against the attempts of recent politicians and planners to bury the familiar contours of the national past in favour of a modern, youthful and 'creative Britain'.[78]

Notes

1 E. Barker, 'The teaching of politics' (1936), reprinted in *The Citizen's Choice* (Cambridge, Cambridge University Press, 1938), p. 161.

2 On the substitution of the concept of 'national community' for the state in Idealist-inspired political thought of the late 1920s and 1930s, see M. Grimley, *Citizenship, Community, and the Church of England: Anglican Theories of the State, c. 1926–1939*, PhD dissertation, University of Oxford, 1998.

3 C. Harvie, 'The moment of British nationalism, 1939–1970', *Political Quarterly*, 71:3 (2000), 328–40; R. Weight and A. Beach (eds), *The Right to Belong: Citizenship and National Identity in Britain, 1930–1960* (London, I. B. Tauris, 1998).

4 A. Bryant, 'London pride', *Illustrated London News* (hereafter *ILN*), 2 November 1940, p. 78.

5 See T. Mowl, *Stylistic Cold Wars: Betjeman Versus Pevsner* (London, John Murray, 2000), pp. 53–4, 98, 104–5.

6 John Betjeman, 'Some comments in wartime', BBC Home Service, 4 July 1940, quoted in Candida Lycett Green (ed.), *John Betjeman: Coming Home* (London, Methuen, 1997), p. 108.

7 A. Bryant, *The Lion and the Unicorn: A Historian's Testament* (London, Collins, 1969), p. 14.

8 A. Bryant, 'Doomed treasures', *ILN*, 30 October 1937, reprinted in *The Lion and the Unicorn*, p. 57.

9 R. F. Delderfield to Bryant, 22 February 1970; Bryant Papers, Liddell Hart Centre for Military Archives, King's College London, E15.

10 A collection of Bryant's *ILN* articles on the Common Market written during 1961 and 1962 was published as *A Choice for Destiny: Commonwealth and Common Market* (London, Collins, 1962). Delderfield sent Bryant a financial contribution to an anti-Common Market campaign. Delderfield to Bryant, 22 February 1970, Bryant Papers, E15.

11 Delderfield to Bryant, 28 April 1967, Bryant Papers, E15.

12 Delderfield to Bryant, 29 August 1967; Bryant Papers, E15.

13 A. Bryant, 'Portrait of the victors', *The Age of Elegance, 1812–1822* (London, Reprint Society, [1950] 1954), ch. 8.

14 A. Bryant, 'Lest we forget', *ILN*, 5 August 1967, reprinted in *The Lion and the Unicorn*, p. 223.

15 A. Bryant, 'To find us in the way', *ILN*, 1 April 1939, reprinted in *The Lion and the Unicorn*, p. 65.

16 A. Bryant, 'The passing of the regiments', *ILN*, 27 November 1965; 10 August 1957; 28 March 1959; 20 August 1968; 25 November 1944; 22 July 1950, reprinted in *The Lion and the Unicorn*, p. 315.

17 A. Bryant, *The Turn of the Tide, 1939–1943* (London, Collins, 1957), p. 266; *Triumph in the West, 1943–1946* (London, Collins, 1959).

18 A. Bryant, *Nelson* (London, Collins, 1970); A. Bryant, *The Great Duke: The Invincible General* (London, Collins, 1971); A. Bryant, *The Man in the Making* (Cambridge, Cambridge University Press, 1933), *The Years of Peril* (Cambridge, Cambridge University Press, 1935) and *The Saviour of the Navy* (Cambridge, Cambridge University Press, 1938).

19 J. J. Lawson, *A Man's Life* (London, Hodder & Stoughton, [1932] 1944), p. 28.

20 J. J. Lawson to Bryant, 28 March 1944; Bryant Papers, D4.

21 J. J. Lawson, 'Sunday postscript', 20 February 1944, Home and Forces programme; typescript in Lawson Papers, Durham University Library, Box 6, First Deposit.

22 Bryant to Lawson, 4 April 1944; Lawson Papers, Second Deposit, Personal Correspondence, *c.* 1900–1960s.

23 Paget also became Principal of Bonar Law College in 1946, a position he retained until 1949.

24 Bryant to Lawson, 25 August 1945; Lawson Papers, Second Deposit.

25 Bryant to Lawson, 16 April 1949 and 18 December 1953; Lawson Papers, Second Deposit.

26 Bryant to Lawson, 27 October 1944; Lawson Papers, Second Deposit. Lawson, *A Man's Life*, ch. 8.

27 J. J. Lawson, *The Man in the Cap: The Life of Herbert Smith* (London, Methuen, 1941).

28 The title was used with considerable irony. The second half of the book traced the decline in national morality following the triumph over Napoleon at Waterloo, pausing to note at one instance of a lack of compassion for the poor that here, 'the nemesis of the contemporary passion for elegance lay: so admirable when as in the eighteenth century it had arisen spontaneously from a widespread love and craving for beauty, so dangerous when it became an obsession, driving men of all classes to a heartless, competitive extravagance'; *The Age of Elegance*, p. 320.

29 A. Bryant, 'Our notebook', *ILN*, 13 December 1947, p. 650.

30 Lawson to Bryant, 28 January 1948; Bryant Papers, D4.

31 Bryant to Lawson, 11 June 1945; Lawson Papers, Second Deposit.

32 Bryant to Lawson, 27 November 1947; Lawson Papers, Box 4.

33 Bryant to Lawson, 11 June 1945 Lawson Papers, Second Deposit.

34 Lawson to Bryant, 23 September 1946; Bryant Papers, D4.

35 Lawson to Bryant, 22 February 1957; Bryant Papers, D4.

36 Bryant to Lawson, 31 May 1949; Lawson Papers, Second Deposit. J. J. Lawson, *Peter Lee* (London, Epworth Press, 1934).

37 J. J. Lawson, 'Something of my philosophy', broadcast on the Home Service, 28 March 1954; Lawson Papers, Box 6.

38 Bryant to Lawson, 2 April 1954; Lawson Papers, Second Deposit.

39 Lawson to Bryant, 12 December 1962 and 12 October 1948; Bryant Papers, D4.

40 Bryant to Lawson, 30 March 1954; Lawson Papers, Second Deposit.

41 Lawson to Bryant, 9 December 1958; Bryant Papers, D4. See also Lawson to Bryant, 16 May 1945; Bryant Papers, D4.

42 Lawson to Bryant, 5 December 1953; Bryant Papers, D4. A. Bryant, *The Story of England: Makers of the Realm* (London, Collins, 1953).

43 As we have seen in Chapter 6 Bryant delivered the Presidential Address to the English Association in 1946, which he entitled 'The art of writing history'. He wrote of history that 'only when it is literature [is it] truly history'; A. Bryant, *The Art of Writing History*, The English Association Presidential Address, 1946 (London, English Association, 1946), p. 14.

44 A. Bryant, 'What democracy is not', *Observer*, 11 July 1937, reprinted in *Humanity in Politics* (London, Hutchinson, 1937), p. 329.

45 James Lees-Milne to Betjeman, 30 May 1965, *John Betjeman: Letters*, 2 vols, II, *1951–1984*, ed, C. Lycett Green (London, Methuen, 1995), p. 292. (Hereafter, *Letters*, II.)

46 Betjeman to the Secretary of the Athenaeum, 3 February 1967; in *Letters*, II, p. 330.

47 Betjeman to A. Pryce-Jones, 17 April 1937, *John Betjeman: Letters*, 2 vols, I, *1926–1951*, ed. C. Lycett Green (London, Methuen, 1994), p. 171. (Hereafter, *Letters*, I.)

48 Betjeman to R. Harrod, 25 March 1939, in *Letters*, I, pp. 223–5.

49 J. Lowe, *The Warden: A Portrait of John Sparrow* (London, Harper Collins, 1998), p. 128.

50 Betjeman, interview with *Picture Post*, July 1964, quoted in *Letters*, II, p. 253.

51 B. Bergonzi, 'Culture and Mr. Betjeman', *The Twentieth Century*, 165 (February, 1959), 133.

52 See his poem 'Beside the seaside', in *Collected Poems*, ed. Lord Birkenhead (London, John Murray, [1958] 1973), pp. 157–65.

53 J. Betjeman, *Ghastly Good Taste: Or a Depressing Story of the Rise and Fall of English Architecture* (London, Chapman & Hall, 1933), p. 13.

54 Betjeman, 'Coming home', in *Coming Home*, pp. 140–1.

55 *Letters*, I, p. 385.

56 Betjeman to Dr Francis Carolus Eeles (Secretary for the Council for the Care of Churches), 29 August 1946, *Letters*, I, p. 397.

57 *Letters*, I, pp. 366–7.

58 *Letters*, I, pp. 422–3.

59 A. L. Rowse, *The English Past: Evocations of Persons and Places* (London, Macmillan, 1951).

60 John Betjeman and John Piper, *Shropshire: A County Guide* (London, Faber, 1951).

61 Betjeman pressed home the inextricability of these three aspects of England for him in his Rede Lecture at Cambridge in 1956: 'There is not a district in England which is not enriched for me by some writer who lived in it: not self-consciously, but because he was part of the place'; Betjeman, *The English Town in the Last Hundred Years* (Cambridge, Cambridge University Press, 1956), p. 8.

62 Betjeman to Walter de la Mare, 1 May 1938; *Letters*, I, p. 210.

63 J. Betjeman, 'Sir Henry Newbolt after a hundred years', in *Coming Home*, pp. 387–91. Betjeman commented that 'Books are, to me, the last link with the beautiful in England' (p. 391).

64 J. Betjeman, 'Hawker of Morwenstow', BBC talk, 7 October 1945, in C. Lycett Green (ed.), *Betjeman's Britain* (London, The Folio Society, 1999), pp. 74–5.

65 J. Betjeman, 'Sabine Baring-Gould', BBC West Region broadcast as 'Western men', 21 September 1945, in *Coming Home*, pp. 164–8.

66 J. Betjeman, 'Theo Marzials', BBC Home Service Broadcast, 24 December 1950, and 'Edmund Blunden', contribution to *Edmund Blunden – Sixty-Five*, ed. Chau Wah Ching (Hong Kong, University of Hong Kong Press, 1961) in *Coming Home*, pp. 231–8, 392–3.

67 J. Betjeman, 'The death of Modernism', *Architectural Review*, December 1931, reprinted in *Coming Home*, p. 21.

68 J. Betjeman, 'Lamp-posts and landscape', *Light and Lighting*, November 1953, in *Coming Home*, p. 309.

69 J. Betjeman, 'High Frecklesby', *Punch*, 27 May 1953, reprinted in *Coming Home*, pp. 246–8.

70 J. Betjeman, Introduction to *English Parish Churches* (London, Collins, 1958), reprinted in *Coming Home*, p. 354.

71 J. Betjeman, 'How to look at a church', *The Listener*, 8 September 1938, reprinted in *Coming Home*, p. 80.

72 J. Betjeman'How to look at books', *The Listener*, 31 August 1939, pp. 98–9.

73 E. Powell, Speech to the Royal Society of St George, 22 April 1961, in J. Wood, *Freedom and Reality* (London, Batsford, 1969), p. 256.

74 J. Betjeman'How to look at a church', p. 76.

75 J. Betjeman'Bristol', BBC talk, 12 April 1937, in *Betjeman's Britain*, pp. 88–9.

76 J. Betjeman'Highworth, Wiltshire', BBC talk, 29 September 1950, in *Betjeman's Britain*, pp. 174–5.

77 J. Betjeman'Sheffield', *Daily Telegraph*, 3 July 1961, in *Betjeman's Britain*, p. 223.

78 C. Smith, *Creative Britain* (London, Faber, 1998). In his recent, apocalyptic account of Britain, the journalist Peter Hitchens quoted Betjeman's acid poem, 'The planster's vision' in attacking the continued despoilation of the British landscape, not least the countryside 'which so many Britons had seen as the symbol of their country's unchanging, rural core'; Hitchens *The Abolition of Britain: The British Cultural Revolution from Lady Chatterley to Tony Blair* (London, Quartet Books, 1999), pp. 95, 97–8. On Bryant as an underrated author see Paul Johnson, 'Revised editions', *Sunday Telegraph*, 9 April 2000 (Review Section), p. 14. Something very close to the Bryant/Betjeman view of England is kept alive by the successful quarterly magazine *This England*, on which see J. Paxman, *The English* (London, Michael Joseph, 1998), ch. 5. The sustained appeal of English churches to the national imagination is evident in Simon Jenkins, *England's Thousand Best Churches* (London, Penguin, 1999).

Part IV

Political intellectuals and the idea of England/Britain, 1945–2000

The distance of postwar political thought from that of the prewar period has been suggested at several points already in the course of this book. We saw Zimmern, at the end of Chapter 5, lamenting the success of Toynbee's *A Study of History* for its role in turning the concept of civilisation into a dangerous 'opiate' and away from the constructive and urgent sense it had acquired in the interwar period when Toynbee had first undertaken the work. In Chapter 3 we noted Lindsay's dismay at the readiness of postwar thinkers such as E. H. Carr to divorce democracy from its association with toleration in a previous age of faith and to recognise as equally valid its basis in proletarian class rule. In Chapter 4 we considered John Strachey's encounter with the postwar 'literature of reaction' and its misguided elevation of the private sphere over the public, albeit in a spiritual void, the traditional religious and moral proportions of which Strachey had now come to appreciate. To these examples we might add Ernest Barker's critical review of Karl Popper's *The Open Society and its Enemies* (1945), which took Plato all too literally and condemned him as a harbinger of the totalitarian state. 'No doubt', Barker argued,

> we English have made too much of Plato, from the days of Sir Thomas More (who learned something different from the 'Republic' from what Mr. Popper finds there) to the days of Nettleship and Cornford. But does it help life, or truth, or scholarship, to find Plato turned into an 'historicist totalitarian,' wishing to arrest political change by a return to the solidarity of the primitive tribe, or to find this transmogrified Plato accused of a love of lies, of treachery to the memory of Socrates, and of a greed for power?[1]

The implications of this remark, as with the other examples above, were that the horizons of postwar political thought had become unduly narrow, and that the public values that had previously been associated with the concept of civilisation, or the pursuit of 'the good life' under the influence of the Greeks, were now at a severe discount.

The suggestion made by Strachey in 1960 that the revulsion for communism had triggered a wider mood of political quiescence among intellectuals was confirmed in the second volume of statements of belief by leading thinkers published by George Allen & Unwin in 1966. Comparing the contemporary intellectual climate with that of a quarter of a century earlier, the Editor – George Unwin – remarked upon two significant changes. First, the 'humanist' contributors in 1966 discussed the 'inward' applications of thought only, eschewing the 'outward' schemes for major social and political transformation which had animated authors such as Auden, Aldous Huxley and Strachey in 1940. This was as true of A. J. Ayer as it was of Barbara Wootton. The latter, despite her role as the arch-exponent of planning after the Second World War, reserved only a small portion of her entry to 'political' issues such as class and inequality, devoting most of her chapter to an attack upon Christianity. Only one contributor – significantly a psychologist, Edward Glover – could be said to combine conviction with 'advocacy': the 'belief not merely in something but for something', which characterised the earlier cohort of writers. Second, George Unwin remarked upon the declining 'authoritativeness' of leading thinkers and – concomitantly – the decline in authority that was bestowed upon them. Intellectual 'giants' belonged to the earlier volume, a quality which had diminished not least because of 'the notorious domesticating influence of modern media of communication'. [2] Certainly, the advent of television in 1949 severely hampered the vision of the founders of the Third Programme three years earlier of quality, educative broadcasting that – through judicious integration with the Light and Home Programmes – would gradually break down the barriers between different listening classes. But by the mid 1950s, too, it had become clear that the limited appeal of the Third Programme had much to do also with its own inaccessibility. In 1957, an internal working party felt compelled to recommend 'an end of those programmes whose real place is . . . in the learned quarterlies'. The distance between the Home Programme and the Third Programme was described by one BBC executive as that 'between Malcolm Muggeridge and Isaiah Berlin'.[3]

However, the diminishing impact of intellectuals on public life that seemed evident to some during the 1950s and 1960s should not be exaggerated. The intellectual fare served up by Muggeridge may not have been as esoteric as Berlin's but given his success in exposing large radio and television audiences to issues and debates of serious import his role as a public intellectual should not be underestimated.[4] Moreover, there were still those who sought a public role for intellect but who envisaged a more indirect means of bringing it to bear than that which had typically prevailed before the War. For example, the political philosopher Michael Oakeshott rejected the call to political commitment that was characteristic of intellectuals in the 1930s. Nevertheless, he emphasised the duty which philosophers, along with artists and poets, performed in 'creat[ing] and recreat[ing] the values of their society'. In an article of 1939 which captured fully the spirit of his postwar political thought, he wrote of these figures that

> It is not their business to come out of a retreat, bringing with them some superior wisdom, and enter the world of political activity, but to stay where they are, remain true to their genius, which is to mitigate a little their society's ignorance of itself.[5]

Furthermore, as the example of Oakeshott on another front makes clear, the increasingly dominant public note of 'scepticism' in postwar political thought was never a nihilistic, disillusioned response[6]; rather, it emphasised the positive, indeed invaluable, role of politics, albeit as simply one among many areas of communal life, and certainly not the most formative. The way in which Oakeshott chose to illustrate this conception of the political realm emphasises well the influence which positive ideals of English historical development made upon the retreat of some intellectuals from political activism after the War. Essentially, they were ideals of a nation which had made its own destiny, hence limiting the scope for a specialised intellectual and political class.

Political activity may have given us Magna Carta and the Bill of Rights, but it did not give us the contents of these documents, which came from a stratum of social thought far too deep to be influenced by the actions of politicians.[7]

These ideals were by no means the only justification for the lower political profile of political intellectuals: Kingsley Amis's sense of the void between the 'ordinary party man' and the intellectual – the latter's hopeless romanticism as a substitute for any real, situational connection to live political causes which were in any case in short supply in the 1950s – would serve equally well.[8] But the essentially English inspiration of Oakeshott's political thought of the 1940s and 1950s was not confined to the right in postwar Britain; it also proved an important influence on the protest that was mounted *against* the mood of apathy on the left – which Amis typified – among thinkers of the early New Left, most notably E. P. Thompson. Here, too, the role of grand theory in politics was brought into question at the same time that 'the peculiarities of the English' were played up and the idea of the national duty and belonging of intellectuals made evident. The loss of empire, the trauma of Suez, the implosion of empire, perceptions of economic decline and fears of American dominance all enhanced earlier attempts during the interwar period and during the Second World War itself to give England, and thereby Britain more widely, a clearer focus and also greater self-confidence. It was not until the 1980s and 1990s that – under the triple influences of multiculturalism, European Union and devolution – supportive explorations of the definitive role of England in British culture and identity in political thought waned appreciably.

These themes form the subject of Chapters 9 and 10 below. But it is worth adding here that, in general, the decline of the informing sense of Englishness in political thought coincided with decreasing enthusiasm among political intellectuals – certainly those who were scholars – for exercising a wider influence in society by shaping the public mind in the widest possible sense (or rather, as Enoch Powell constantly insisted, articulating pre-existing identities). If they sought to address directly a wider audience than those who shared their own specialist academic field, it was now likely to be in conjunction with a role in think tanks and other lobbying organisations, or simply through networking with individual politicians and businessmen at a personal level, the assumption being that the 'public' or nation is defined in and through elites, government policy and services. Indeed, resurgent forms of Englishness in the 1980s and 1990s have themselves tended to be transmitted in these 'top-down' ways,[9] so changed had the political and intellectual climate become in the last quarter of the twentieth century (although equally there are still cases where more popular interpretations and methods of diffusion have been a priority, one being that of the historian Raphael Samuel, who is briefly considered at the end of Chapter 9).

Notes

1   E. Barker, 'From Plato to Popper', *The Sunday Times*, 18 November 1945, p. 4b. Review of K. R. Popper, *The Open Society and its Enemies*, (London, Routledge, 1945).

2   G. Unwin (ed.), *What I Believe* (London, George Allen & Unwin, 1966), p. 8.

3   H. Carpenter, *The Envy of the World: Fifty Years of the BBC Third Programme and Radio 3, 1946–1996* (London, Weidenfeld & Nicolson, 1996), pp. 9, 168, 170.

4   See, for example, M. Muggeridge, *Muggeridge through the Microphone: BBC Radio and Television* (London, British Broadcasting Corporation, 1966).

5   M. Oakeshott, 'The claims of politics', *Scrutiny*, 8 (1939–40), in T. Fuller (ed.), *Religion, Politics, and the Moral Life* (New Haven, Yale University Press, 1993), pp. 95–6.

6   Oakeshott's positive concept of political activity, as realised in 'civil association' and civil association alone, has been well explored by Glenn Worthington in 'Oakeshott's claims of politics', *Political Studies*, 45:4 (1997), 727–38.

7   Oakeshott, 'The claims of politics', p. 93.

8   K. Amis, *Socialism and the Intellectuals* (London, The Fabian Society, 1957).

9   See, for example, the historian Corelli Barnett's statement of whom he most seeks to influence through his books on how the pursuit of 'unrealistic ambitions and ideals' blew England/Britain off its historic course of industrial competitiveness, particularly in the postwar period. R. English and M. Kenny (eds), *Rethinking British Decline* (London, Macmillan, 2000), p. 48.

9

Political scepticism and cultural affirmation, 1945–80

I

The chapters in Part III followed the path of political and cultural reflection in the work of popular historical and literary writers during the middle decades of the twentieth century who took the idea of England/Britain as their principal protagonist. This chapter turns to the development of political thought in more recognisably academic and political settings after the Second World War. In particular, it considers the public, and particularly national, identities that continued to be disseminated at this intellectual level, despite the notes of caution and scepticism its practitioners increasingly struck concerning what was attainable in the political realm.

II

As Professor of Modern History at Cambridge from 1944–63, and then Regius Professor from 1963–68, Herbert Butterfield might seem an unlikely candidate with which to begin a discussion of notable public intellectuals in postwar Britain. However, as Maurice Cowling has pointed out, his later writings indicate his clear possession of a 'doctrine', and doctrines naturally require the broadest dissemination.[1] Moreover, all of Butterfield's writings were deeply rooted in an historiographical bias against the actions and thoughts of elites in history, the confusion of minority movements such as the Renaissance and Enlightenment with the trend of history at large. Indeed, he readily embraced the Marxist perception that 'bourgeois' historians are so obsessed with individuals, and the ideas by which they are assumed to be guided, that the wider thrust of the history of a society is lost from sight.[2] Finally, for Butterfield history had to serve an educational as much as a scientific function, and indeed he believed that the latter constituted a serious threat to the former the more developed it became. He found himself wondering, in 1961 – significantly in the A. D. Lindsay Memorial Lecture at Keele University – whether

170

the older type of historical narrative, as written by English writers such as Macaulay, was not a better training for life and politics (because of the kind of reflection it contained) than the more modern form of historical writing, though the more modern will contain fewer errors of facts.

As this example he made of Macaulay well indicates, his animus against history that was unduly skewed towards the actions and thoughts of the privileged few did not rule out the history of government. On the contrary, it was essential for social classes who were newcomers to the exercise of political power to learn the 'structure of political conflict' and to 'measure contemporary movements against deeper long-term tendencies'. The most instructive means for doing so was afforded by the study of past struggles, where 'the controversy is over, the story completed, the passion spent'.[3]

In accordance with these beliefs and approaches, Butterfield increasingly sought a wide audience for his views. This can be seen in his contribution to Ernest Barker's series of short books entitled 'Current problems' in 1944, *The Englishman and his History*. The jacket of each book described 'Current problems' as 'A new series of books for general reading; concise, expert, setting out all the necessary material for a full understanding of certain urgent political, social, and international problems'. Butterfield's role as a publicist can also be seen in his broadcasting endeavours, most notably the six lectures he delivered on the Third Programme in 1949 entitled *Christianity and History*, and which were published by the Methodist publishing house, The Epworth Press.

Yet Butterfield's political message was essentially one of quiescence, forged out of a number of interlocking themes in his mature work: that Christianity had been one of the great stabilising and civilising forces in modern European history, particularly English history; that the transition from the medieval to the modern world was embodied in the Scientific Revolution of the seventeenth century, not in the tradition-bound movements of the Renaissance and Reformation, or an Enlightenment heavily dependent upon previous and more impressive ruptures in thought;[4] and that the way forward lay in the restraint of ideological passion and self-rightousness that Christian influences alone could ensure. Above all, Butterfield was imbued with the idea of British politics as embodying a laudable tradition of 'practice', free from the bigoted and doctrinaire approach which prevailed over much of the European continent. He never made explicitly 'anti-intellectual' statements, but there was plenty of evidence in his writings that he – like his Cambridge teachers, Canon Smyth and Bernard Lord Manning – found the liberal intelligentsia insufferably arrogant in its misplaced optimism about human nature and human affairs.[5]

As the great critic of Whig history in the 1930s, Butterfield had attacked partisanship in historical study as the enemy of truth.[6] This he continued to do in the 1940s in his capacity as a professional historian, maintaining in his inaugural lecture of 1944 that liberation from dogmatic beliefs – such as the belief that the century before 1919 bore witness to the ineluctable growth of democracy, thus generating expectations of its sustained momentum – was essential in order to understand 'the flight from liberalism and the spread in Europe of the totali-tarian idea'.[7] At the same time, however, Butterfield abandoned his attack upon Whig history, emphasising its supreme serviceability to a nation now united by the threat which had been posed to its very survival in 1940. The attainment of 'truth' was now only considered to be one of several functions of historical study. Another – and at some periods the more essential task – was to impart a unify-ing conception of a society to itself. In this endeavour, truth was of secondary importance.

In *The Englishman and his History*, Butterfield emphasised how – duly mod-ified after the excesses of the seventeenth century, in which Whiggism shut out all influences from virtuous English history bar that of an exclusive, parliamen-tary cause – Whig history gradually entered into the heart of all Englishmen.[8] While for the French in the eighteenth century, medieval history was read all too accurately as harbouring rights against monarchs that were exclusive to semi-feudal potentates, and therefore had to be abolished with those potentates, the English middle classes had forestalled such a possibility in the previous century by appealing to 'rights' that were (wrongfully) assumed to be universal to all Englishmen. They thus kept history on their side.[9] The role of Whig history was no longer to bind, rigidly, the present to the past through an anachronistic reading of the latter, but to encourage co-operation with 'providence', the adap-tation to new pressures while keeping an identifiable inheritance intact. The English past was infinitely flexible. For the sake of its survival, generosity towards one's political opponents was an ingrained political ethic in Britain, as was the settlement of disputes by discussion rather than violence, and compro-mise before conflict and hatred erupted. This quintessentially 'Whig' attitude had triumphed most recently in 1940, when England 'resumed contact with her traditions'.

It is obvious why Butterfield attached so much significance to this date in reviving Whiggism as the form of history and politics most dear to the national heart. Clearly, he was cheered by the spirit of compromise and alliance implicit in the Churchill/Attlee coalition, to the aid of which, argued Cowling, he attempted to bring Asquitheanism.[10] But also he wanted to stress the peculiar-ities of the English – most clearly reflected in their history – which distinguished them from their enemies and emphasis upon which was called forth by Dunkirk. English history was undeniably the story of liberty, even if gross liberties were often taken in the recounting of that story. Criticising himself, as much – pos-sibly – as a new school of Marxist history that had developed in the interwar period, he cautioned against those who, 'perhaps in the misguided austerity of youth, wish to drive out that whig interpretation (that particular thesis which controls our abridgement of English history) [and who] are sweeping a room which humanly speaking cannot long remain empty'.[11] For all its defects, argued Butterfield, Whig history was itself an historical fact, 'part of the landscape of English life, such as our country lanes or our November mists or our historic inns'.[12] In the last resort, however, Whiggism was a question of statesmanship.

As Butterfield rhetorically asked, 'who amongst us would exchange the long line of amiable or prudent statesmen in English history, for all those masterful and awe-inspiring geniuses who have imposed themselves on France and Germany in modern times?'[13] Flawed though Whiggism was as an interpretation of history, it had thus proved infinitely more beneficial than 'technical history', with its vastly superior basis in fact. This was recognised by the *Times Literary Supplement*, which took the unusual step of publishing a poem which had been inspired by Butterfield's book.[14]

Yet technical history continued to have its merits, not least in emphasising how each generation possessed its own order and purpose, and was not a mere 'stepping stone' to the present. Butterfield made this point in his lectures on *Christianity and History*, in which he developed the political and theological ideas which were to inform all of his future work. His intention in doing so was to underline the providential nature of history (although not the prophetic nature of historical study: the book was, clearly a broadside against the later volumes of Toynbee's *A Study of History*[15]), insight into which narrative history could never attain. In this sense, each generation was 'equidistant from eternity'.[16] It was very necessary to grasp the idea of history as a divine process in order to expose the folly of those in history who had sought to impose their own providential order on to the future: without exception, they had been subject to 'the hardest strokes of heaven'. For Butterfield, history was the bearer of the supreme cautionary message in politics, that mankind is empowered to undertake small things only and that the future must be left flexible. This belief, in turn, rested on a view of the ineradicable sinfulness of human beings, and which thus annulled all utopian plans for the improvement of the world.[17] Butterfield held up for admiration the example of the ancient Hebrews, who more perfectly represented the point at which religion and history intersected than any other people.[18] This was because, while the Old Testament identified them as a 'chosen people', it constantly dwelt upon their failings rather than their righteousness. Nonetheless, although Butterfield cast our 'modern patriotic histories' in a poor light besides this shining example, he was imbued with the notion of the English people's greater public godliness than any other nation in Europe, and the beneficial consequences of this for their history. At the end of *The Englishman and his History*, he stressed how the absence of militant 'paganism' in modern English history had helped to undermine the tendency elsewhere of 'making gods out of things of this world'.[19]

Clearly, throughout his career, Butterfield felt painfully the weight of the tension that existed between 'technical' history on the one hand, and history with a theological moral to which English history most closely corresponded, on the other. His attempts at reconciliation were not persuasive. The balance of his sympathy lay clearly with the latter, despite repeated attempts to further the cause of the former. This can be seen in his commentary upon Trevelyan's achievement just before the latter's death in 1962: for all the technical weaknesses of Trevelyan's histories, he maintained, they were nevertheless elevated, not only by the 'qualities of sheer intellect' but also by those associated with the author's 'grandeur of the soul'.[20] This may have been something to which Butterfield himself aspired, and never achieved. But he recognised fully the intellectual's duty to raise the standards of moral and cultural awareness in society by addressing issues of public concern in terms of widely held values and identities.

III

Butterfield's pessimistic view of human nature and history was by no means shared by other professional historians. Maurice Powicke, for one, was made distinctly uneasy by Butterfield's importing of theological doctrines into the study of history, particularly doctrines which discounted the more positive and constructive side of human nature that most other Christians, he maintained, would readily avow.[21] But there was considerable ideological affinity between Butterfield and another seminal Cambridge figure, Michael Oakeshott, who jointly edited the *Cambridge Historical Journal* with Butterfield. Oakeshott shared none of Butterfield's ambitions to reach a popular audience, desiring instead to influence the specialist activity of political philosophy, and on a long-term basis at that.[22] He steered well clear of the Third Programme, and a not inconsiderable part of his work from the immediate postwar period did not appear in print until after his death in 1990. Nevertheless, there is much congruence between his published and unpublished work of this period, and it is significant that in one of his unpublished essays, he drew specifically on Butterfield's *The Englishman and his History*. While advancing a highly theoretical view of the character of modern European politics, the experience of English politics – as understood by Oakeshott and supported by Butterfield – was particularly influential in shaping it.[23] In *The Politics of Faith and the Politics of Scepticism* – drafted in the immediate postwar years and completed in 1952 – Oakeshott contrasted two styles of political conduct that had wrestled for supremacy in the transition to modernity. Those who advocated the politics of faith – as its designation suggests – were never entirely happy about the late medieval separation of the spheres of religion and politics, and sought through the latter the fulfilment of the millenarium and other high hopes of the former. Their cause was immensely strengthened by the increasing opportunities for the exercise of political power afforded by the development of a separate office of government from the previous basis of authority in the 'intensified private rights' of the monarch.[24] But the antithesis of the politics of faith – the politics of scepticism – harked backwards in its response to the circumstances which begat the politics of faith, to a medieval understanding of government as fundamentally judicial rather than transformative in nature. England, Oakeshott maintained, 'has been peculiarly the home of this understanding of government'. It was informed, fundamentally, by 'a suspicion of government invested with overwhelming power, and a recognition of the unavoidable arbitrariness of most'.[25] Following Butterfield, Oakeshott maintained that the medieval legacy underlining the politics of scepticism was most successfully modernised towards the end of the seventeenth century with Halifax. This endeavour was sustained in the eighteenth century through the work of Hume and Burke. These writers and politicians ensured that scepticism was not exclusive to any one party: indeed, scepticism easily overran its natural, conservative domain and became the basis of a style of politics – the radical republicanism of Paine, Price and Bentham – with which its essence was wholly incompatible. These '*mesalliances*' were as interesting to Oakeshott as the purer expressions of sceptical politics, representing, as they did, the 'inspiration' – albeit negative – it had represented in England during the last century and a half, 'elicited for the most part from some of the ancient traditions of English politics, patiently considered and reconsidered in each generation and applied to the current situations of the world'.[26]

Oakeshott was fully aware of the low ebb which the politics of scepticism had reached in the postwar world. In the current 'activist climate'[27] of English politics, it was only natural that this political style would be abjured, condemned by its lack of ambition to set the world to rights, beyond that of adjudicating between individuals whose pursuits and interests had fallen foul of each other. But even in circumstances in which the politics of faith had reached a new, highwater mark in pursuing comprehensive, inevitably centralised social welfare, Oakeshott was optimistic that 'in a society, such as ours, which has not yet lost the understanding of government as the prevention of coercion, as the power which holds in check the overmighty subject, as the protector of minorities against the power of majorities', there was scope for its revival.[28] In this way, Oakeshott's work struck at the idealism which had underlined much of the political thought and commitment of the interwar period, and which had reached full fruition in the postwar Labour government, albeit in the form of a mass of restrictions and controls on consumption and production.[29] Idealism, for Oakeshott, was very often a mask for 'counterfeit piety'. At the best of times, he maintained, 'political activity seems to encourage many of the less agreeable traits of human nature'.[30] But while politics was often a sordid business, on the rare occasions when it was confined to the limited task of enforcing rules of conduct which ensured to all individuals the maximum scope for pursuing their own, freely chosen goals, it was a vital human activity. Most emphatically, however, the action of free individuals takes place within the context of a social whole, with whose 'protection and occasional modification' a political system was fundamentally charged. If the 'law and custom and tradition' of the social whole were not guarded in this way, individual liberty would be gravely threatened.[31]

The political philosophy of Oakeshott was therefore far from negative in its appraisal of government. Moreover, a key source of the value he attached to government lies in what he understood as the British intellectual and political traditions and their singularity. Oakeshott's conception of the singularity of the British intellectual tradition is evident as early as 1932 in a piece he wrote about Bentham. In reviewing C. W. Everett's *The Education of Jeremy Bentham* (1931), it was obvious to Oakeshott why Bentham's *ideas* – as opposed to his proposals for reform – had made a far greater impact on the continent than in England. This was because Bentham was essentially a *philosophe*, the character of which was utterly 'foreign to the English character'. The essence of the *philosophe* was to make a fetish out of knowledge such that all knowledge was valued indiscriminately, 'in a way which we [the British] find difficult to understand – we who have long ago lost this confidence'. Far from representing a paragon of modernity, Bentham's system of philosophy was fatally flawed by its immaturity. *Philosophisme*, according to Oakeshott, 'can make no serious contribution to our store of knowledge; it denies the traditions of the past and attempts to fasten no new traditions on the future'.[32]

Oakeshott's interlocking conception of the singularity and value of the British tradition was equally apparent in his postwar polemics against the Labour government. In an article of 1947–48, he emphasised that democracy in Britain had not been the product of 'abstract thought' but rather of a 'way of living' that had emerged in the Middle Ages. Parliamentary institutions had developed out of judicial procedures in enforcing the 'common law rights and duties of Englishmen', an achievement which was unsurpassed. As a 'living method of social integration' parliamentary institutions constituted 'the most civilized and the most effective method ever invented by mankind'.[33] Oakeshott eschewed all essentialist concepts of human nature,[34] which would naturally extend to the idea of innate 'national characters'. If he subscribed to a notion of British exceptionalism, this certainly did not embrace a notion of intrinsic national difference. Even followers of Oakeshott who have been less coy in associating British liberty with British national character have framed the latter in terms of a 'morality' – one in which the 'vigorous virtues' of self-sufficiency, energy and adventurousness have always assumed pride of place – rather than a genetic constitution.[35]

Commentators on Oakeshott were not slow to recognise the patriotic roots of his political thought. For example, W. H. Greenleaf revealingly emphasised Oakeshott's 'deep and genuine patriotism'. But he also noted its 'rarity' in 1966.[36] One powerful factor in the assumption by such 'national' intellectuals of an antagonistic mantle after 1945 was the ascendancy of a materialistic, sociological notion of citizenship which T. H. Marshall articulated in 1950, and which was wholly at odds with Oakeshott's – centred as it was upon common loyalty to a national parliamentary tradition that was essentially judicial in character.[37] Certainly, in the case of Britain at least, the decline of political philosophy after 1945 in terms of both its imaginative range and its authority might be linked directly to the decline of the stimulus – both negative and positive – which the *patria* had provided to theorists earlier in the twentieth century. W. J. M. Mackenzie – a staunch critic of Oakeshott – tried to sidestep this aspect of things when he wrote in 1977 of the importance of reassessing such Victorian 'Knights of the textbooks' as Fitzjames Stephen, James Bryce, Dicey, Pollock and Maitland, who had dominated the education, but negatively influenced the interwar generation of political scientists to whom he belonged. Only Fitzjames Stephen, he asserted, would have taken at face value the ironic lines of Kipling's 'Song of the English' but there was much value, nevertheless, in the insistence of these distinctively non-Marxist intellectuals on studying the *detail* of a society through its legal face.[38] Mackenzie's piece was a considerable indictment of the Marxist and scientistic inroads into British social science in postwar Britain which had done much to undermine the patriotism which informed Oakeshott's thought, as well as marking the influence of imperial decline on the changing nature of this field of inquiry. Still, Mackenzie, a Scotsman, could not bring himself to explore the inspiration of England/Britain on the masters of English legal history to which, not just Oakeshott, but Politics as an academic discipline generally in Britain – here much indebted to Germany – owed so much. Not surprisingly, it can be no coincidence that the thinkers of both right and left who privileged British character or traditions or institutions, or made them central to the elucidation of political concepts, remained marginal in intellectual circles in the 1950s and 1960s. This holds especially true of F. A. Hayek.

IV

Hayek sought wide public influence for his ideas concerning the importance of returning to classical liberal values after the Second World War, not least by serialising his book, *The Road to Serfdom* in the *Reader's Digest*. This was because he sensed – correctly – that his views would be reviled by the political and intellectual establishment, the 'professional economists and civil servants, the academic philosophers and social scientists' whom Hayek had in mind in dedicating the book to 'the socialists of all parties'.[39] Few were more aware than Hayek of the careless attitudes towards liberty among British intellectuals in the 1930s. He gave numerous instances of this, from Laski, to E. H. Carr, C. H. Waddington and the Webbs. But the root of the problem was a more basic contempt for country. Certainly, among those who attacked him – Barbara Wootton, for example[40] – few looked beyond the polemic against planning, which they took to be the core of the book, to Hayek's lament for the decline of British civilisation and character by which it was more fundamentally informed.

There are clear autobiographical reasons for this deeper concern. Of Austrian descent, Hayek had taken out British citizenship in 1938. He had arrived in Britain in 1931, delivering lectures at the London School of Economics in response to an invitation by Lionel Robbins and remaining as the Tooke Professor of Economic Science and Studies from 1932 to 1949. In his reminiscences, he wrote of the ease with which he became absorbed in English life from the start: 'Somehow the whole mood and intellectual atmosphere of the country had at once proved extraordinarily attractive to me'. This process of assimilation was completed during the years of the Second World War: had not been for the circumstances surrounding his divorce, he maintained, 'I should never have wished to leave the country again'.[41]

Not surprisingly, therefore, *The Road to Serfdom* was written very 'definitely in an English frame of reference'.[42] In the book, he argued that collectivism had not only undermined a set of political attitudes rooted in the priority of economic liberty, but more seriously a morality which had raised a whole people above most others in the world. He laid much of the blame for this decline at the door of the left intelligentsia, who for too long had 'worshipped foreign gods' and looked with disdain upon British institutions and traditions.[43] Hayek's intellectual and cultural cornerstone was the liberal world before the First World War, led by such luminaries as Acton, Mill, Dicey and Morley. Since then, however, the British ruling class's loss of confidence in the nation had generated a reluctance among its intellectual representatives to stress and prize the characteristics which distinguished England from other countries: 'independence, self-reliance, individual initiative and local responsibility, the sucessful reliance on voluntary activity, non-interference with one's neighbour and tolerance of the difference and queer, respect for custom and tradition, and a healthy suspicion of power and authority'.[44] Under the influence of a collectivism of largely foreign – and specifically German – extraction,[45] the 'British moral genius' was being progressively destroyed. Hayek made special mention of the ineffectiveness of British propaganda during the Second World War, largely on account of its compromising attitude towards national values and propensity to concede too much to enemy states.[46] But he did not merely beat the patriotic drum. There was a wealth of sophisticated social and political philosophy inspired by his experience of British political, cultural and intellectual life. This was as evident in *The Road to Serfdom* as it was in later works such as *The Constitution of Liberty* in which Hayek further developed his theory of freedom in society. His biographers select a passage to illustrate Hayek's theoretical perceptiveness which includes the following:

> To 'plan' or 'organize' the growth of mind, or, for that matter, progress in general, is a contradiction in terms. The idea that the human mind ought 'consciously' to control its own development confuses individual reason, which alone can 'consciously control anything', with the interpersonal process to which its growth is due. By attempting to control it we are merely setting bounds to its development and must sooner or later produce a stagnation of thought and a decline of reason.[47]

Hayek's following lay well outside a growing consensus of opinion in favour of planning and the expansion of public welfare. He was greatly admired in the Cobdenite business circles which joined forces with anti-statist lawyers and writers in the Society of Individualists, later to become the Society for Individual Freedom. Their manifesto of 1942 pledged unity 'in the desire to restore to British public life that spirit of individual liberty and responsibility which characterized its period of greatness and which is today gravely threatened'.[48] But among like-minded dissidents in established intellectual and political circles Hayek found little favour. Indeed, quite the opposite, he encountered outright hostility. Oakeshott's contemptuous dismissal of Hayek's 'plan to resist all planning' is by now notorious.[49] Isaiah Berlin also failed to recognise an ally when he saw one: for all the high regard he shared with Hayek for Britain in general, and English liberalism in particular, he dismissed *The Road to Serfdom* as mere fuel for Wall Street agitation against Keynesianism.[50] He managed to touch an always raw liberal nerve with his fellow economist, J. M. Keynes, who took *The Road to Serfdom* far more seriously than his own followers. Yet for all Keynes's sensitivity to the need for caution in applying planning mechanisms, his basic trust in English good sense in these matters underlined the complacency among British intellectuals that so concerned Hayek.[51] Another figure from whom close association might have been expected was Enoch Powell. But while Powell was much inspired by the publication of Hayek's *The Constitution of Liberty*, he was too much of a loner to link his own political agenda to that of others, however sympathetic. He finally resigned from Hayek's Mont Pelerin Society in 1980, declaring to Ralph Harris his unease at belonging to an organisation that had tended to become 'a Hayek adulation society, with a minor niche for Friedman'. Equally significant, however, was his further declaration of 'dislike' for Hayek's 'teutonic habit of telling the English, whom he does not in the least understand, how to set about governing themselves'.[52] Hayek was evidently handicapped in British intellectual life by an 'alien' status which had not been resolved by his naturalisation in 1938.

V

Powell's refusal of all political alignment, however, was indicative of an intense individualism that reinforced the libertarian philosophy of Hayek and Oakeshott alike. Moreover, he took the English sympathies that accompanied the libertarianism in the writings of these two thinkers to a new extreme of romantic nationalism. On account of the latter trait, Powell's political thought emphasises further the central theme of this chapter – the positive side of the distrust of political faiths which Strachey and others characterised as the general, negative temper of postwar political thought. While Powell was first and foremost a professional politician after 1945, he wrote and delivered speeches of the highest intellectual calibre. They hence merit attention in this study of the ideas of political intellectuals. Furthermore, although much inspired by Nietzsche, Powell's individualism derived considerable shape from his conceptions – forcefully portrayed – of English national character and history. Unlike Oakeshott and to a lesser extent, Hayek, Powell believed in the capacity of virtually all individuals – certainly in Britain – to pursue their own initiatives. Perhaps because as a politician he could ill afford to, he had little of Oakeshott's sense of the rarity of the individual in modern history, and the constant threat which the latter figure encountered of being reined in by the 'anti-individual'. He certainly did not brave a repetition of Oakeshott's assertion that free speech was of only marginal importance in a free society because 'the major part of mankind has nothing to say'.[53] This was because, like Hayek, he accorded as much importance to economic as political structures in fostering a climate of liberty, even while insisting that the free market economy was more valuable as the necessary condition of all other types of freedom – free speech, free thought and action – than on account of the prosperity it made possible.[54] Powell's preferred definition of 'Powellism' was 'an almost unlimited faith in the ability of people to get what they want through peace, capital, profit and a competitive market'.[55] The rule of law and market activity were mutually sustaining in this respect. This is why Powell was so vocal in attacking voluntary prices and incomes policies in the 1960s, as an affront to the rule of law whose authority alone citizens were required to recognise.[56] Market activity, perhaps more than any other in Powell's view, sustained the individual's sense of self, and of his or her autonomy. Powell laid the blame for the current loss of national morale squarely on politicians, whose incompetence in mismanaging the economy they tried to evade by shifting responsibility on to the profligacy of the people themselves. He suggested in one of his speeches of 1966 that the propensity of the British people to comply in this condemnation of themselves had become habitual in 'former days of power and lush abundance, such as the penitential verses in Kipling's *Recessional*'. In the competitive climate of the present, however, it militated against the 'brashness and self-confidence' with which the British now had to assert themselves.[57] He could not but regret that a people 'in some ways so shrewd and sophisticated' had fallen for the 'old stone age trick' of shouldering blame where it had been erroneously placed by the villains themselves.[58]

It has often been alleged that Powell's individualism and his conception of organic nationhood stood in direct contradiction to one another.[59] Certainly the sources of the two could not have been more disparate, the one the legacy of the influence of Nietzsche on Powell's philosophical thought and classical studies prior to the Second World War, and the other the product of his increasingly vocal resistance to immigration after the passage of the 1948 Nationality Act, and his transition from 'imperialist to nationalist'.[60] In Nietzsche he had found a model of the intellectual which he was to make his own: courageous, aloof and highly appreciative of the nobility of the Greeks on the basis of their conception of the sheer force of human personality which Christianity had subsequently crushed.[61] Increasingly, however, Powell combined this influence with a practising allegiance to the Anglican Church and an unparalleled depth of concern for the fortunes of the English people in a period of imperial and industrial decline. Nietzsche's contempt for all things English is notorious, particularly English Christianity, which he characterised as a 'subtler poison' against an individualism that presented itself primarily as vulgarity.[62] However, this double blow to English pride Powell chose to ignore, and turned the English into a lonely, heroic and embattled nation, resisting the pressure towards political integration into alien, essentially manufactured, entities such as the Common Market, composed of states which had come into existence 'no more than a century or a century and a half ago – within the memory of two lifetimes'.[63]

As for the Anglican Church, Powell valued it as much for the tribal totem it represented as its role as a secure anchor for his re-emerging religious belief in 1949. Indeed, the two were inseparably intertwined. Christianity, he believed, could survive textual criticism of the accounts of miracles in the Gospels.[64] But the worship of God that remained seemed an impoverished activity without the ancestor worship afforded by English village churches. He regarded the latter as national shrines – vital points of contact between the English people across generations and centuries. In his speech before the Royal Society of St George in 1961, he spoke hauntingly of how the post-imperial English could find true affinity with the 'old English', who lay

> beneath the tall tracery of a perpendicular East window and the coffered ceiling of the chantry chapel. From brass and stone, from line and effigy, their eyes would look at us, and we gaze into them, as if we would win some answer from their inscrutable silence.

Powell urged these relics to disclose 'what it is that binds us together'.[65] Apart from the landscape, which Powell depicted in almost lyrical terms, he emphasised the importance of parliament as the unifying force of the nation, created by the monarch who was both 'symbol, yet source' of power. 'Take parliament out of the history of England and that history becomes meaningless', he proclaimed, in campaigning against Common Market membership in 1970 and the inevitable erosion of national sovereignty to which he believed it would lead.[66] It was a point on which the Labour left – particularly represented by Michael Foot and Tony Benn – were to concur with Powell as the European Communities Bill was pushed through the House of Commons in 1972: their 'instincts and reasoning' impressed him as 'exactly as nationalistic, not to say patriotic, as my own'.[67] The continuity of monarchy and of the institution it established in order to conduct a dialogue with the nation and to dispense a uniform system of justice was for Powell 'a phenomenon unique in history'. From the continuous nature of the nation's existence sprang all that was peculiar in its gifts and achievements: 'its laws, its literature, its freedom, its self-discipline'.[68] However, according to this account, the homogeneity which the English people derived from parliament was not the product of racial essentialism but of an unrivalled zealousness for the freedom and rights of the individual, culturally and politically acted upon. In other words, Powell's individualism and nationalism can only be regarded as contradictory elements in his outlook if the latter is wrongly assumed to be based on a racially absolutist notion of the English,[69] rather than a fiercely independent outlook which brought national homogeneity in its train.

It is apparent at the end of the address that Powell was aware that this heritage of kingship in parliament as the basis of English nationhood was under increasing threat. He made reference to the 'sham' notion of both monarchy *and* citizenship entailed by the 1953 Royal Titles Act, which eliminated the word 'British' from the Commonwealth and tacked on 'her other realms and territories' to the United Kingdom in which the Queen was recognised as 'Head'. For Powell, citizenship was fundamentally rooted in the principle of allegiance; it could not be acquired indirectly through an identity which alien parliaments had bestowed on their people, as in the 1948 Nationality Act. The new entity created by the 1953 Act was wholly fictitious, especially when taken in conjunction with the resolve of Commonwealth leaders after Indian independence to recognise India's continuing membership, but without enforcing any pledge of allegiance to the Sovereign at the Commonwealth's heart. So absurd a situation Powell expressed in terms of the analogy of his recognition of 'the Rt Hon Member for Walthamstow West [Mr Attlee] as leader of the Opposition, but that does not make me a Member of the Opposition'. Sorely lacking in the new conception of the Commonwealth was 'that basic, instinctive recognition of belonging to a greater whole which involves the ultimate consequence in certain circumstances of self-sacrifice in the interests of the whole'.[70] Citizenship, in other words, had become a right without associated obligations. The element of 'instinct' was to recur often in Powell's political speeches, for it was – in his view – in instinct rooted in history and tradition that the force of English national identity chiefly lay: he declared, in 1961, that 'the deepest instinct of the Englishman . . . is for continuity'. Instinct was invoked as a highly exclusionary concept, which would nonetheless have been entirely unremarkable before the postwar implosion of the Commonwealth. But Powell clearly felt that it was time for the national identity to become far more expressive, if not assertive. It was currently endangered not so much by 'violence and force' as 'indifference and humbug'. While he concluded that his thoughts were not 'thoughts for every day, nor words for every company', it was with an evident sense of the inadequacy of the gesture that he appealed to his audience to consider whether, 'on St. George's Eve, in the Society of St. George, . . . we [may] not think and speak them, to renew and strengthen in ourselves the resolves and the loyalties which English reserve keeps otherwise and best in silence'.[71]

Powell firmly denied that he was a racist, and was proud of his record of equal service to all his constituents, of whatever racial origin.[72] He found it alarming that to raise concerns about the number of immigrants coming in to Britain was to be branded a 'racist'.[73] He was a vociferous and sincere opponent of the practice of racial discrimination, proclaiming, in 1964, with striking biblical emphasis, that 'I have set and I always will set my face like flint against making any difference between one citizen and another on grounds of his origin'.[74] He was not opposed to immigration *per se* so long as it was in numbers small enough to make possible the kind of assimilation achieved by the Jews in Britain at the end of the nineteenth century.[75] When asked, after the famous Birmingham speech of 1968, whether he was a racialist, he replied in terms of the numbers of coloured immigrants he regarded as tolerable. 'Do I object to one coloured person in this country? No. To 100? No. To 1,000? No. To a million? A Query. To five million? Definitely'.[76] He took the opportunity in one speech – at the time of the 1970 General Election – to emphasise that 'like the overwhelming majority of my fellow countrymen, I hold no man inferior because he is of different origin'.[77] What did trigger his alarm, however, was the disintegrating effect of mass immigration, especially when accompanied by the development of communalism and the organisation of immigrant groups into successful lobbies, claiming rights and privileges different from the mainstream nation. This, coupled with the powers that the Race Relations Act of 1968 gave to investigate 'private actions' which allegedly discriminated against the immigrant, augered ill for a nation whose identity was rooted in freedom. It was the Second Reading of the Bill which eventually became the 1968 Act that provoked Powell's infamous reference to 'rivers of blood' in the Birmingham speech. However intemperate and insensitive a reaction it represented, the latter highlighted a permanent danger in race relations legislation of giving 'the stranger, the disgruntled and the *agent provocateur* the power to pillory [the existing population] for their private actions'.[78] Moreover, the concern to foster racial awareness that began with the passage of the Act has often heightened racial identity in ways that for Powell would have detracted from national unity.

VI

Powell was not alone among political thinkers in the 1960s in addressing the immigration issue and its implications for English national identity and political traditions. It also rated high on the agenda of the New Left – although from an opposite perspective that showed an early concern for the diversification of Britain. But the New Left itself was notoriously divided, and within this seemingly unpromising territory, much succour was given to the idea of English nationhood. This developed out of a key battlefront between advocates of a rigid Marxist model of historical development in which the singularity of the English case represented a problem, and those – E. P. Thompson especially – who insisted upon the importance of tailoring Marxist theory to English practice as the basis of a new, 'socialist humanism'. In doing so, Thompson could hardly conceal his sympathy with the English practices and traditions he wished Marxism to recognise as authentic and not distorted forms of political experience. But – in common with his counterparts on the right who were equally sensitive to English culture – Thompson found himself marginalised: the momentum in the New Left moved decisively towards continental, particularly French, forms of Marxism espoused by Perry Anderson and Tom Nairn, and – from his point of view – the irrelevant cultural Marxism of Raymond Williams.

Thompson always maintained – against the accusations of Nairn – that he was no insular 'English nationalist' but a 'socialist internationalist' for whom the national character of the past was an inescapable fact.[79] He certainly distanced himself from establishment versions of Englishness and the English 'idiom' of empiricism which he associated with Popper, Hayek, Max Beloff and Sir Geoffrey Elton.[80] But his high regard for English dissent yielded a vociferous defence of the democratic structures and humane temper of the country which had given it quarter.[81] For all Thompson's harsh words against Orwell and Koestler for discrediting the cause of communism and, with that, fostering disillusion with politics more generally, he himself pursued Orwell's strategy of grounding the spirit of the left in native thinkers and intellectual and cultural traditions. Indeed, in castigating his contemporary thinkers on the left who grounded their critique of capitalism in foreign revolutionary models, he could openly don Orwell's mantle.[82] He made much of the Romantic contribution to English socialism, from Blake to Morris, and he defended unequivocally the communist movement in Britain of the 1930s whose importance – he maintained – far outstretched the few celebrity intellectuals who eventually betrayed it.[83] A recent study of the early New Left by Michael Kenny has perceptively situated Thompson's patriotism in his wartime experience of a united country in the face of a common and deadly enemy.[84] This was not an experience which his younger rivals within the New Left shared; hence their dismissal of his idealism, nationalism and empiricism, and their attraction to foreign intellectual icons.

Kenny emphasises the shortcomings of Thompson's socialist humanism by comparison with the New Right, many of whose assumptions it shared: for example, a distrust of the bureaucratic state and a belief in the moral autonomy of the individual. If Thompson is compared specifically with Hayek, then the basis of their libertarian thought in indigenous traditions of liberalism and radicalism represents another common area of discourse, however differently they conceived the social, political and economic implications of those traditions. Yet the New Right was much more successful in mobilising popular opinion in its favour.[85]

However, Thompson's search for a socialist humanism that was rooted in presumptions of *agency* on the part of individuals whose context was significantly national was to find similar echoes among historians such as Raphael Samuel in the 1980s and 1990s. For the latter, English patriotism was not a bourgeois snare but a sentimental reality, and nowhere more so than among the people on the streets (and in the fields).[86] However much Samuel strove to emphasise the conservative force of 'people's history' – particularly with its acceptance of local attachments – and notwithstanding his thinly veiled criticism of Thompson in this respect,[87] his concern just before his death in 1998 to assert the left's interest in 'heritage' was barely distinguishable from establishment attempts to legitimise the latter in the interests of the fake spirit of national homogeneity and stability that he wanted to denounce.[88]

Notes

1   M. Cowling, *Religion and Public Doctrine in Modern England* (Cambridge, Cambridge University Press, 1980), pp. 220–1. Butterfield's work has been sensitively explored by Reba Soffer in 'The Conservative historical imagination in the twentieth century', *Albion*, 28 (1996), 1–17; and 'British Conservative historiography and the Second World War', in B. Stuchtey and P. Wende (eds), *British and German Historiography, 1750–1950: Traditions, Perceptions and Transfers* (London, Oxford University Press, 2000), pp. 373–99.

2 Cowling, *Religion and Public Doctrine*, pp. 224–5.

3 H. Butterfield, *The Universities and Education*, the A. D. Lindsay Memorial Lectures, 1961 (London, Routledge, 1962), p. 109.

4 H. Butterfield, 'A bridge between the arts and the sciences', *The Listener*, 15 July 1948, pp. 95–6.

5 See Cowling, *Religion and Public Doctrine*, pp. 200, 226.

6 H. Butterfield, *The Whig Interpretation of History* (London, Bell, 1931).

7 H. Butterfield, *The Study of Modern History* (London, Bell, 1944), pp. 29–30.

8 Cowling recounts the origins of *The Englishman and his History* in lectures which Butterfield gave in German universities in 1938. Butterfield was invited by the cultural attaché at the German Embassy in London to give an account of how the Whig interpretation 'came about'; *Religion and Public Doctrine*, p. 227, n. 1.

9 H. Butterfield, *The Englishman and his History* (Cambridge, Cambridge University Press, 1944), p. 9.

10 Cowling, *Religion and Public Doctrine*, p. 229.

11 Butterfield, *The Englishman and his History*, pp. 3–4.

12 Butterfield, *The Englishman and his History*, p. 2.

13 Butterfield, *The Englishman and his History*, p. 99.

14 C. W. B, 'Two histories', *Times Literary Supplement*, 8 July 1944, p. 332.

15 C. Navari, 'Arnold Toynbee (1889–1975): prophecy and civilization', *Review of International Studies*, 26 (2000), 296.

16 H. Butterfield, *Christianity and History* (London, Bell, 1949), pp. 65–6.

17 Butterfield, *Christianity and History*, p. 104.

18 H. Butterfield, *Christianity and History*, p. 73.

19 Butterfield, *The Englishman and his History*, p. 128.

20 Quoted in D. Cannadine, *G. M. Trevelyan: A Life in History* (London, Harper Collins, 1992), p. 212.

21 M. Powicke, 'Two books about history', *History* (October 1950), p. 197.

22 T. Fuller, Introduction to M. Oakeshott, *The Politics of Faith and the Politics of Scepticism* (New Haven and London, Yale University Press, 1996), p. x.

23 This English inspiration is somewhat overlooked in the otherwise interesting article by Luke O'Sullivan, 'Michael Oakeshott on European political history', *History of Political Thought*, 21:1 (2000), 132–51.

24 Oakeshott, *The Politics of Faith*, p. 75.

25 Oakeshott, *The Politics of Faith*, pp. 80–1.

26 Oakeshott, *The Politics of Faith*, p. 89.

27 Oakeshott, *The Politics of Faith*, p. 109.

28 M. Oakeshott, 'The political economy of freedom' (1949), in T. Fuller (ed.), *Rationalism in Politics and Other Essays*, new and expanded edition (Indianapolis, Liberty Press, 1991), p. 406.

29 For details, see J. Jewkes, *Ordeal by Planning* (London, Macmillan, 1948).

30 Oakeshott, *The Politics of Faith*, p. 20.

31 M. Oakeshott, *Religion, Politics, and the Moral Life* (New Haven, Yale University Press, 1993), pp. 8–9.

32 M. Oakeshott, 'The new Bentham', *Scrutiny*, 1 (1932), reprinted in Fuller (ed.), *Rationalism in Politics*, pp. 138–40.

33 M. Oakeshott, 'Contemporary British politics', *The Cambridge Journal*, 1 (1947–48), p. 490.

34   R. Grant, *Oakeshott* (London, Claridge Press, 1990), p. 75.
35   S. R. Letwin, *The Anatomy of Thatcherism* (London, Fontana, 1992), p. 336.
36   W. H. Greenleaf, *Oakeshott's Philosophical Politics* (London, Longmans, 1966), p. 84.
37   On Marshall see E. Low, 'Class and conceptualization of citizenship in twentieth-century Britain', *History of Political Thought*, 21:1 (2000), 114–51.
38   W. J. M. Mackenzie, 'The knights of the textbooks', in R. Frankenberg (ed.), *Custom and Conflict in British Society* (Manchester, Manchester University Press, 1982), pp. 36–49.The paper had been written five years earlier in 1977. Mackenzie wrote despairingly in 1955 of Oakeshott's refuge against the dangers of ideological politics in 'nationalism, scepticism, and pessimism'; Mackenzie, 'Political theory and political education', in *Explorations in Government: Collected Papers, 1951–1968* (London, Macmillan, 1975), pp. 25–9.
39   S. Kresge and L. Wenar (eds), *Hayek on Hayek: An Autobiographical Dialogue* (London, Routledge, 1994), pp. 19–21, 102–3.
40   B. Wootton, *Freedom under Planning* (London, George Allen & Unwin, 1945).
41   Kresge and Wenar (eds), *Hayek on Hayek*, pp. 75–6, 98.
42   Kresge and Wenar (eds), *Hayek on Hayek*, p. 102.
43   F. A. Hayek, *The Road to Serfdom* (London, Routledge, [1944] 1986), p. 160.
44   Hayek, *The Road to Serfdom*, p. 159.
45   Hayek, *The Road to Serfdom*, pp. 16, 6–7. It is true that, once Germany started forging ahead with plans for European Unity in the postwar world, the Labour Party sought to distance itself from such attempts at supranational planning as the Schuman Plan. The grounds on which it did so were full of exceptionalist rhetoric. See *European Unity: A Statement by the National Executive Committee of the British Labour Party* (London, The Labour Party, 1950). However, Hayek showed how, at the turn of the century, the German model of socialism was the most advanced in Europe, inspiring not just western European models but the Soviet model which – in turn – became the beacon of socialist hope in the interwar period, not least in Britain. Labour Party intellectuals helped to give the Soviet model – and the German model on which it was based – its authority, but only so long as it was confined within single national contexts. When attempts were made to overreach these contexts, the statist socialism of Cripps, Laski and Strachey reacted powerfully with the 'nationalist' socialism of figures such as Lawson and Attlee.
46   This is certainly confirmed by the experience of Francis Brett Young with the Ministry of Information on the outbreak of the War, on which see Chapter 6, pp. 121–2.
47   Kresge and Wenar (eds), *Hayek on Hayek*, pp. 19–20; Hayek, *The Road to Serfdom*, pp. 122–3.
48   D. Abel, *Ernest Benn: Counsel for Liberty* (London, Ernest Benn, 1960), p. 110.
49   M. Oakeshott, 'Rationalism in politics' (1947), in *Rationalism in Politics and Other Essays* (London, Methuen, 1962), p. 21.
50   M. Ignatieff, *Isaiah Berlin: A Life* (London, Chatto & Windus, 1998), p. 128.
51   R. Skidelsky, *John Maynard Keynes*, Volume 3, *Fighting for Britain, 1937–1946* (London, Macmillan, 2000), pp. 284–6.
52   S. Heffer, *Like the Roman: The Life of Enoch Powell* (London, Weidenfeld & Nicolson, 1998), pp. 266, 644–5.
53   Oakeshott, 'The political economy of freedom', p. 391.

54   E. Powell, speech delivered on 21 April 1964, in *A Nation not Afraid: The Thinking of Enoch Powell*, ed. J. Wood (London, Batsford, 1965), p. 25.

55   E. Powell, 'Conservatism and social problems', in *Swinton Journal* (1968), quoted in W. H. Greenleaf, *The British Political Tradition*, vol. II, *The Ideological Heritage* (London, Routledge, [1983] 1988), p. 320.

56   See the 1966 speech which became known as 'Enoch's point', reprinted in J. Wood (ed.), *J. Enoch Powell, Freedom and Reality* (London, Batsford, 1969), pp. 94–8.

57   E. Powell, speech at Blackpool, 24 September 1966, in *Freedom and Reality*, p. 129.

58   E. Powell, speech at Bristol, 29 September 1966, in *Freedom and Reality*, p. 139.

59   This argument was levelled by William Rees-Mogg (see Heffer, *Like the Roman*, p. 381); Tom Nairn, *The Break-Up of Britain: Crisis and Neo-Nationalism* (London, New Left Books, 1977), pp. 283–4; and Rodney Barker, *Politics, Peoples and Government* (London, Macmillan, 1994), p. 125. Barker compared Powell with Orwell thus: 'In both cases, the description of England finds them at their most allusive and lyrical, and at their farthest remove from their usual arguments about the conduct of government and politics.'

60   Heffer, *Like the Roman*, p. 185.

61   Heffer, *Like the Roman*, p. 23.

62   F. Nietzsche, *Beyond Good and Evil* (London, Penguin, [1886] 1973), pp. 164–5.

63   E. Powell, 'Britain and Europe', speech delivered at Lyon on 12 February 1971, in M. Holmes (ed.), *The Eurosceptical Reader* (London, Macmillan, 1996), p. 85.

64   Heffer, *Like the Roman*, p. 136.

65   E. Powell, speech to the Royal Society of St George, 22 April 1961 (Heffer points out that J. Wood erroneously dates the speech 22 April 1964 – *Like the Roman*, p. 982), in *Freedom and Reality*, p. 256.

66   E. Powell, 'Britain and Europe', p. 85.

67   Heffer, *Like the Roman*, p. 631. These shared sympathies emphasise that if – as has been argued recently – Powell's (re)conception of British national identity was inimical to the task of 'modernisation' in the 1970s, then socialism as much as conservatism suffered the same fate. See Peter Lynch, *The Politics of Nationhood: Sovereignty, Britishness, and Conservative Politics* (London, Macmillan, 1999), p. 46.

68   E. Powell, speech to the Royal Society of St George, 22 April 1961, p. 257.

69   This is imputed to Powell in Chris Waters, '"Dark strangers" in our midst: discourses of race and nation in Britain, 1947–1963', *Journal of British Studies*, 36 (April 1997), p. 237. Besides race, Powell also ruled out geography as a determinant of nationhood; hence his staunch support for Ulster which began to be manifested in the late 1960s, but which was based upon a long-held conviction that 'if geography made a nation, there would not be two nations in Ireland to-day'; A. Maude and J. Enoch Powell, *Biography of a Nation: A Short History of Britain* (London, John Baker, [1955] 1970), p. 7.

70   E. Powell, Speech in the House of Commons, 3 March 1953, in *Freedom and Reality*, pp. 194–5.

71   E. Powell, Speech to the Royal Society of St. George, in *Freedom and Reality*, p. 257.

72   E. Powell, speech on immigration at Wolverhampton, 11 June 1970, in J. Wood (ed.) *Powell and the 1970 General Election: Enoch Powell's Five Election Speeches* (London, Elliot Right Way Books, 1970), p. 103.

73   E. Powell, speech at Birmingham, 13 June 1970, in Wood (ed.), *Powell and the 1970 General Election*, p. 109.

74   Heffer, *Like the Roman*, p. 361. Isaiah 50:4–7.
75   Heffer, *Like the Roman*, p. 361.
76   Heffer, *Like the Roman*, p. 474.
77   Powell, speech at Wolverhampton, p. 103.
78   Powell, speech at Birmingham, 20 April 1968, in *Freedom and Reality*, p. 217.
79   E. P. Thompson, Foreword to *The Poverty of Theory* (London, Merlin Press, 1978), pp. iii-iv.
80   E. P. Thompson, 'The peculiarities of the English', (1965), in *The Poverty of Theory*, pp. 63–4.
81   Thompson, 'The peculiarities of the English', pp. 56, 69.
82   M. Kenny, 'Reputations: Edward Palmer (E. P.) Thompson', *Political Quarterly*, 7:3 (1999), 325.
83   E. P. Thompson, 'Outside the whale' (1960), in *The Poverty of Theory*, p. 17.
84   M. Kenny, *The First New Left: British Intellectuals after Stalin* (London, Lawrence & Wishart, 1995), p. 181.
85   Kenny, *The First New Left*, p. 83.
86   R. Samuel, 'Preface' to *Patriotism: The Making and Unmaking of British National Identity*, 3 vols, I, *History and Politics* (London, Routledge, 1989), p. xii.
87   R. Samuel, 'Introduction: exciting to be English', in *History and Politics*, p. xlix.
88   See S. Collini, *English Pasts: Essays in History and Culture* (Oxford, Oxford University Press, 1999), pp. 100–2.

10

Political theory, cultural diversity and Britishness in the early twenty-first century

I

The tradition in Britain of thinking about politics in terms of the images and culture of a relatively homogeneous English/British *patrie* declined markedly at the end of the twentieth century. Indeed, so much was this the case that the longer-term process of erosion, and sometimes also its adverse consequences for their subject, was brought sharply to the attention of political theorists.[1] This concluding chapter considers some of the pressures behind recent developments and defends the perspective that is now rapidly falling out of favour.

II

Not the least challenge to Englishness as the cornerstone of public identity in Britain has been multiculturalist demands that the institutions and values of society 'reflect' the various ethnic communities they claim to represent. In response, political theorists have castigated the idea that single nations – however large – within composite communities should be dominant in any way and consequently tempted to 'absolutise' themselves.[2] For the multiculturalists the tendency towards such national arrogance has been associated most obviously with the assimilationist approach to postwar immigration of Enoch Powell. This is the view that the identities of ethnic minorities should remain purely private, largely confined to the sphere of religion, while public, official culture in any reasonably stable, cohesive society must be shaped by the values and traditions of the majority nation. From the multicultural perspective the liberal, or integrationist approach, which looked more favourably on cultural difference, was certainly an improvement, but was still ambiguous about the relationship of minority cultures to that of the majority.[3]

The undermining of assimilationism was fuelled not only by the assertiveness of minority cultures within Britain but, in addition, by deep dissatisfaction with what seemed to be the purely passive notion of citizenship as 'subjecthood' upon which it was premissed. The subsumption of the former in the latter signified common allegiance to the Crown as the principal criterion of the status of British nationality.[4] This allegiance was sealed, on the one hand, by the possession of a limited set of rights and, on the other, by the duty of self-sacrifice, not least the sacrifice of life itself in the event of war.[5] Moreover, throughout most of the twentieth century, theorists of citizenship stressed its *individual* basis. While they accepted that the strength of the bond between individuals and the state depended upon the mediation of smaller group loyalties and identities, ultimately they assumed that those 'partial' loyalties would give way. For example, in the theoretical framework of Idealism earlier in the century, citizenship meant sameness, despite being filtered through a multitude of different organisations. Citizenship represented the transcendence, at the same time as the harmonisation of, its various associative mediums in society.[6] At an imperial level, common citizenship could not be founded upon a patchwork of heterogeneous loyalties; it presumed instead a clear and unifying, although ultimately voluntary, cultural backbone, this being Christian in character for Ernest Barker and one which for John Henry Muirhead was constituted by 'European ties of truth and justice, . . . and European science'.[7]

On the basis of this inheritance, the concept of citizenship in the 1970s and 1980s had developed in such a way that it appeared to have become too amenable to the arguments of the right favouring a racially exclusive and anti-statist polity for the concept itself to bear serious consideration. However, when the left became interested in the rejuvenation of civil society – in the face of its perceived weakening by the bureaucratic impulses of 'old' socialism and authoritarian conservatism alike – it made a new bid for the conceptual terrain of citizenship. Now, instead of denoting a status that was grounded in cultural inheritance, citizenship was redefined in terms of 'empowerment'. No longer was citizenship to be construed in the narrow conservative sense of lending legitimacy to an established order of power and property; rather, it was to be achieved through the development of wide-ranging and enforceable liberties and rights – enshrined in a written constitution – so that all individuals, regardless of class, race or creed, might leave their hitherto private mark on the public face of society. Citizenship, then, came to mean active political participation, on the one hand, and diversity, on the other. Its new champions stressed its roots in mere convention rather than 'nature' and its infinite rather than finite scope for inclusion.[8] It remains to be seen whether New Labour proposals to initiate 'citizenship ceremonies' for successful applicants for British citizenship will retain the oath of allegiance to the Queen and her 'heirs and successors', let alone one which the candidate swears by 'Almighty God'.[9]

Political theorists who have been influenced by multiculturalism recognise the importance of national identity to the success of this new ideal of citizenship. They accept that social unity and equal citizenship are heavily dependent upon the spirit of common nationhood that entrenched and relatively monolithic national cultures were able to generate in the past. They consider that bare constitutional patriotism of the kind pursued in Germany – anxious to escape from the burden of the national past by embracing universal political values – is an inadequate basis for citizenship in complex modern societies.[10] This is despite the defence of constitutional patriotism recently in the work of Habermas and in a more classical Republican form by Viroli which allows for particular cultural attachments.[11] Nevertheless, critics of constitutional patriotism emphasise the inability of the *traditional* nation to generate the loyalty and sense of commonality with which it was previously associated. For David Miller, it is essential that the inherited nation makes room for minority communities in setting its political and cultural contours. Miller takes one step back from full-blooded multiculturalism, maintaining that the civic education which is to be the cornerstone of diverse national communities must contain a 'unitary core', in addition to a 'periphery that is flexible enough to serve the needs of minorities'.[12] Yet like the multiculturalists he believes that citizenship is mediated through a welter of communal identities and is always provisional, both in terms of its internal structure and the allegiance it can command.

Bikhu Parekh has been one of the most insistent protagonists of multiculturalism in Britain in recent years. He has emphasised, in particular, the importance of eroding the boundary between public and private spheres as far as cultural identity is concerned, thereby creating new channels of communication across multicultural divides.[13] Social intercourse and cultural fusion between the various communities of Britain that have taken place at the level of such humdrum pastimes as eating and recreation could be greatly enhanced, and to the benefit of all in society, by public recognition of such developments. This would take the form of both a much fuller integration of such communities into the policy process at all levels than exists at present, and through bringing the influence of their culture to bear on wider social practices and beliefs. The process would be assisted by the creation of 'cultural rights', enabling all cultural communities and their members to sustain and develop their traditions and identities, although in a relationship of continuous dialogue with, rather than seclusion from, one another.[14] Needless to say, and opening up much scope for the exercise of arbitrary, inevitably bureaucratic judgement, not all minority groups and individuals would benefit equally from such largesse. Some – those deemed to be especially disadvantaged in some way – would require 'not only different but also additional rights' such as 'special or disproportionate representation in parliament, the cabinet and other government bodies and the right to consultation and even perhaps a veto over laws relating to them'.[15]

Moreover, while Parekh now invokes national identity as the basis of citizenship, he continues to echo his earlier beliefs about the purely formal and political, as opposed to 'ethno-cultural', nature of the modern state.[16] This is difficult to reconcile, especially when he discusses citizenship in terms of such potentially emotive and exclusionary criteria as the sense of 'common belonging' and 'common self-understanding'. Moreover, while he concedes that the 'long-established culture' of a society can never be entirely eliminated, he maintains that its 'inbuilt advantages . . . should be minimized'. However, this concession is effectively annulled by the more uncompromising claim that even established political values should not be treated as non-negotiable. If they can be shown to be unfairly biased against certain cultures or to exclude other equally worthwhile political values, a critical dialogue on them should be welcomed as a step towards a richer moral culture enjoying a broad consensus.[17]

Although he professes a dislike of the ideology of liberalism for its arrogance in monopolising liberal values and vilifying 'other' political languages in which those values are given different articulations,[18] the suspicion which he casts over all aspects of the received political culture is reminiscent of the spirit of radicalism which brought his ideological antagonist into being. Indeed, Parekh here epitomises the instrumental approach to patriotism which was well castigated by Oakeshott in 1956 in the course of characterising friendship: in both cases, Oakeshott argued, 'the tie is one of familiarity, not usefulness; the disposition engaged is conservative, not "progressive"'.[19]

Indeed, for all Parekh's concern to soothe and harmonise, to encourage the taking of pleasure in difference rather than the adoption of an attitude of hostility, there is a tendency in multiculturalism more widely to demonise the inherited culture. There is a tendency to exaggerate the inherited culture's exclusiveness and its sense of the 'otherness' of the *ethnicities* it allegedly oppresses. This in turn seems to license the exaggeration of *its* 'otherness' in relation to those groups resisting their alleged 'marginalisation' in this way, as in *Braveheart*. There is, in addition, a tendency to emphasise the provincialism and sectarianism of what is perceived as the dominant culture's defendants.

This process has been aided by the Cultural Studies industry, anxious to submit all notions of 'England' and 'Englishness' to the caustic process of 'deconstruction'. A recent anthology in this vein maintains that all such notions hold interest only as the expression of 'a particular social group who sought to define the national character in their own exclusive terms'.[20] But is it really the case that, for example, the 'England' which H. V. Morton went in search of in 1927 was merely a figment of his own narrow class imagination?[21] Surely the phenomenal demand for his book – thirty-six editions in the following twenty years – suggests that the term 'class' would have to be used so widely in this case as to be meaningless. The Macpherson Report on policing of February 1999 is particularly symptomatic of this antagonistic side to multiculturalism, with its contention that an 'institutionalised racism' prevails throughout British society. The report's ethos stands in stark contrast to the comforting belief that the English, at least, have about themselves – recently articulated by the historian Sir Geoffrey Elton – that 'toleration of variety' is one of their defining virtues.[22]

In the light of the Macpherson Report, and the pressures towards multiculturalism which political theorists have been instrumental in bringing to bear, it is appropriate to consider an anthology of literature and verse published in 1997 which emphasises that Britain has always been a 'melting pot of diverse cultural influences'.[23] The Editor – the writer Caryl Phillips – explains that the aim of the book is to challenge long-standing perceptions of the 'exclusiveness' of the British. This he attempts to do by demonstrating the equally long-standing condition of racial and national heterogeneity among the population of the British Isles, a condition which served to produce a 'vigorous and dynamic' literature. His criterion for inclusion is that of being a writer born outside of Britain, but nevertheless having made seminal contributions to the canon of 'English' literature. On the whole, the book strikes an even balance across the range of feelings which 'Britain' has evoked in the literary imagination of the last two centuries. There is hence the contempt of Orwell, Thackeray, Durrell and Naipaul for the *sine qua non* of acceptance in England: the keeping up of appearances. There is the thorough alienation of writers of African descent such as Ben Okri, projected in a macabre fantasy world wrought by the abjectness of their central characters. There is confrontation with the racial violence which has become an intermittent expression of national identity in post-colonial Britain, as depicted by E. R. Braithwaite and Christopher Hope. There is the fascination and disillusion of colonial encounters with the reality of a 'mythical' England as dramatised by Anitai Desai and George Lamming, and Shiva Naipaul and Abdulrazack Gurnah, respectively. At the other end of the scale, there is Conrad's admiration of an England characterised by enduring fortitude: 'The great flagship of the race; stronger than the storms! and anchored in the open sea'. There is Kipling's staunch defence of the English flag and the benefits it has bestowed worldwide. There is Kazuo Ishiguro's contemplation of the 'greatness' of Britain as a function of the undramatic but nevertheless powerful beauty of the land. There is the longing to belong (T. S. Eliot). And finally, there are accounts of the innumerable obstacles to assimilation posed by the absence of detailed 'local knowledge' – more needful here than elsewhere? – (Lively and Rhys).

Many of these contributions cast doubt upon the Editor's claim that Britain has been a notably receptive culture, however much the hostility they describe has been absorbed into the canon of English literature. In Doris Lessing's essay of 1987 defending the cosmopolitan world of the London Underground, the famous receptivity of England/Britain to diversity is attributed exclusively to immigrant, not native culture in Britain. Of the latter, she raises despairing questions:

> Surely the mourners of old London must applaud the Japanese, who are never, ever, scruffy or careless? Probably not: in that other London there were no foreigners, only English, pink-grey as Shaw said, always chez-nous, for the Empire had not imploded, the world had not invaded, and while every family had at least one relative abroad administering colonies or dominions, or being soldiers, that was abroad, it was there, not here, the colonies had not come home to roost.[24]

It may just be a question of time-lag here: given the truly global mix of the people of Britain now, the process of integration will inevitably take longer than it has done in the past. It is also the case that conceptions of integration have changed considerably in recent years, mere 'assimilation' being judged inadequate to the unparalleled diversity of modern British society, as we have seen above. Phillips

quotes Daniel Defoe's poem on 'The true-born Englishman' (1701) as a model
for the 'mongrelised' Britain whose recognition he seeks. But it is not an entirely
appropriate model for the multicultural perspective with which he – and others
such as Miller, who also make use of the poem for similar ends – view the needs
and values of contemporary Britain. For in the lines which follow, Defoe seems
to be extolling (albeit through satirising those who stressed the myth of British
racial supriority and implicitly its purity) the success of the English in moulding
the disparate peoples of the British Isles into one nation: its own.

> The Scot, Pict, Briton, Roman, Dane, submit
> And with the English Saxon all unite:
> And these the mixture have so close pursued,
> The very name and memory's subdued;
> No Roman now, no Briton does remain;
> Wales strove to separate, but strove in vain:
> The silent nations undistinguis'd fall,
> And Englishman's the common name for all.
> Fate jumbled them together, God knows how;
> What'er they were, they're true-born English now.[25]

The poem, in other words, is anglo-centric – although not xenophobic and intol-
erant – to the core. This is true of the similar celebration of the 'mongrel
Englishman' in Kipling's children's story *Puck of Pook's Hill*, which – significantly – was lauded by the anti-racist writer and relative of Kipling, Colin
MacInnes in the 1960s:

> *Puck*'s message to the young is that England's essential nature, throughout its
> history, is to be constantly invaded by new races which the older settlers first
> resisted, and then accepted once the genius of each race became fused in a fresh
> form of the English soul. *Puck*'s lesson is that hostility to the invading race is
> natural, but equally so the wholehearted acceptance of its presence once it has
> lost its alien nature and is contributing to the mongrel glory of the English
> people.[26]

Not surprisingly, Kipling himself was a great admirer of Defoe's poem, using it
on the occasion of his address to the Royal Society of St George in 1920 to correct
the assembled company's rather narrow and racist conception of England – not
least in relation to the sister nations of the United Kingdom – but in order to
enhance rather than diminish their national pride.[27]

III

Miller and other political theorists who have taken up the case of multiculturalism have been much exercised also by the problem of the several nationalisms
within Britain, and particularly the way in which England has virtually defined
the wider cultural and political unit at the expense of the less favoured component nations. For a more equitable model of 'British' nationhood and under the
influence of the pioneering work of the historian Linda Colley, they emphasise

the 'forging' of such a nation at the turn of the eighteenth century. United by a vigorous protestantism, the threat of American secession and the conduct of war with France, a free Britain was the hearty toast of its John Bulls the country over.[28]

However, Colley's work has come under considerable fire. One critic, the historian Adrian Hastings, has doubted whether 'Britain' as an object of patriotic loyalty ever usurped the place of England, even in times of crisis. Indeed, it would be difficult to see how it could ever have done so when the vein of patriotic loyalty in Britain, centred on the *English* nation, ran as far back as the age of Bede. Even if Hastings's claim is as historically questionable as that of Colley, his scepticism that 'the Colley thesis adequately respects the continued emotional, intellectual and political dominance of the concept of England over that of Britain' is persuasive.[29] This can be illustrated in the case of Scotland before the intensification of Scottish nationalism in the 1960s. In the 1930s, for example, the influential Scottish (albeit lowland) businessman and man of letters, F. S. Oliver, wrote that:

> The notion that a subordination, or any abatement of national pretensions, is implied in the use of 'England' or 'English' to denote the great incorporating Union and the things appertaining thereto, must provoke a smile on the face of anyone who knows his fellow-countrymen on both sides of the Border. There are few Scotsmen, I imagine, who *love* the Union – by whatever name they may choose to call it – so well as they *love* Scotland; but there are many of us to whom the word 'England' conveys the idea of that Union, and of the loyalty that is due to it, as clearly as the word 'Britain', but with a richer harmony and a nobler tradition.[30]

Other scholars have also questioned whether 'Britishness' was ever a free-standing political identity, independently of the English core which, over the centuries, played a preponderant, although not exclusive, role in giving it form and definition. This is true not least with respect to the centrality of Protestantism to the notion of England as an 'elect' nation in the sixteenth century, before translating to Britishness in the eighteenth century.[31] Sometimes that core took a merely 'civic' form, in which formal associative values such as universalism and inclusion prevailed over more selective 'ethnic' notions of kinship and character.[32] But it is important to recognise that the conception of the United Kingdom as a nation bound together by civic bonds was itself borne of a conception of English nationhood as vitally expressed in institutions, and therefore unreflective in the same way as Scottish nationalism. It was quite amenable, too, that meant, and unusually so, to the leadership of other nationals:

> A Scotsman, a Welshman, a Jew, may become the political leader of the English people; an Irishman such as Wellington may command its armies, and another Irishman (a Swift or a Shaw) may lash its foibles by his satire. [English nationality] remains the same; and if it attains to so much reflection, it will only murmur to itself that 'the English constitution might be worse, and England, after all, is not a bad country'.[33]

The English core was substantiated in part by legends of the ancient Britons in attempts to wrest that legacy from the Celtic nations. Rebecca Langlands has maintained that, whatever 'Britishness' may become in the new era of devolution now unfolding, historically it has acted as an overarching identity which has often denoted more than simply common political allegiance. Although driven by 'bureaucratic incorporation' of the four nations into one – a key illustration being the integration of the Scottish Highland regiments into the British Army from the mid eighteenth century – this process 'entailed a considerable measure of accommodation, cultural fusion, and social intermingling'. Never has 'Britishness' been an 'invention' wrought by the ideological needs of the state at any one moment; its meaning and significance have been the subject of constant change and development, not as something 'superimposed' over, but *in relation to*, the loyalties and identities of its four component parts.[34]

IV

Finally, the notion of Englishness as the principal conduit of Britishness has been undermined by attempts to construct a federal European polity with associated ideals of European citizenship that draw upon, but transcend, the cultural and political resources of individual European nations. The unquestioned assumption of many leading political thinkers in Britain at the present time is that federal union is inevitable, especially given the control of the French administrative class over European policy, which sees integration as a means of, on the one hand, ensuring its national frontiers against a greatly enlarged Germany and, on the other, resisting American influence in Europe. But there is a strong conviction too that European federalism is a desirable outcome, especially when conceived in terms of accommodating maximum diversity rather than the current trend of imposing a unitary state. The main concern of such thinkers is to consider how, given the inexorable drive towards the federal goal, European integration can be shaped by the peoples as much as the governments of Europe through securing the broadest consent to a written constitution along American lines – on their own admittance, a long-term project.[35]

But in the understanding of 'peoples', nations do not figure largely; national sovereignty still less, for all that – somewhat confusingly – fine civic traditions are accredited to old-style nation-states rather than, for example, regions.[36] Richard Bellamy discounts 'civic nationalists' as much as 'cosmopolitans' in constructing a Republican model of European polity which gives maximum scope for participation in the furthering of all interests and minimum scope to the domination of powerful blocs within the system. Neither set of protagonists, he claims, 'will work for a pluralist polity in which such norms have to be constructed piecemeal from amongst often conflicting values by multiple *demoi* working in diverse situations'.[37] In his alternative model of 'cosmopolitan communitarianism', groups of varying purposes, identities and persuasions engage in a process of continuous dialogue, out of which the desired consensus supporting European Union emerges. While he is concerned to defend national identities against supranational or post-national polities in this approach, the weight of his argument falls on more local or minor attachments. National identities – certainly old, hegemonic ones – are far too monolithic to support his pluralist ideal of Europe. The idea that the resultant 'associationalism' can act as a foil against the bureaucratic tide of the European Union – especially when the public funding he envisages to empower groups will require considerable administration both to collect and assign – is also questionable, and is intrinsically at odds with those nations whose innate distrust of government still runs deep.[38] Finally, whether associationalism can raise the level of European citizenship above the alleged 'instrumentalism' of its cosmopolitan and civic nationalist opponents, to the higher level of allegiance, obligation and self-sacrifice commanded certainly by the latter, remains to be seen. The obituaries of Second World War heroes continue to give ample testimony to the effectiveness of historic nation-states in marshalling the survival instincts – often at great individual risk – of communities under threat, the basis of which lies in the existence of a quiet, unarticulated patriotism through years of peacetime previously.[39] This is a hard act for an 'associational' model of political society to follow. Nor are such examples of heroism and courage best interpreted as relatively uninformed attempts 'to protect their country's religious or ethnic or cultural unity':[40] as was argued at the end of Chapter 1, it is extremely difficult to dissociate a people's conception of their unity from their conception of a shared, and often ancestral, enjoyment of liberty.

In this light it is refreshing to read the work of David Archard, who recognises the non-negotiable nature of nationalism; that is, its subconscious roots in myths, feelings and attitudes which transcend and overcome the physical boundaries of the communities thereby 'imagined'. On this account, the campaign to 'modernise' national identity is flawed because it fails to take account of the implicit rather than express structures of belief which bind a people together. Archard questions in particular those friendly critics of nationalism who, while recognising the value of nations in providing a solution to the 'collectivist deficit' in modern times, nevertheless seek to expose the beliefs that national communities have about themselves to 'collective critical deliberation' so that any superiority complexes and other undesirable features of their self-consciousness may be eradicated. As Archard maintains, 'if national myths are to function in the beneficial way that they currently do, they cannot be the subject of an on-going, sceptical, critical reason. Nor can the civic education which serves to reproduce a national identity be constituted by such a reason'.[41]

V

While political theorists have strained every nerve of nationalist theory in efforts to adapt it to the needs of plural societies, there has been some attempt, too, to emphasise the congruity of the work of eminent political thinkers in the past with the modern 'politics of recognition' at the heart of multicultural concerns.

David Boucher, for example, concedes that 'the vocabulary of human rights and multiculturalism did not enter into' the writings of Collingwood. Nevertheless, he maintains that Collingwood's work is helpful in clarifying the issues which such vocabulary raises. In particular, he emphasises the scope in Collingwood's conception of the civilising process for extending the practice of civility to those previously excluded from its favour. This could apply, argues Boucher, as much to minorities within a dominant culture as to relations between sovereign political bodies. Essentially, the practice of civility entails eliminating force in the conduct of social relations, resolving differences through consensus and compromise, and hence acknowledging the capacity for free choice in those who are recognised as members of the 'social community'. Boucher emphasises that to deny such a capacity is tantamount to undermining the self-respect of the persons concerned. Failure to act with civility towards others is hence to inflict psychological damage upon them, as well as – frequently – physical damage too.[42] Boucher makes a convincing case for the immense potential of Collingwood's notion of the moral community and its expansive nature – not least the store it sets by comparative history in the self-understanding necessary to civilised life. Nevertheless, it is arguable that this notion is of limited use in resolving the conflicts and differences that arise in societies where minority status across a wide range of fronts is actively cultivated. There are grounds for maintaining that the condition of radical diversity in contemporary societies has a tendency to produce a public culture that is too heterogeneous and shallow to foster a common sense of identity and discipline, so participative that it becomes – in Collingwood's terms – 'cristical' rather than 'dialectical'; that is, confrontational rather than conciliatory. It may concede so much to minority communities that citizenship becomes a means to narrow, sectional ends rather than a common end in itself.

Earlier political theorists in Britain were alive to the importance of national and cultural difference, and emphasised the benefits of contact and fusion. However, they were wary of politicising 'difference', believing in an English/British model of the state which had kept such matters largely under political wraps. Naturally, they could afford to do so as their nation was not at risk of being subsumed by one more dominant than itself. However, they sensed well enough the dangers of fragmentation and conflict that would inevitably accompany the ascendancy of groups whose aims were limited and whose methods were belligerent: the *débâcle* of Ireland in the early twentieth century was instrumental in the development of this aspect of their political and cultural consciousness. They confined their enthusiasm for 'difference' to the (by now) relatively mundane level of 'liberal pluralism' – the right to maintain an identity that has been largely constructed out of resources internal to it, but within a wider public configuration in which it can expect to find few echoes. Their legacy will hold little interest to those who seek to grapple with the question of identity at deeper, 'symbolic' levels,[43] or through the theory of the psychological 'gaze' which holds that dominant cultures, races and genders deliberately distort and violate the identities of those they seek to subdue, and fashion their own identity in opposition to such negative projections. However, the sense of caution, distrust of excessive particularism and wider public role for the political intellectual that such a devotion to England/Britain inspired is worth remembering, even at this late juncture for 'old Britain'.

Notes

1 Margaret Canovan, for example, has remarked on how, for at least the past half century, 'most anglophone political theorists have turned their backs on the whole business [of nationalism] and gone on talking about their preferred topics – democracy (for example), social justice, freedom, rights, even community – as if nationalism were an irrelevance'; *Nationalism and Political Theory* (Cheltenham, Edward Elgar, 1996), p. 1.

2 B. Parekh, 'Theorizing political theory', in N. O'Sullivan (ed.), *Political Theory in Transition* (London, Routledge, 2000), p. 256.

3 B. Parekh, 'British citizenship and cultural difference', in G. Andrews (ed.), *Citizenship* (London, Lawrence & Wishart, 1991), pp. 183–204.

4 Citizenship as 'subjecthood' based on the principle of 'indelible' allegiance to the Crown was established in Calvin's case of 1608. The Naturalisation Act of 1870 significantly modified the notion of 'indelible' allegiance, but not the principle of allegiance itself as the basis of citizenship, and in 1914 it was given statutory definition in the Common Code, thus binding together the empire in the face of the common enemy. See A. Dummett and A. Nichol, *Subjects, Citizens, Aliens and Others: Nationality and Immigration Law* (London, Weidenfeld & Nicolson, 1990), pp. 88, 124–5.

5 The importance of 'sacrifice' was stressed by the campaign group 'Education for Citizenship' in the 1930s, an uneasy alliance of (mainly progressive) intellectuals and public figures under the leadership of the Liberal MP Sir Ernest Simon, who sought to strengthen democracy in Britain against the threat of dictatorship. The element of 'sacrifice' was envisaged within a framework of 'free citizenship', in contrast to the continental understanding of the term as slavishness to a party and leader through rigorous 'drilling'. See E. Simon and E. Hubback, *Training for Citizenship* (London, Oxford University Press, 1935), pp. 16, 20, 48.

6 See Bernard Bosanquet's Introduction to the second edition of his *The Philosophical Theory of the State* (London, Macmillan, [1899] 1910), pp. lviii, lix.

7 E. Barker, 'The contact of colours and civilisations', *The Contemporary Review* (1930), 585; and 'The conception of empire', in C. Bailey (ed.), *The Legacy of Rome* (Oxford, Clarendon Press, 1924), p. 65; See also J. H. Muirhead, 'What imperialism means' (1900), in D. Boucher (ed.), *The British Idealists* (Cambridge, Cambridge University Press, 1997), p. 239.

8 See Andrews (ed.), *Citizenship*, esp. Introduction; D. Held, 'Between state and civil society: citizenship'; and Parekh, 'British citizenship and cultural difference'.

9 T. Utley, 'Citizenship ceremonies to make the blood run cold', *Daily Telegraph*, 13 September 2000.

10 D. Miller, *On Nationality* (Oxford, Clarendon Press, 1995), p. 163.

11 See M. Viroli, *For Love of Country: An Essay on Patriotism and Nationalism* (Oxford, Clarendon Press, 1995), Epilogue.

12 Miller, *On Nationality*, pp. 189, 181.

13 B. Parekh, 'Common citizenship in a multicultural society', *The Round Table*, 88:351 (1999), p. 457.

14 On the contrast between Parekh's 'civic' brand of multiculturalism in this respect and other varieties see S. Tempelman, 'Constructions of cultural identity: multiculturalism and exclusion', *Political Studies*, 47:1 (1999), 17–31.

15 B. Parekh, *Rethinking Multiculturalism: Cultural Diversity and Political Theory* (London, Macmillan, 2000), p. 262.

16 B. Parekh, 'Defining British national identity', *Political Quarterly*, 71:1 (2000), 8. David Miller has remarked upon the contrast between the spartan conception of political community in Parekh's early essay on 'The "New Right" and the politics of nationhood' (in G. Cohen *et al.*, *The New Right: Image and Reality* (London, The Runnymede Trust, 1986)) and his recent writings in *On Nationality*, p. 175, n. 31.

17 Parekh, 'Common citizenship in a multicultural society', pp. 456–8.

18 Parekh, 'Theorizing political theory', p. 253.

19 M. Oakeshott, 'On being conservative', *Rationalism in Politics and Other Essays* (London, Methuen, 1962), p. 177.

20 J. Giles and T. Middleton (eds), *Writing Englishness, 1900–1950: An Introductory Sourcebook on National Identity* (London, Routledge, 1995), p. 5.

21 H. V. Morton, *In Search of England* (London, Methuen, 1927).

22 G. Elton, *The English* (Oxford, Blackwell, 1992), p. 235.

23 C. Phillips (ed.), *Extravagant Strangers: A Literature of Belonging* (London, Faber & Faber, 1997), p. xi.

24 D. Lessing, 'In defence of the underground', in Phillips (ed.), *Extravagant Strangers*, pp. 96–7.

25 D. Defoe, *Works*, V (London, Bohm, 1865), p. 442.

26 C. MacInnes, *Out of the Way* (1979), quoted in A. Lycett, *Rudyard Kipling* (London, Weidenfeld & Nicolson, 1999), p. 381.

27 Lycett, *Rudyard Kipling*, p. 502.

28 L. Colley, *Britons: Forging the Nation, 1707–1837* (New Haven, Yale University Press, 1992).

29 A. Hastings, *The Construction of Nationhood: Ethnicity, Religion and Nationalism* (Cambridge, Cambridge University Press, 1997), p. 63.

30 F. S. Oliver, *The Endless Adventure*, 3 vols, I (1931), p. 44, quoted in E. Grigg, *The Faith of an Englishman* (London, Macmillan, 1936), p. viii.

31 R. Langlands, 'Britishness or Englishness? The historical problem of national identity in Britain', *Nations and Nationalism*, 5:1 (1999), 54, 57, 61–2, 64.

32 For an excellent account of such oscillations in British history, see H. Kearney, 'The importance of being British', *Political Quarterly*, 71:1 (2000), 15–25.

33 E. Barker, *National Character and the Factors in its Formation* (London, Methuen, [1927] 1928), p. 194. On the importance of a stable national core, and the English achievement in providing one for Britain that both preserved its own identity while allowing other national identities to flourish, see P. Langford, *Englishness Identified: Manners and Character, 1650–1850* (Oxford, Oxford University Press, 2000), pp. 14, 319.

34 Langlands, 'Britishness or Englishness?', 54, 61–2, 64.

35 L. Siedentop, *Democracy in Europe* (London, Allen Lane/The Penguin Press, 2000).

36 Siedentop, *Democracy in Europe*, pp. 28, 231.

37   R. Bellamy, 'Citizenship beyond the nation-state: the case of Europe', in O'Sullivan (ed.), *Political Theory in Transition*, p. 104.
38   Rodney Barker has made a similar point about pluralism as a doctrine of government when he asks, 'is it not open to Oscar Wilde's jibe that the trouble with socialism was that it did "cut into one's evenings so dreadfully" and to the accusation that liberty depends not on the proliferation of government, but in its limitation?'; 'Pluralism, revenant or recessive?', in J. Hayward, B. Barry and A. Brown (eds), *The British Study of Politics* (Oxford, Oxford University Press, 1999), p. 142.
39   See, for example, the obituary of Daphne Pearson, GC, *The Times*, 26 July 2000, p. 19.
40   Viroli, *For Love of Country*, p. 185.
41   D. Archard, 'Nationalism and political theory', in O'Sullivan (ed.), *Political Theory in Transition*, p. 166.
42   D. Boucher, 'Tocqueville, Collingwood, history and extending the moral community', *British Journal of Politics and International Relations*, 2:3 (2000), 331, 337–8.
43   See M. Patrick, 'Identity, diversity and the politics of recognition', in O'Sullivan (ed.), *Political Theory in Transition*, pp. 33–46.

Manuscript sources

Arthur Bryant Papers, Liddell Hart Centre for Military History, King's College London.
Herbert Butterfield Papers, Cambridge University Library.
Central Zionist Archives, Jerusalem.
Neville Chamberlain Papers, Birmingham University Library.
R. G. Collingwood Papers, Bodleian Library, Oxford.
J. C. C. Davidson Papers, House of Lords' Record Office (The Parliamentary Archives).
Geoffrey Dawson Papers, Bodleian Library, Oxford.
Foreign Office Papers, Public Record Office, Kew.
Felix Frankfurter Papers, Library of Congress, Washington, DC.
Oliver Wendell Holmes Papers, Harvard Law School Library.
Horace Meyer Kallen Papers, YIVO Institute for Jewish Research, New York.
Lord Lawson Papers, Durham University Library.
Lord Lindsay Papers, Keele University Library.
Walter Lippmann Papers, Yale University Library.
Violet Markham Papers, British Library of Political and Economic Science, London.
F. S. Marvin Papers, Bodleian Library, Oxford.
Gilbert Murray Papers, Bodleian Library, Oxford.
Oxford University Archives, Bodleian Library, Oxford.
Passfield Papers, British Library of Political and Economic Science, London.
William Plomer Papers, Durham University Library.
Maurice Reckitt Papers, Sussex University Library, Brighton.
Round Table Papers, Bodleian Library, Oxford.
R. W. Seton-Watson Papers, School of Slavonic and East European Studies, University of London.
Arnold Toynbee Papers, Bodleian Library, Oxford.
Graham Wallas Papers, British Library of Political and Economic Science, London.
Chaim Weizmann Papers, The Weizmann Institute of Science, Rehovot, Israel.
Francis Brett Young Papers, Birmingham University Library.
Alfred Zimmern Papers, Bodleian Library, Oxford.

Select bibliography

Primary sources

Books and pamphlets

Amis, K., *Socialism and the Intellectuals* (London, The Fabian Society, 1957).

Anson, W. et al., *Rights of Citizenship: A Survey of Safeguards for the People* (London, Frederick Warne, 1912).

Auden, W. H. et al., *I Believe: Nineteen Personal Philosophies* (London, George Allen & Unwin, 1940).

Barker, E., *Political Thought from Spencer to the Present Day* (London, Williams & Norgate, 1915).

Barker, E., *National Character and the Factors in its Formation* (London, Methuen, [1927] 1928).

Barker, E., *The Uses of Leisure* (London, World Association for Adult Education, 1936).

Barker, E., *The Citizen's Choice* (Cambridge, Cambridge University Press, 1937).

Barker, E., *Change and Continuity*, The Ramsay Muir Memorial Lecture (London, Gollancz, 1949).

Benda, J., *The Betrayal of the Intellectuals*, trs. R. Aldington (Boston, The Beacon Press, [1927] 1955).

Betjeman, J., *Ghastly Good Taste: Or a Depressing Story of the Rise and Fall of English Architecture* (London, Chapman & Hall, 1933).

Betjeman, J., *The English Town in the Last Hundred Years*, The Rede Lecture (Cambridge, Cambridge University Press, 1956).

Betjeman, J., *John Betjeman: Letters*, Volume One: 1926–1951, ed. C. Lycett Green (London, Methuen, 1994).

Betjeman, J., *John Betjeman: Letters*, Volume Two: 1951–1984, ed. C. Lycett Green (London, Methuen, 1995).

Betjeman, J., *John Betjeman: Coming Home*, ed. C. Lycett Green (London, Methuen, 1997).

Boucher, D., (ed.), *Essays in Political Philosophy: R. G. Collingwood* (Oxford, Clarendon Press, 1989).

Boucher, D., (ed.), *The British Idealists* (Cambridge, Cambridge University Press, 1997).

Brennan, E., J. T., (ed.), *Education for National Efficiency: The Contribution of Sidney and Beatrice Webb* (London, Athlone Press, 1975).

Brodnick, G. C. et al., *Essays on Reform* (London, Macmillan, 1867).

Bryant, A., *Humanity in Politics* (London, Hutchinson for The National Book Association, 1937).

Bryant, A., *Unfinished Victory* (London, Macmillan, 1940).

Bryant, A., *English Saga (1840–1940)* (London, Fontana, [1940] 1953).

Bryant, A., *The Art of Writing History*, The English Association Presidential Address, 1946 (London, English Association, 1946).

Bryant, A., *The Age of Elegance, 1812–1822* (London, Reprint Society, [1950] 1954).

Bryant, A., *The Turn of the Tide, 1939–1943* (London, Collins, 1957).

Bryant, A., *A Choice for Destiny: Commonwealth and Common Market* (London, Collins, 1962).

Bryant, A., *The Lion and the Unicorn: A Historian's Testament* (London, Collins, 1969).

Bryce, J., *Studies in Contemporary Biography* (New York, Macmillan, 1903).

Bryce, J., *The Hindrances to Good Citizenship* (New Haven, Yale University Press, 1909).

Butterfield, H., *The Whig Interpretation of History* (London, Bell, 1931).

Butterfield, H., *The Englishman and his History* (Cambridge, Cambridge University Press, 1944).

Butterfield, H., *The Study of Modern History* (London, Bell, 1944).

Butterfield, H., *Christianity and History* (London, Bell, 1949).

Butterfield, H., *The Universities and Education*, The A. D. Lindsay Memorial Lectures, 1961 (London, Routledge, 1962).

Cain, P. (ed.), *Empire and Imperialism: The Debate of the 1870s* (South Bend, Indiana, St. Augustine's Press, 1999).

Carr, E. H., *Democracy in International Affairs*, Cust Foundation Lecture, 1945 (Nottingham: University of Nottingham, 1945).

Cecil, H., *Liberty and Authority* (London, Edward Arnold, 1910).

Cecil, H., *Conservatism* (London, Williams & Norgate, 1912).

Chamberlain, N., *The Struggle for Peace*, ed., A. Bryant (London, Hutchinson, 1939).

Dawson, C., *Beyond Politics* (New York, Sheed & Ward, 1939).

Dicey, A. V., *Lectures on the Relation between Law and Public Opinion in England during the Nineteenth Century* (London, Macmillan, [1905] 1914).

Duncan, D., *The Life and Letters of Herbert Spencer* (London, Methuen, 1908).

Durbin, E. F. M., *The Politics of Democratic Socialism: An Essay on Social Policy* (London, Routledge, 1940).

Eliot, T. S., *The Idea of a Christian Society and other Writings*, intro. by D. Edwards (London, Faber & Faber, [1939] 1982).

Figgis, J. N., *Studies of Political Thought from Gerson to Grotius, 1414–1625* (Cambridge Cambridge University Press, [1907] 1916).

Figgis, J. N., *Churches in the Modern State* (London, Longman, 1913).

Fisher, H. A. L., *James Bryce (Viscount Bryce of Dechmont, O.M.)* 2 vols (London, Macmillan, 1927).

Forster, E. M., *Two Cheers for Democracy* (Harmondsworth, Penguin, [1951] 1965).

Forster, E. M., *The Prince's Tale and Other Uncollected Writings*, ed. P. N. Furbank (London, Andre Deutsche, 1998).

Goodwin, M. (ed.), *Nineteenth Century Opinion: An Anthology of Extracts from the First Fifty Volumes of The Nineteenth Century, 1877–1901* (Harmondsworth, Penguin, 1951).

Hayek, F. A., *The Road to Serfdom* (London, Routledge, [1944] 1986).

Hayek, F. A., *Hayek on Hayek: An Autobiographical Dialogue*, ed. S. Kresge and L. Wenar (London, Routledge, 1994).

Hichens, W. L., *Some Problems of Modern Industry: The Watt Anniversary Lecture* (London, Nisbet & Co., 1918).

Hyde, D., *I Believed: The Autobiography of a Former British Communist* (London, William Heinemann, 1951).

Lawson, J. J., *A Man's Life* (London, Hodder & Stoughton, [1932] 1944).

Lindsay, A. D., *Christianity and Economics* (London, Macmillan, 1933).

Lindsay, A. D., *The Churches and Democracy*, The Social Service Lecture (London, Epworth, 1934).

Lindsay, A. D., *I Believe in Democracy*, addresses broadcast in the BBC Empire Programme (London, Oxford University Press, 1940).

Lindsay, A. D., *Toleration and Democracy*, The Lucien Wolff Memorial Lecture (London, Oxford University Press, 1942).

Lindsay, A. D., *Religion, Science and Society* (Oxford, Oxford University Press, 1943).

Lindsay, A. D., *The Modern Democratic State* (London, Oxford University Press, 1943).

Lindsay, A. D., *The Good and the Clever*, The Founders Memorial Lecture, (Cambridge, Cambridge University Press, 1945).

Mackenzie, W. J. M., *Explorations in Government: Collected Papers, 1951–1968* (London, Macmillan, 1975).

Marvin, F. S. (ed.), *The Unity of Western Civilization* (London, Oxford University Press, 1915).

Massingham, H. J., *A Mirror of England: An Anthology of the Writings of H. J. Massingham*, ed. E. Abelson (Bideford, Green Books, 1985).

Meadowcroft, J. (ed.), *L. T. Hobhouse: Liberalism and Other Writings* (Cambridge, Cambridge University Press, 1994).

Morley, J., *On Compromise*, ed. J. Powell (Edinburgh, Keele University Press, [1874] 1997).

Muggeridge, M., *Muggeridge through the Microphone: BBC Radio and Television* (London, British Broadcasting Corporation, 1966).

Muggeridge, M., *Chronicles of Wasted Time*, 2 vols, II, *The Infernal Grove* (London, Collins, 1973).

Muirhead, J. H., *Reflections by a Journeyman in Philosophy on the Movements of Thought and Practice in his Time* (London, George Allen & Unwin, 1942).

Oakeshott, M., *Rationalism in Politics and Other Essays*, new and expanded edition ed. T. Fuller (Indianapolis, Liberty Press, [1962] 1991).

Oakeshott, M., *Religion, Politics, and the Moral Life*, ed. T. Fuller (New Haven, Yale University Press, 1993).

Oakeshott, M., *The Politics of Faith and the Politics of Scepticism*, ed. T. Fuller (New Haven and London, Yale University Press, 1996).

Orwell, G., *The Lion and the Unicorn: Socialism and the English Genius* (London, Penguin [1941], 1982).

Percy, E., Greenwood, A., Dover Wilson, J., Seton-Watson, R. W. and Zimmern, A. E., *The War and Democracy* (London, Macmillan, 1914).

Powell, J. E., *A Nation not Afraid: The Thinking of Enoch Powell*, ed. J. Wood (London, Batsford, 1965).

Powell, J. E., *Freedom and Reality*, ed. J. Wood (London, Batsford, 1969).

Powell, J. E., *Powell and the 1970 General Election: Enoch Powell's Five Election Speeches*, ed. J. Wood (London, Elliot Right Way Books, 1970).

Pyle, A. (ed.), *Liberty: Contemporary Responses to John Stuart Mill* (Bristol, Thoemmes Press, 1994).

Quiller-Couch, A., *The Poet as Citizen and Other Papers* (Cambridge, Cambridge University Press, 1934).

Rowse, A. L., *Politics and the Younger Generation* (London, Faber & Faber, 1931).

Rowse, A. L., *The English Spirit: Essays in History and Literature* (London, Macmillan, 1945).

Rowse, A. L., *The Use of History* (London, Hodder & Stoughton, 1946).

Rowse, A. L., *The End of an Epoch: Reflections on Contemporary History* (London, Macmillan, 1947).

Rowse, A. L., *The English Past: Evocations of Persons and Places* (London, Macmillan, 1951).

Rowse, A. L., *A New Elizabethan Age?*, Presidential Address to the English Association, 1952 (London, English Association, 1952).

Rowse, A. L., *Historians I Have Known* (London, Duckworth, 1995).

Seeley, J. R., *The Expansion of England: Two Courses of Lectures* (London, Macmillan, [1883] 1897).

Snow, C. P., *The Two Cultures*, ed. S. Collini (Cambridge, Cambridge University Press, [1959] 1994).

Spencer, H., *An Autobiography*, 2 vols (London, Watts & Co., 1904).

Stapleton, J. (ed.), *Liberalism, Democracy, and the State in Britain: Five Essays, 1862–1891* (Bristol, Thoemmes Press, 1997).

Stephen, J. F., *Liberty, Equality, Fraternity* (Chicago, University of Chicago Press, [1873] 1991).

Stephen, L., *The Life of Sir James Fitzjames Stephen* (London, Smith, Elder & Co., 1895).

Strachey, J., *The Coming Struggle for Power* (London, Victor Gollancz, [1932] 1934).

Strachey, J., *The Theory and Practice of Socialism* (London, Victor Gollancz, 1936).

Strachey, J., *The Strangled Cry and Other Unparliamentary Papers* (London, Bodley Head, 1962).

Thompson, E. P., *The Poverty of Theory* (London, Merlin Press, 1978).

Trevelyan, G. M., *English Literature and its Readers*, The English Association Presidential Address (London, English Association, 1951).

Unwin, G. (ed.), *What I Believe* (London, George Allen & Unwin, 1966).

Von Hügel, F., *The German Soul in its Attitude towards Ethics and Christianity, the State and War* (London, J. M. Dent, 1916).

Wallas, G., *Human Nature in Politics* (London, Constable, [1908] 1929).

Wallas, G., *The Great Society: A Psychological Analysis* (New York, Macmillan, [1914] 1921).

Wallas, G., *Men and Ideas: Essays by Graham Wallas*, ed. M. Wallas (London, Allen & Unwin, 1940).

Webb, S. and Webb, B., *The Prevention of Destitution* (London, Longman, 1911).

Webb, S and Webb, B., *The Decay of Capitalist Civilisation* (London, The Fabian Society, 1923).

Webb, B., *The Diary of Beatrice Webb*, ed. N. and J. Mackenzie, 4 vols (London, Virago, 1982–85).

What is Democracy?, Peace Aims Pamphlet no. 38 (London, 1946).

Wilson Harris, H. (ed.), *Christianity and Communism* (Oxford, Basil Blackwell, 1937).

Young, F. B., *The Island* (London, Heinemann, 1944).

Zimmern, A. E., *The Greek Commonwealth: Politics and Economics in Fifth-Century Athens* (Oxford, Clarendon Press, [1911] 1924).

Zimmern, A. E., *Nationality and Government with other War-Time Essays* (London, Chatto & Windus, 1918).
Zimmern, A. E., *Learning and Leadership* (London, Oxford University Press, 1928).
Zimmern, A. E., *The Study of International Relations* (Oxford, Clarendon Press, 1931).
Zimmern, A. E., *The Prospects of Democracy* (London, Chatto & Windus, 1932).
Zimmern, A. E., *The League of Nations and the Rule of Law* (London, Macmillan, [1936] 1939).
Zimmern, A. E., *Spiritual Values and World Affairs* (Oxford, Clarendon Press, 1939).

Articles and chapters

Barker, E., 'The discredited state', *Political Quarterly*, (February 1915), 101–21.
Lindsay, A. D., 'The Church's concern', in William Temple, *et al.*, (eds), *The Crisis of the Western World and Other Broadcast Talks* (London, George Allen & Unwin, 1944), 1–14.
Lindsay, A. D., 'Christian individualism and scientific individualism', in T. F. Woodlock (ed.), *Democracy: Should it Survive?* (London, Dennis Dobson, 1946), 118–26.
Lindsay, A. D., 'The philosophy of the British Labour Government', in F. C. S. Northrop (ed.), *Ideological Differences and World Order: Studies in the Philosophy and Science of the World's Cultures* (New Haven, Yale University Press, 1949), 250–68.
Lindsay, A. D., 'Democracy in the world today', in R. McKeon (ed.), *Democracy in a World of Tension* (Chicago, University of Chicago Press, 1951), 172–85.
Lindsay, A. D., 'Philosophy as criticism of standards', a paper read at the Jubilee Meeting of the Scots Philosophical Club, 29 September 1950, in E. V. Lindsay (ed.), *A. D. Lindsay, 1879–1952: Selected Addresses* (E. V. Lindsay, Cumberland, 1957), pp. 127–54.
Mackenzie, W. J. M., 'The knights of the textbooks', in R. Frankenberg (ed.), *Custom and Conflict in British Society* (Manchester, Manchester University Press, 1982), 36–49.
Oakeshott, M., 'Contemporary British politics', *The Cambridge Journal*, 1 (1947–48), 474–90.
Powell, J. E., 'Britain and Europe', speech delivered at Lyon on 12 February 1971, in M. Holmes (ed.), *The Eurosceptical Reader* (London, Macmillan, 1996), pp. 75–87.
Seeley, J., 'Ethics and religion', in The Society of Ethical Propagandists (ed.), *Ethics and Religion* (London, Swan Sonnenschein, 1900), pp. 1–30.
Trevelyan, G. M., 'The calls and claims of natural beauty', The Rickman Godlee Lecture for 1931, reprinted in *An Autobiography and Other Essays* (London, Longmans, 1949), 92–106.
Zimmern, A. E., 'Oxford in the new century', *Independent Review*, III (1906), 95–104.
Zimmern, A. E., 'The evolution of the citizen', in O. Stanley (ed.), *The Way Out: Essays on the Meaning and Purpose of Adult Education* (London, Oxford University Press, 1923), 20–47.

Secondary sources

Books

Allen, P., *The Cambridge Apostles: The Early Years* (Cambridge, Cambridge University Press, 1979).
Annan, N., *Our Age: The Generation that Made Postwar Britain* (London, Fontana, [1990] 1991).
Annan, N., *The Dons: Mentors, Eccentrics, Geniuses* (London, Harper Collins, 1999).

Biagini, E. F. (ed.), *Citizenship and Community: Liberals, Radicals and Collective Identities in the British Isles, 1865–1931* (Cambridge, Cambridge University Press, 1996).

Blaazer, D., *The Popular Front and the Progressive Tradition: Socialists, Liberals, and the Quest for Unity, 1884–1939* (Cambridge, Cambridge University Press, 1992).

Burrow, J. W., *Whigs and Liberals: Continuity and Change in English Political Thought* (Oxford, Clarendon Press, 1988).

Cannadine, D., *G. M. Trevelyan: A Life in History* (London, Harper Collins, 1992).

Carpenter, C., *The Envy of the World: Fifty Years of the BBC Third Programme and Radio 3, 1946–1996* (London, Weidenfeld & Nicolson, 1996).

Colley, L., *Britons: Forging the Nation, 1707–1837* (New Haven, Yale University Press, 1992).

Collini, S., *Liberalism and Sociology: L. T. Hobhouse and Political Argument in England, 1880–1914* (Cambridge, Cambridge University Press, 1979).

Collini, S., *Public Moralists: Political Thought and Intellectual Life in Britain, 1850–1930* (Oxford, Clarendon Press, 1991).

Collini, S., *English Pasts: Essays in History and Culture* (Oxford, Oxford University Press, 1999).

Cowling, M., *Religion and Public Doctrine in Modern England* (Cambridge, Cambridge University Press, 1980).

Dummett, A. and Nicol, A. (eds), *Subjects, Citizens, Aliens and Others: Nationality and Immigration Law* (London, Weidenfeld & Nicolson, 1990).

English, R. and Kenny, M. (eds.), *Rethinking British Decline* (London, Macmillan, 2000).

Eyck, F., *G. P. Gooch: A Study in History and Politics* (London, Macmillan, 1982).

Feske, V., *From Belloc to Churchill: Private Scholars, Public Culture, and the Crisis of British Liberalism, 1900–1939* (Chapel Hill, University of North Carolina, 1996).

Grainger, J. H., *Character and Style in English Politics* (Cambridge, Cambridge University Press, 1969).

Grainger, J. H., *Patriotisms: Britain 1900–1940* (London, Routledge, 1986).

Grant, R., *Oakeshott* (London, Claridge Press, 1990).

Greenleaf, W. H., *Oakeshott's Philosophical Politics* (London, Longman, 1966).

Greenleaf, W. H., *The British Political Tradition*, 3 vols, 2, *The Ideological Heritage* (London, Routledge, [1983] 1988).

Harris, J., *Private Lives, Public Spirit: A Social History of Britain, 1870–1914* (Oxford, Oxford University Press, 1993).

Harvie, C., *The Lights of Liberalism: University Liberals and the Challenge of Democracy, 1860–1885* (London, Allen Lane, 1976).

Hastings, A., *The Construction of Nationhood: Ethnicity, Religion and Nationalism* (Cambridge, Cambridge University Press, 1997).

Heffer, S., *Like the Roman: The Life of Enoch Powell* (London, Weidenfeld & Nicolson, 1998).

Heffer, S., *Nor Shall My Sword: The Reinvention of England* (London, Weidenfeld & Nicolson, 1999).

Hill, R., *Lord Acton* (New Haven, Yale University Press, 2000).

Hitchens, P., *The Abolition of Britain* (London, Quartet Books, 1999).

Ignatieff, M., *Isaiah Berlin: A Life* (London, Chatto & Windus, 1998).

Ironside, P., *The Social and Political Thought of Bertrand Russell* (Cambridge, Cambridge University Press, 1996).

Jann, R., *The Art and Science of Victorian History* (Columbus, Ohio State University Press, 1985).

Jennings, J. and Kemp-Welch, A. *Intellectuals in Politics: From the Dreyfus Affair to Salmon Rushdie* (London, Routledge, 1997).

Jones, H. S., *Victorian Political Thought* (London, Macmillan, 2000).

Kenny, M., *The First New Left: British Intellectuals after Stalin* (London, Lawrence & Wishart, 1995).

Kojecky, R., *T. S. Eliot's Social Criticism* (London, Faber & Faber, 1971).

Kramnick, I., and Sherman, B., *Harold Laski: A Life on the Left* (London, Hamish Hamilton, 1993).

Langford, P., *Englishness Identified: Manners and Character, 1650–1850* (Oxford, Oxford University Press, 2000).

Lasch, C., *The Revolt of the Elites and the Betrayal of Democracy* (New York, W.W. Norton, 1995).

Lavin, D., *From Empire to International Commonwealth: A Biography of Lionel Curtis* (Oxford, Clarendon Press, 1995).

Lowe, J., *The Warden: A Portrait of John Sparrow* (London, Harper Collins, 1998).

Lubenow, W. C., *The Cambridge Apostles, 1820–1914: Liberalism, Imagination, and Friendship in British Intellectual and Professional Life* (Cambridge, Cambridge University Press, 1998).

Lycett, A., *Rudyard Kipling* (London, Weidenfeld & Nicolson, 1999).

Mackenzie, J., *The Children of the Souls: A Tragedy of the First World War* (London, Chatto & Windus, 1986).

Mandler, P., *The Fall and Rise of the Stately Home* (New Haven, Yale University Press, 1997).

Mandler, P. and Pederson, S. (eds), *After the Victorians: Private Conscience and Public Duty in Modern Britain: Essays in Memory of John Clive* (London, Routledge, 1994).

McCrillis, N. R., *The British Conservative Party in the Age of Universal Suffrage: Popular Conservatism, 1918–1929* (Columbus, Ohio State University Press, 1999).

McLaine, I., *Ministry of Morale: Home Front Morale and the Ministry of Information in World War II* (London, George Allen & Unwin, 1979).

Meadowcroft, M., *Conceptualizing the State: Innovation and Dispute in British Political Thought 1880–1914* (Oxford, Clarendon Press, 1995).

Miller, D., *On Nationality* (Oxford, Clarendon Press, 1995).

Mowl, T., *Stylistic Cold Wars: Betjeman Versus Pevsner* (London, John Murray, 2000).

Nicholls, D., *The Pluralist State: The Political Ideas of J. N. Figgis and his Contemporaries*, (London, Macmillan, [1975] 1994).

Ollard, R., *A Man of Contradictions: A Life of A. L. Rowse* (London, Allen Lane, 1999).

Parekh, B. *Rethinking Multiculturalism: Cultural Diversity and Political Theory* (London, Macmillan, 2000).

Phillips, C. (ed.), *Extravagant Strangers: A Literature of Belonging* (London, Faber & Faber, 1997).

Ritschel, D., *The Politics of Planning: the debate on Economic Planning in Britain in the 1930s* (Oxford, Clarendon Press, 1997).

Roberts, A., *Eminent Churchillians* (London, Phoenix, [1994] 1995).

Roberts, E. A., *The Anglo-Marxists: A Study in Ideology and Culture* (Lanham, Ma. Rowman & Littlefield, 1997).

Rose, N., *The Cliveden Set: Portrait of an Exclusive Fraternity* (London, Jonathan Cape, 2000).

Rothblatt, S., *Tradition and Change in English Liberal Education: An essay in History and Culture* (London, Faber, 1976).

Runciman, D., *Pluralism and the Personality of the State* (Cambridge, Cambridge University Press, 1997).

Said, E., *Representations of the Intellectual: The 1993 Reith Lectures* (London, Vintage, 1994).

Samuel, R. (ed.), *Patriotism: The Making and Unmaking of British National Identity*, 3 vols, I, *History and Politics* (London, Routledge, 1989).

Sanderson, M., *The Universities and British Industry, 1850–1970* (London, Routledge, 1972).

Scott, D., *A. D. Lindsay: A Biography* (Oxford, Blackwell, 1971).

Scruton, R., *England: An Elegy* (London, Chatto & Windus, 2000).

Searle, G. R., *The Quest for National Efficiency: A Study in British Politics and Political Thought, 1899–1914* (Oxford, Basil Blackwell, 1971).

Searle, G. R., *Morality and the Market in Victorian Britain* (Oxford, Clarendon Press, 1998).

Siedentop, L., *Democracy in Europe* (London, Allen Lane/The Penguin Press, 2000).

Soffer, R. N., *Discipline and Power: The University, History, and the Making of an English Elite, 1870–1930* (Stanford, Stanford University Press, 1994).

Stapleton, J., *Englishness and the Study of Politics: The Social and Political Thought of Ernest Barker* (Cambridge, Cambridge University Press, 1994).

Stray, C., *Classics Transformed: Schools, Universities, and Society in England, 1830–1960* (Oxford, Clarendon Press, 1998).

Strum, P., *Louis D. Brandeis: Justice for the People* (Cambridge, Ma., Harvard University Press, 1984).

Thomas, H., *John Strachey* (London, Eyre/Methuen, 1973).

Thompson, N., *John Strachey: An Intellectual Biography* (London, Macmillan, 1993).

Turner, F. M., *The Greek Heritage in Victorian Britain* (New Haven, Yale University Press, 1981).

Vellacott, J., *Bertrand Russell and the Pacifists in the First World War* (Brighton, Harvester, 1980).

Viroli, M., *For Love of Country: An Essay on Patriotism and Nationalism* (Oxford, Clarendon Press, 1995).

Von Arx, J. P., *Progress and Pessimism: Religion, Politics, and History in Late Nineteenth Century Britain* (Cambridge, MA, Harvard University Press, 1985).

Wallace, S., *War and the Image of Germany: British Academics, 1914–1918* (Edinburgh, John Donald, 1988).

Wedderburn Cannan, M., *Grey Ghosts and Voices* (Kineton, The Roundwood Press, 1976).

Weight, R. and Beach, A. (eds), *The Right to Belong: Citizenship and National Identity in Britain, 1930–1960* (London, I. B. Tauris, 1998).

Wiener, M. J., *Between Two Worlds: The Political Thought of Graham Wallas* (Oxford, Clarendon Press, 1971).

Williamson, P., *Stanley Baldwin: Conservative Leadership and National Values* (Cambridge, Cambridge University Press, 1999).

Wood, N., *Communism and British Intellectuals* (London, Gollancz, 1959).

Wormell, D., *Sir John Seeley and the Uses of History* (Cambridge, Cambridge University Press, 1980).

Wright, T. R., *The Religion of Morality: The Impact of Comtean Positivism on Victorian Britain* (Cambridge, Cambridge University Press, 1986).

Zastoupil, L., *John Stuart Mill and India* (Stanford, Stanford University Press, 1994).

Articles and chapters

Archard, D., 'Nationalism and political theory', in N. O'Sullivan (ed.), *Political Theory in Transition* (London, Routledge, 2000), 155–71.

Barker, R., 'Pluralism, revenant or recessive?', in J. Hayward, B. Barry, and A. Brown (eds), *The British Study of Politics* (Oxford, Oxford University Press, 1999), 117–46.

Bell, P., 'A historical cast of mind: some eminent English historians and attitudes to continental Europe in the middle of the twentieth century', *Journal of European Integration*, 2 (1996), 5–19.

Bellamy, R., 'Citizenship beyond the nation-state: the case of Europe', in N. O'Sullivan (ed.), *Political Theory in Transition* (London, Routledge, 2000), 91–112.

Boucher, D., 'The place of education in civilization', in D. Boucher, J. Connelly, and T. Modood (eds), *Philosophy, History and Civilization: Interdisciplinary Perspectives on R. G. Collingwood* (Cardiff, University of Wales Press, 1995), 269–99.

Boucher, D., 'Tocqueville, Collingwood, history and extending the moral community', *The British Journal of Politics and International Relations*, 2:3 (2000), 326–51.

Dean, D., 'The dilemmas of an academic liberal historian in Lloyd George's government: H. A. L. Fisher at the Board of Education, 1916–1922', *History*, 79 (1994), 57–81.

Den Otter, S., '"Thinking in communities": late nineteenth-century liberals, idealists and the retrieval of community', in E. H. H. Green (ed.), *An Age of Transition: British Politics 1880–1914* (Edinburgh, Edinburgh University Press, 1997), 67–84.

Engel, A., 'The English universities and professional education', in K. H. Jarausch (ed.), *The Transformation of Higher Learning, 1860–1930: Expansion, Diversification, Social Opening, and Professionalization in England, Germany, Russia, and the United States* (Chicago, University of Chicago Press, 1983), 293–305.

Gibbins, J. R., 'Liberalism, nationalism and the British Idealists', *History of European Ideas*, 15:6 (1992), 491–7.

Harris, J., 'Political thought and the state', in S. J. D. Green and R. C. Whiting (eds), *The Boundaries of the State in Modern Britain* (Cambridge, Cambridge University Press, 1996), 15–28.

Harvie, C., 'The moment of British nationalism, 1939–1970', *Political Quarterly*, 71:3 (2000), 328–40.

Hernon, J. M., Jr, 'The last Whig historian and consensus history: George Macaulay Trevelyan, 1876–1962', *American Historical Review*, 81:1 (1976), 66–97.

Heyck, T. W., 'Myths and meanings of intellectuals in twentieth-century British national identity', *Journal of British Studies*, 37:2 (1998), 192–221.

Ignatieff, M., 'The decline and fall of the public intellectual', *Queen's Quarterly*, 104 (1997), 395–403.

Kearney, H., 'The importance of being British', *Political Quarterly*, 71:1 (2000), 15–25.

Kenny, J., 'Reputations: Edward Palmer (E. P.) Thompson', *Political Quarterly*, 7:3 (1999), 319–27.

Kidd, A. J., 'The state and moral progress: the Webbs' case for social reform, c. 1905–1940', *Twentieth Century British History*, 7:2 (1996), 189–205.

Langlands, R., 'Britishness or Englishness? The historical problem of national identity in Britain', *Nations and Nationalism*, 5:1 (1999), 53–69.

Loughlin, J., 'Joseph Chamberlain, English nationalism and the Ulster question', *History*, 77:250 (1992), 202–19.

Low, E., 'Class and conceptualization of citizenship in twentieth-century Britain', *History of Political Thought*, 21:1 (2000), 114–51.

Maddox, G., 'Skirmishers in advance: A. D. Lindsay and modern democratic theory', *Balliol College Annual Record* (1997), 11–18.

Mandler, P., 'Against "Englishness": English culture and the limits to rural nostalgia, 1850–1940', *Transactions of the Royal Historical Society*, 6th series, vol. 7 (1997), 155–75.

Mandler, P., '"Race" and "nation" in mid-victorian thought', in S. Collini, R. Whatmore, and B. Young (eds), *History, Religion, and Culture: British Intellectual History 1750–1950* (Cambridge, Cambridge University Press, 2000), 224–44.

Mandler, P., 'The consciousness of modernity? liberalism and the English "national character", 1850–1940', in M. Daunton and B. Rieger (eds), *Meanings of Modernity: Britain from the Late-Victorian Era to World War II* (Oxford, Berg, 2001), 119–440.

Markwell, D. J., 'Sir Alfred Zimmern revisited', *Review of International Studies*, 12 (1986), 279–92.

Marwick, A., 'Middle opinion in the thirties: planning, progress and political "agreement"', *The English Historical Review*, 79:311 (1964), 285–98.

Mauriello, C. E., 'The strange death of the public intellectual: liberal intellectual identity and the "field of cultural production"', *Journal of Victorian Culture* (6:2001), 1–26.

Meadowcroft, J. and Taylor, M., 'Liberalism and the referendum in British political thought 1890–1914', *Twentieth Century British History*, 1 (1990), 35–57.

Navari, C., 'Arnold Toynbee (1889–1975): prophecy and civilization', *Review of International Studies*, 26 (2000), 289–301.

Nicholas, S., '"Sly demagogues" and wartime radio: J. B. Priestley and the BBC', *Twentieth Century British History*, 6:3 (1995), 247–66.

O'Sullivan, L., 'Michael Oakeshott on European political history', *History of Political Thought*, 21:1 (2000), 132–51.

Parekh, B., 'British citizenship and cultural difference', in G. Andrews (ed.), *Citizenship* (London, Lawrence & Wishart, 1991), 183–204.

Parekh, B.,'Common citizenship in a multicultural society', *The Round Table*, 88: 351 (1999), 449–60.

Parekh, B., ' Theorizing political theory', in N. O'Sullivan (ed.), *Political Theory in Transition* (London, Routledge, 2000), 242–59.

Parekh, B., 'Defining British national identity', *Political Quarterly*, 71:1 (2000), 4–14.

Qvortrup, M., 'A. V. Dicey: the referendum as the people's veto', *History of Political Thought*, 20:3 (1999), 531–46.

Roach, J., 'Liberalism and the Victorian intelligentsia' (1957), reprinted in P. Stansky (ed.), *Government and Society in Victoria's Britain* (New York, New Viewpoints, 1973), 323–53.

Soffer, R. N., 'Authority in the university: Balliol, Newnham and the new mythology', in R. Porter (ed.), *Myths of the English* (Cambridge, Polity Press, 1992), 192–215.

Soffer, R. N., 'History and religion: J. R. Seeley and the burden of the past', in R. W. Davis and R. J. Helmstadter (eds), *Religion and Irreligion in Victorian Society* (London, Routledge, 1992), 133–50.

Soffer, R. N., 'The conservative historical imagination in the twentieth century', *Albion*, 28:1 (1996), 1–17.

Soffer, R. N., 'The historian, catholicism, global history, and national singularity', *Storia della Storiografia*, 35 (1999), 113–27.

Soffer, R. N., 'British Conservative historiography and the Second World War', in B. Stuchtey and P. Wende (eds), *British and German Historiography, 1750–1950: Traditions, Perceptions and Transfers* (London, Oxford University Press, 2000), 373–99.

Soffer, R. N., 'The long nineteenth century of conservative thought', in G. K. Behlmer and F. M. Leventhal (eds), *Singular Continuities: Tradition, Nostalgia, and Identity in Modern British Culture* (Stanford, Stanford University Press, 2000), 143–62.

Stapleton, J., 'Localism versus centralism in the Webbs' political thought', *History of Political Thought*, 12:1 (1991), 147–65.

Stapleton, J., 'English pluralism as cultural definition: the social and political thought of George Unwin', *Journal of the History of Ideas*, 52:4 (1991), 665–85.

Stapleton, J., 'James Fitzjames Stephen: liberalism, patriotism, and English liberty', *Victorian Studies*, 41:4 (1998), 244–61.

Stapleton, J., 'Resisting the centre at the extremes: "English" liberalism in the political thought of interwar Britain', *British Journal of Politics and International Relations*, 1:3 (1999), 270–92.

Stapleton, J., 'Political thought and national identity in Britain, 1850–1950', in S. Collini, R. Whatmore and B. Young (eds), *History, Religion, and Culture: British Intellectual History, 1750–1950* (Cambridge, Cambridge University Press, 2000), 245–69.

Stapleton, J., 'Cultural conservatism and the public intellectual in Britain, 1930–1970', *The European Legacy*, 5:6 (2000), 797–815.

Waters, C., '"Dark strangers" in our midst: discourses of race and nation in Britain, 1947–1963', *Journal of British Studies*, 36 (April 1997), 207–38.

Williamson, P., 'Christian Conservatives and the totalitarian challenge, 1933–1940', *English Historical Review*, 115:462 (2000), 607–42.

Worthington, G., 'Oakeshott's claims of politics', *Political Studies*, 45:4 (1997), 727–38.

Unpublished PhD theses

Grimley, M., *Citizenship, Community, and the Church of England: Anglican Theories of the State, c. 1926–1939*, PhD thesis, University of Oxford, 1998.

Scott, N., *The Influence of British Political Thought in China and India: The Cases of Sun Yat-Sen, Mahatma Gandhi and Jawaharlal Nehru*, PhD thesis, University of Durham, 2001.

Stapleton, J., *Academic Political Thought and the Development of Political Studies in Britain, 1900–1950*, PhD thesis, University of Sussex, 1986.

Worsley, D. J. *Sir John Robert Seeley and his Intellectual Legacy: Religion, Imperialism, and Nationalism in Victorian and Post-Victorian Britain*, PhD thesis, University of Manchester, 2001.

Index

Note: literary works can be found under authors' names; 'n.' after a page reference indicates the number of a note on that page.